PAIDEIA AGONISTES

The Lost Soul of Modern Education

John E. Grote

University Press of America, ® Inc.
Lanham • New York • Oxford

Copyright © 2000 by
University Press of America, ® Inc.
4720 Boston Way
Lanham, Maryland 20706

12 Hid's Copse Rd.
Cumnor Hill, Oxford OX2 9JJ

Library of Congress Cataloging-in-Publication Data

Grote, John E.
Paideia agonistes : the lost soul of modern education / John E. Grote.
p. cm.
Includes bibliographical references and index.
1. Education, Humanistic—United States. 2. Education—Aims and
objectives—United States. 3. Educational change—United States. I. Title:
Lost soul of modern education. II. Title.
LC1011 .G76   2000   370.11'2—dc21   00-039290 CIP

ISBN 0-7618-1726-3 (pbk: alk. ppr.)

⊖™ The paper used in this publication meets the minimum
requirements of American National Standard for Information
Sciences—Permanence of Paper for Printed Library Materials,
ANSI Z39.48—1984

This work is dedicated to
Those without whom it could not have been written:
To my parents, who supported me without reason,
My professor, Arthur Wirth, who could see only the good in my work,
My wife who believed in the book on faith alone,
And my children who finished it for me.

Acknowledgements

"Dr. Sigmund Freud Discovers the Sea Shell", **Collected Poems 1917-1982** by Archibald MacLeish. Copyright © 1985 by The Estate of Archibald MacLeish. Reprinted by permission of Houghton Mifflin Co. All rights reserved.

Excerpt from **To The Lighthouse** by Virginia Woolf, copyright © 1927 by Harcourt Brace & Company and renewed 1954 by Leonard Woolf, reprinted by permission of the publisher and by The Society of Authors, on behalf of the Virginia Woolf Estate.

Extracts from "A Prayer for Old Age", "Lapis Lazuli", and "The Circus Animals Desertion" are taken from **The Collected Poems of W.B. Yeats,** revised and edited by Richard Finneran, with the permissions of A.P.Watt Ltd on behalf of Michael Yeats and of Scribner, a Division of Simon & Schuster. Copyright © 1940 by Georgie Yeats; copyright renewed 1968 by Bertha Georgie Yeats, Michael Yeats, and Anne Yeats.

Excerpts from **The Human Cycle** by Colin Turnbull reprinted with the permissions of Simon & Schuster and Jonathan Cape (publisher). Copyright © 1983 by Colin Turnbull.

Table of Contents

Introduction

Cultures define the larger world in which humans live. In doing so they give shape and substance to our conceptions of the world and of ourselves. This theme is as pervasive and foundational to modern thought as fate was to Greek drama. No matter how skilled, thoughtful, tenacious, and heroic an individual effort, neither the culture nor fate can be ignored or avoided. Only by passing through them is there a chance of change or salvation, and even then success is possible only through the intervention of a great leader or a hero or the actions of the gods.

Culture and fate are different, though, in one important way. Fate is the work of forces beyond the human realm, both inscrutable and impervious to our entreaties or plight. Humans stand before it as Job before God: uncomprehending, powerless, and suffering. With culture it is different. While to those who are born into a culture it may seem as remote, powerful, and untouchable as fate or God, it is by its nature, in fact and by definition, a human creation. Because something in us humans needs certainty and a fixed universe of truth and value, we reify, even sanctify, our cultures. We do so, I think, because we understand how quickly the immutable and eternal universe created by our culture may dissolve amid the transitions of individual and social life. This strikes all groups sharply and regularly in their need to educate their young. Here the group discovers that the world it inhabits is dependent upon its efforts, and particularly its efforts to educate the young into the world defined by its culture. Most would prefer their culture were somehow built into the order of things, an integument of the physical and spiritual universe transmitted at birth as instincts are in animals. Regardless of how painstakingly cultures strive to convince their members they are part of a natural order, the flow of an aleatory existence makes them aware of the fact that culture is not a gift of the gods or of nature but of the tribe, people, race, or specific time and place and its particular substance and spirit.

It is this connection of culture and education that will be at the center of this book. Cultures require education to transmit their world views and prepare the young for the everyday demands of life in their society. Education, in turn, requires culture to give it form and content. If we wish to understand education, then we must begin with this wedding of education and culture. We also must understand that the marriage may not be healthy, happy, or productive. As in marriage, the source of problems is usually in one or the other parties or in their relationship. It is the same in this. The problem either resides in the culture or in the educational system or in the particular relationship that exists between them. Wherever the problem resides, it is the inseparability of the two that is important.[1]

During the current decade long debate over the problems of education in the U.S. much of the discussion has centered on one side of this relationship of education and culture. The primary focus has been on the schools as the source of the decline and as the means of reversing it. The discussion, as a result, has centered on the shortcomings and failures of our schools. The solution, accordingly, has been to reform the schools and thereby improve their quality and effectiveness. For some this has meant going back to the way schools were when they were good and scores were high; for others it has lead to the creation of new ways of educating appropriate for our times.

Some in this debate, however, have directed their fire toward the culture. They see the problem as a problem of the larger culture. As do those who focus on schools, these critics vary in their complaints and in their specific understandings of the shortcomings of our culture. But all of them, strange companions that they often are, locate the primary problem in a failure in the general modern culture that shapes both the general lives we live in modern American society and the specific life of the schools.

A good, and I think representative, example of this approach is an essay by the political scientist Benjamin Barber about our current problems in education. He argues that the education debate of the last decade "reeks of hypocrisy." We condemn the schools and moralize at the young for doing and being just what the larger society is. The young understand our culture better, or at least are more honest and open about it, than all the pontificating scholars and critics who attack teachers, students, administrators, parents, and politicians in defense of high, literate culture. The young learn from the streets, television, advertising, movies, public policy, consumer patterns, and salary scales what we value and live for. Barber insists that the problem is not that the young don't know anything but that they know too well what we adults and our world are all about. They don't learn it, though, in schools but by looking at "television, in the boardroom, around Washington, on Madison Avenue, in Hollywood." The real lessons are the "deeds and reward structures" of our society which teach that "we honor greed, we celebrate materialism, we worship acquisitiveness, we cherish success, and we commercialize the classroom—and then we bark at the young about the gentle arts of the spirit." If the schools teach a curriculum whose aim and content is in opposition to these lessons of the culture, they will have a hard time of it and most likely little effect on the young. The young already know what they must do to be successful. The problem, therefore, is not in our schools, but in ourselves and the culture we have created. Progress in improving education is possible, in Barber's view, only through an honest examination of our culture and a genuine commitment to the nobler ideals of our tradition.[2]

Barber's point is Margaret Mead's at the end of **Growing Up in New Guinea**:

> Not until we realize that a poor culture will never become rich, though it be filtered through the expert methods of unnumbered pedagogues, and that a rich culture with no system of education at all will leave its children better off than a poor culture with the best system in the world, will we begin to solve our educational problems.[3]

If she is correct and Barber is accurate in his depiction of the condition of our culture, then all the talk and effort aimed at reforming schools will fail. The problem is with the culture and unless we turn our attention to the more fundamental and difficult task of reforming, reconceiving, revitalizing it, all our efforts will be in vain.

We in the U.S. have a long history of seeking solutions in the wrong places and of shifting responsibilities away from their primary sources. It has been easier and safer to assume the basic culture is healthy and turn instead to tinkering with its methods of operation or its inefficiency than to run the risks associated with a closer consideration of its nature. The school system has been one way our culture has avoided looking closely at itself. When problems have arisen the schools have been called upon to fix them. Expanded responsibilities, new programs, and a steady rise in importance as a social institution have placed it at the center of current discussions of how to address our current economic and social problems. Our faith in schools is so great that when they fail to solve our problems we are convinced that we merely need to adjust the schools so that they will accomplish what we need done.[4]

Whether or not this faith can carry us through this time depends in part on what we want the schools to fix. Our current problems are compounded by the fact we are not clear about exactly what we want to accomplish. If we want to be more competitive with Asian and European companies, then we may be able to adjust the schools so they can produce the workforce we need in order to compete. If we are worried about what and how much the young know about the world in which they live, then we can have the schools teach it to them and through grades and tests push them to learn it. If it is our cultural heritage we wish instilled, then we can restore the older core curriculum built upon the "great tradition." If it is the values and behaviors of the young we are concerned about, then we can intensify civics education, teach the basic republican virtues of the nineteenth century school, and create moral education programs suited to our time. They are each difficult, but they are possible. And in fixing them we may solve the problem: the graduates of our schools will be able to staff the economy, understand the way the world works, understand their culture, have our values, and behave themselves well enough to keep things running. But when we are done and assess our success, the problem will still be with us because Mead is correct. All the teachers and pedagogy, curriculum and equipment, money and time, can't put back together again a school system whose underlying cultural foundation is poor.

This is only to say what many have said. Our problems lie deeper than we are willing to admit in our efforts at reform. Unless we consider the condition of our culture, which is for me the deeper source, we will continue to produce superficial and short term solutions while the real problem roams among us, unattended and unknown, endangering not only our reforms but the framework of our educational and social system. And more than these, and more important, it threatens the lives of the young by denying them an education and a life within a rich and whole culture.

In the next chapter I will describe the deeper problems of our culture that make it too poor to provide, either in school or out, a good education to the young. But before doing so, I want to be clear about the tenor or tone of what I have and will say. There is a certain grimness in these introductory remarks, in both the topic and my attitude toward it. The theme is the poverty of our culture and the specific ways in which it fails our society and each of its members, and in particular its failure to truly and completely, in the best, grandest, noblest sense, educate the young. But my sense of this is not apocalyptic, as it often is in works dealing with this subject in this way. I am not claiming we have reached a moment of decision on which hangs the destiny of America or the West. Nor do I think we have arrived at a watershed in history, one of the great turning points in the course of events and civilization. The force of history is not at our backs pushing us to act or perish. We can, I imagine, go on as we have, experiencing the normal troubles and changes, for a long time. Perhaps we cannot and the flood will come soon. I don't know. What I do know and what propels this work is the belief that something is wrong with the way we live, something that lies at the heart of our culture, and that until we understand it and change it we will remain a poor culture hopelessly attempting, against all the odds, to educate our children into the greater and richer possibilities and gifts of the life that all our modern wealth and power should have made possible for us, but haven't.

Chapter One
The Problem

Modern man is the victim of his own disillusionment; he has been
disinherited by his own analytic strength.[5]

Ernest Becker

The first and greatest problem of the modern world is this: we have
created the means of disillusioning ourselves without the countervailing
power to affirm new beliefs with confidence and certainty. The
withering gaze of our modern analytical, critical, empirical methods
and mentality have impaled us on the central conundrum of our time:
the modern critical temper permits us neither our ancient securities nor
new ones. We are stranded, unable to create a new world view and
society, and torn between the appeal of a past unacceptable to our
modern mind and a present we can't clearly define or accept.

Regardless of where people fall on the virtues and vices of modern
thought, they are nearly all concerned about the failure of the age to
create some new order. Some are more upset than others, seeing it as a
Faustian bargain that will damn us, while others see only a natural
process through which we must and will move. But they agree that a
condition exists and are disturbed about its immediate consequences for
our culture and lives. Generally, the fear is that in our efforts to escape
the too deeply cut channels of pre-modern thought we have lost the
ability to cut channels at all. For Robert Pirsig "the stream of our
common consciousness seems to be obliterating its banks, losing its
central direction and purpose, flooding the lowlands, disconnecting and
isolating the highlands and to no particular purpose other than wasteful
fulfillment of its own internal momentum."[6] Specifically, the problem

is that we don't know where the momentum is carrying us or whether it is carrying us any where at all. If it is creating some new world we wonder how we will live in it, if the transition has become a permanent condition we worry that we won't be able to tolerate it. Consequentially, we moderns don't know what we believe or how to order our lives or in what to put our faith, confidence, and commitment.

This disillusionment isn't, though, what troubles us most. It is, rather, that we suffer from an infirmity of our hearts or souls or spirits, of the invisible core of our lives and our selves. So much in the modern way of thinking and living ignores or discounts this realm of our existence or misconceives away the delicacies of its designs and the power of its needs. But it is difficult to give it a name and to grasp it firmly enough to bring our powers of observation to bear upon all its insubstantiality, to force it under a microscope to find out what it is made of, what it can do, what it really is. We have tried to fix it within our modern ways of thinking, but usually have failed, concluding in the end that either the something that we thought there is insignificant, refusing as it does to offer the hard data necessary to earn it standing in science's eye, or that it isn't there at all. Our modern reason, the reason of the head, cannot understand it, cannot penetrate it and know it, yet it cannot leave it alone; it cannot accept a separate realm of knowledge and knowing, one with its own way of knowing and being, with its own principles and truths that will not permit themselves to be impugned by our modern reason.

This modern reason, when unbridled, partially blinds us. It limits, distorts, or undermines our vision and so blinkers us that we cannot sense the powerful and evanescent world that moves beyond its sight, a world that bumps and bruises our hearts. What troubles this modern rationality is the suggestion that these reasons of the heart may be primary and that from them we derive the first principles of our human existence. But modern reason is not troubled. It has usually won and in victory condemned its competitor to the disreputable fringes and obscure reaches of the modern world. Only the steady whisper of the heart, like the murmur of a seashell, remains to remind us and to keep us attentive to all the "common things that crave."[7]

I

Teach me, teach me to believe,
For to believe's to be.[8]

Edwin Muir

Of all the things we crave, there is nothing so important to us and so pressing in our everyday lives as the matter of our beliefs. Our lives are shaped most by the answers we give to a simple question: What do I believe? Answers to this question arise from the circumstances of our existence as inhabitants of particular times and places, and from our general and peculiar human nature and condition. They address nearly all aspects of our lives, from the great issues to the mundane matters of everyday life, from questions about God, the purpose of our lives, the faith we affirm, and the ideals we honor, to the friends we keep, the activities that fill our days, and all the particulars that together constitute our lives.

It is particularly difficult for us late modern Americans to define and settle these matters of belief. Most of the time, we can't settle them, so we change the subject, shuffle around, and go on living. We are unsettled by our inability to believe and act deliberately and with conviction, and by the difficulties we face in navigating a course for our lives without a fixed reference or compass of belief.

Even in the best of times humans have struggled with what to believe and how to live. It comes with our humanness. For some periods of history it is more difficult than others. Ours is, I think, such a period. How can we of the modern enlightened age expect individuals to believe and have faith if the societies in which they live, that raise them and shape them, are without any agreed upon belief and lack any effective means of arriving at one. The historian Carl Becker claimed that our modern age is notable for its having lost or discarded or destroyed the first premises upon which to build itself and with which to explain and justify its ways to itself. Modern man has become, in his view, a "foundling in the cosmos abandoned by the forces that created him. Unparented, unassisted and undirected by omniscient or benevolent authority, he must fend for himself, and with the aid of his own limited intelligence find his way about in an indifferent universe."[9]

Much of modern thought arises from this modern condition. The Existentialists, both theistic and atheistic, have bemoaned this sad fact of our modern life. Their modern man is the representative characters in modern literature, the typical patient of psychotherapy, and the faceless, anomic, alienated individual of sociology; all are tormented by a modern world unable to satisfy their needs for a firm foundation for their lives, a secure and safe mooring in belief, an orderly and comprehensible world, and a sense that life has a meaning and purpose that transcends the trivial pursuits of daily life.

The world has been saved, so far, the full effects of the torments and dislocations of such social changes and the periodic dissolutions of beliefs by the stability and faith of the common people who are truer and more steadfast in their convictions than the upper classes and intellectuals whose minds are too easily captivated by the new thinking and who too often became rootless and uncertain, for all their knowledge and insight, about themselves and the world. The British television program "Upstairs, Downstairs" captured this. It described a post-war Britain in which the serving classes upheld the old values and beliefs while the ruling classes wavered and were lost amid the turmoil and change brought by the war. Tolstoy's work, too, contrasts the sophistication and emptiness of much of upper class society to the firmness, simplicity and faith of the peasants.

For us, though, the effects of change and the disruption of the system of belief are more egalitarian. Michael Harrington in his book **Politics at God's Funeral** claims that the singular quality of our late twentieth century world is "that masses of people in the West no longer know what they believe."[10] People don't know because the culture is, in fundamental ways, disordered and lost amid the welter and confusion of all the ideas and facts it so prolifically produces. Allan Bloom, representing an altogether different tradition of thought from Harrington, nevertheless sees the same disturbing characteristics in the young: thoughtlessness, shallowness, passionlessness, and convictionlessness.[11] Ernest Becker, a social scientist who wrote during the 1960s, drives the point further with his contention that "modern man is not 'wiser' than men at other times; rather, he is almost wholly without ideals....We live in an epoch that has almost wholly abandoned the quest for the ideal."[12] Ideals are the blooms on systems of thought and belief, from which come the finest fruits of human life: deep commitment, a sense of duty, devotion to a cause and its truths, a belief in the purposefulness and meaningfulness of life. It is precisely these that our age of analysis and disillusionment has been unable to create. It is these we associate with the ideals and energy of earlier ages and which make us long to have what they had and lament the barrenness of the modern world we have created. It is this inability to define and affirm first premises and ideals with which to create a new system of belief and a modern life of passionate devotion and human, and cosmic, significance that makes our land of plenty seem so like a waste land.

This may seem surprising in an age racked by culture wars fought by armed camps and wandering bands of zealots fervently committed to their beliefs and to the destruction of one another. But behind the bombast and the battling of these groups, usually small and loud and amplified by the media, sit the rest of us, wavering, a little confused, waiting for something to believe, seeking some order that transcends the guerrilla wars and the shifting currents of a mixed-up age, wanting beyond all else a world ordered and whole in which to sink roots, grow and blossom. These are the ones who lament, in their darkest moments, the world we have created, the world T. S. Eliot laments in his poetry:

> What are the roots that clutch, what branches grow
> Out of this stony rubbish? Son of man,
> You cannot say, or guess, for you know only
> A heap of broken images, where the sun beats,
> And the dead tree gives no shelter, the cricket no relief,
> And the dry stone no sound of water.[13]

Poets write to expose us to this reality, we wish to avoid it, knowing we cannot bear it. We cannot escape it, though. We find it in the everyday lives we live and in the world around us. The reality is still there: the images are still broken, the soil is still dry and lifeless, and we are still without shelter and roots.

I have seen this fact of contemporary life in my teaching. It has been a regular experience of mine that students who have many and strong opinions can not, when ask to define their basic beliefs, do so. When I put questions to them about their beliefs, questions like "What are the basic beliefs of our American culture?" or "What do you, as an American, believe?", they have difficulty answering (they are upper level undergraduate and graduate students). Even with some guidance and explanation the responses come without much clarity or conviction or confidence. The initial response is silence, then some struggle to figure out an acceptable and respectable response, some declarations and fulminations from those few who have strong convictions, and then slowly a fumbling toward a platitudinous declaration noteworthy for its tentative and rudimentary nature. It is almost always the case that they don't know because they have never really thought much about it as a matter of belief, only as some content in a course (for those who have taken such courses) or the empty rhetoric of politicians or religious leaders (for the cynical).

It is much the same situation when I discuss with students the ethics of teaching, a subject, particularly for graduate students most of whom are teachers, that should be less academic and abstract, closer to home, work, and everyday life. Most students, after some initial confusion and resistance, find the ethics interesting and can apply them to their teaching. They do so, though, only after demonstrating two things: all ethics are relative and matters of opinion and they are usually irrelevant to the practice of teaching because most ethical issues are best resolved by technical or managerial means. As often as possible, and it seems to be nearly always possible, ethical dilemmas will be skirted by reordering the situation so that the dilemma will disappear. While this is reasonable, the determination and consistency with which students employ it as the preferred method reflects the dominance of the rational-technical approaches at the expense of social-ethical-philosophical ones. The dominance of this way of thinking in our schools and society explains such responses, but not completely. They are also the result of students' uneasiness with and inability to work with the other approaches. Invariably, the first responses to the case studies I give them consider technical solution without ethical content, an approach which requires no ethical deliberation. Only when pushed do some of the students acquiesce to the idea that there are fundamental issues of conduct and belief at the center of the cases. And for these it often becomes uncomfortably clear that they have little idea what beliefs they have and how they apply to the practices of their current or future teaching. The responses of these midwestern and very traditional students are interesting because they are drawn from a region and population that is not crippled, supposedly, as directly or severely by the dilemmas of modern thought and culture to which I have been attaching responsibility for this situation.

The pervasiveness of this condition was exemplified for me recently when I attended a lecture on race relations. The lecturer, a prominent researcher and surveyor of the American mind, had been part of a project that created and administered a survey to determine the attitudes of Americans on race issues. He had used the latest and most sophisticated instruments, ones capable, he was convinced, of getting behind the public postures and dissemblings on the sensitive issues surrounding race in our society. One of his findings was of particular interest. The reigning view in public opinion scholarship is that of all our attitudes those about race are some of the firmest and most deeply held. To test this the surveyors decided that they would do more than merely ascertain individual attitudes. They would also present counterarguments for each position taken by a respondent. They found, and this is the interesting finding, that forty four percent, nearly half, could be persuaded by these arguments to alter their position. To the lecturer and his associates this was heartening in that it meant race relations and attitudes were fluid enough to permit change. We weren't destined, like characters in a Greek tragedy, to live out a script set by our long-standing and destructive racial attitudes, fated to fulfill the curse laid upon us by our previous sins. To me it says something in addition to this, something different and disheartening. It is something I have seen in my teaching in both the secondary school and the university. Many of us aren't certain what we believe about anything. When we have consciously held beliefs at all, they are so shallow that even moderate disturbances at the surface churn up the water all the way to the bottom. When we do believe in something it is with very little certainty, confidence, or commitment, so little we cannot withstand challenges to it and aren't willing to venture, in its defense, any action that might entail risk, sacrifice, or sustained and arduous effort. Too many of us, more than the forty four percent found in this survey, both adults and children, can't pull our experiences and ideas together into beliefs that guide and give purpose to our lives. We are mixed-up in that we can't seem to get things straight and firmly set in an order that can both persuade us of their value and truth and persevere in the face of new experience and different ideas.

Two things are assumed here. One is that belief is necessary to us as human beings and is, as Muir's epigraph to this section insists, part of our nature as humans, as essential to us as our autonomic system and as instincts and programmed behaviors are to animals. This necessity arises in part from the fact that we do not possess those characteristics of animals that build them into their physical and social environments, and we therefore are by nature creatures whose world is open and uncertain,. In this condition we are condemned, or blessed, by the unavoidable experience of perplexity and doubt (which is a natural part of our existence and not the invention of modern thought and Descartes), and by the demand such a nature and condition place upon us to order the world for ourselves and create for ourselves a place in nature, society, and the universe. To be human, then, requires we create and believe, for creation shapes itself according to vision, which is, when conscious, the articulation of our deepest and most important beliefs. To act at all demands choice among the possibilities presented to us, and to choose, when something vital is at stake, is to act on the basis of belief: for us, as William James said, "there is some believing tendency whenever there is willingness to act at all."[14]

This everyday and inescapable need to believe, finding itself in an age congenitally incapable of satisfying it, has become the root of our problem. The natural human habitat, the place that we arrange for ourselves and call home, is of the mind, and the mind, always vaporous and elusive, achieves its integrity and force from the structures of belief that give it form and content. Without these we are homeless. The requirement, though, is not simply whether to believe or not to believe, for, as James says above, we certainly act and therefore believe. To live at all it is impossible not to. Our particular modern problem lies, rather, in a certain class or level of beliefs addressing, using Tillich's name for it, our ultimate concerns or, for James, the momentous decisions and beliefs of life.

When Muir in the epigraph weds believing and being he is considering these ultimate, momentous matters of human life and belief. In the closing lines of his autobiography he tells us where his believing carried him: "To comprehend that [the infinite web of things and events] is not given to us, and to think of it is to recognize a mystery, and to acknowledge the necessity of faith."[15] It is in these indispensable matters that our present problem of belief lies. Muir's faith is the highest and the greatest human passion, without which we are less than human and prey to the meaner devices of a world that is content, even satisfied, when we are being less than human. Whatever hope is possible for him is vouchsafed him through this faith and the belief that it makes possible. Whatever home is available for him is built out of them. Here alone is a home for the human heart. Here only can he be fully human.

It is impossible to escape the religious or spiritual tone of these ideas. It is also difficult to avoid the conclusion that this view of human life calls each individual to a higher life—to the pursuit of the ideal, the rigors of the active life, and the call to the heroic. Even if this is beyond the abilities of each individual, and it isn't in my opinion, it must still be a fundamental constituent of the social or cultural world in which all individuals live. A call to this higher life is the essence of what we call religion. It describes what is essentially a religious conception of human life.

This religious conception takes many forms, including secular ones. When it does it has, I think, the same source and the same nature. An example is Andre Gide's foreword to the novel **Night Flight** by Antoine de Saint-Exupery. In it he offers a vision of human life that is secular yet shaped by the human needs I have described. Gide declares that "man's happiness lies not in freedom but in his acceptance of a duty.... Man is not to seek an end within himself but to submit and sacrifice his all to some strange thing that commands him and lives through him."[16] In Gide's man, the poet Muir with his mystical conception becomes the active and engaged partisan and pilot Saint-Exupery wearing a flight jacket and running mail across the Andes or fighting against the Nazis; here it happens not in the mind alone but "in a marrow-bone," in the active rather than contemplative life.[17] Gide's man becomes, in the classical humanistic tradition, noble and heroic, both more than man and the quintessence of being human.

In Saint-Exupery, too, we find another vision of the religious life. He talks of spiritual decay, of humanity's long descent into a dark abyss, an abyss filled with "refrigerators, politics, card games, and cross-word puzzles." In his **Wartime Writings** he dreads the results of this descent, and in particular the effects of World War II on all he cherishes:

> But what will remain of what I have loved? By that I mean not just people but customs, certain indispensable intonations, a certain spiritual radiance. What will remain of the farmhouse lunch under olive trees of Provence, or of Handel? The things that endure, damn it. What is valuable is a certain ordering of things. Civilization has to do not with things but with the invisible ties that join one thing to another.[18]

What we love, the web of affections and sympathies that are the tangible forms of our deepest, most fundamental beliefs, those invisible beliefs that tie the world and experience together, are endangered in the modern age. Without them we will be lost, homeless, less than human. Saint-Exupery is lamenting the slow dissolution of the commitments, devotions, and actions that makes such a life possible for us and through which we are fully alive and human. These carry us beyond ourselves in service to something greater than ourselves. In the forms of everyday life, Exupery's customs and small enduring orderings of our lives, give a radiance and a substance to the airy essentials of our minds and hearts.

The nineteenth century British art critic and essayist John Ruskin embodies this kinship of the secular and religious visions. Born and raised a strict methodist, in mid-life he had a profound experience of doubt and rejection while visiting a small church in Italy. From this experience forward he was no longer a professing Christian; he was instead an ex-Christian whose heart was, and remained, tempered by an essentially religious disposition. What remained, the residue of his former faith, took the form of an unrelenting attack upon the English culture of the mid-nineteenth century. At its heart was the demand that life be lived for something higher, something containing the capacity for faith, belief, duty, and the passionate pursuit of an ideal. His denunciation took the form of a question that contains most of what has been said above: "Now, lastly, will you tell me what we worship, and what we build?"[19] This seems a religious question, or a question containing a specifically religious content, demanding an answer only a religious person would be capable of answering. But it is so only in the sense that all basic questions about human life are religious, for religion and the religious, regardless of their sources and the authority of their claims, are inescapably human concerns, distilled by the alembic of the human soul and mind, into the answers we require to be fully human in our world and life.

Even John Dewey, no friend of the transcendent, theism, or religion, called for a common faith based upon the ideals of individuals and communities, and he called it a religious enterprise. This faith unifies and guides human experience. Through it our experience and our lives become   meaningful and complete. His modern view undoubtedly narrowed the materials with which to conceive and construct this faith, and his dynamic and evolutionary philosophy of experience contributed to the fragmentation and uncertainty of modern life and to the dissolution of the encompassing and unifying faiths characteristic of ancient and medieval civilizations. But the important point about Dewey, one that is often overlooked, is that his work both tears down the old structures of belief and insists that a new foundation be laid, one which unifies human experience on the basis of the beliefs and ideals of a common faith. For Dewey, too, the questions at the heart of human experience and life are what we believe, what we worship, what devours us, and to what we dutifully commit our lives.

The issue is, therefore, not religion and not whether the ideas presented so far, centering on belief and faith, are incompatible with modern secular society and life. The capacity for creating belief and faith exists today, as it has at all times in human existence. It is an indelible attribute of our nature. The issue, instead, is whether we modern people believe in much of anything, whether we have much or any faith, and whether, when we do manage to have either one or the other or both, they are able to do for us the things Muir, Gide, Exupery, Ruskin, and Dewey insist they must do. I contend, and this is the premise of this book, that we modern Americans, both individually and collectively, live without these beliefs, ideals, and common faith, and that the modern world we have created for ourselves is too weak and unstable to bear the full weight of our human need.

Is this too severe a verdict on our times? We have churches, a generally accepted political philosophy and system, a general, if often contested, code of public morality, and a system of laws and institutions that embodies the contents of all of these. Moreover, all of these are the products of the cultural traditions and history that, regardless of the debates that center on them currently, have shaped us and, in some form, will probably continue to do so in the future. We are anything but empty vessels; it would be easier to argue we suffer from a surfeit of beliefs and faiths rather than a dearth. We are overwhelmed by new beliefs, new lifestyles, movements, philosophies; and the old ones are continuously reborn or reformulated for the new mass markets of television or radio or self-help books. If we have all of these, how can the grim picture above be accurate?[20]

I grant the oddity, perhaps irony, of our situation. Being richer in so many ways, richer than all the past tribes and nations, chieftains, pharaohs, popes and emperors that have come before us, we are at the same time poorer than they were. How can we explain this situation? Great wealth, of itself, builds only great expectations, but nothing more. Children of the wealthy, afforded abundant opportunities, can and do fail to achieve wealth of their own—in money, accomplishments, talents, character, position, or respect; for all of their assets they are poor. So it is with us as a society. But why? Because, in part, our heads have been turned by the plenty that surrounds us—the materialism of the marketplace has seeped into our souls—and has led us to believe that quantity and variety are both enough and good for us. It has muted the voice within us that asks the questions. In part, too, it is that the answers we get are too many and too confusing and the authorities no longer command our respect or have the ability to convince us that their ways of ordering and explaining things are credible or worthy of our commitments. We are like shoppers at a mall who cannot figure out what to buy because of all the choices and claims. All that was solid has indeed melted into air, leaving us with more, but less certain and valuable, objects of belief and faith. The old guidelines, the maps we need to chart a course through the world, have either disappeared or multiplied, and in either case we find ourselves confused and unsettled.[21]

II

The problem of belief is also present in our changing conceptions of the hero and the heroic in our culture. Northrope Frye contends that European literature has for fifteen hundred years moved from the mythic and romantic image of the hero to the enervated, confused, diffident modern ironic anti-hero. The change is more than a change in literary convention. It is a matter of culture. Literature reflects and expresses the condition of the culture that produces it. It helps define the culture's image of itself. Our attitude toward heroes and the particular heroes we create for ourselves reflect something fundamental about who we are as individuals and as a culture. The modern anti-hero, a lost, confused soul, able to see through all the pretensions and the sham but unable to be clear about what to believe and how to live, finds some solace in being honest about his plight. They achieve a sort of salvation in standing against the illusions and deceptions of the world they live in. As Shakespeare's fools are often wise, these irresolute, often pathetic characters are often heroic in their ironic, unheroic, modern way.

Heroes should represent the ideals of the culture, not its banalities. Ours, therefore, should be those appropriate to a modern, industrial, and democratic society built upon the republican and Judeo-Christian ideals of the ancient and western traditions that once inspired, harnessed, and guided its dynamic energies. Throughout our history we have produced a pantheon of such heroes, from the intrepid explorers and faithful and persevering settlers to the defenders of liberty and the titans of industry. All were honored for their distinctive virtues and their heroic deeds, some for steadfastness in faith, some for physical courage, some for knowledge and skill, and some for their distinctive entrepreneurial virtues of drive, hard work, inventiveness, determination, pluck, and discipline. This modern model of the heroic is based upon an ideal of character, a vision of the good life, and a belief that the struggle for success, either earthly or heavenly, was a worthy, even noble, undertaking. Society held these before the young as a light with which to see and guide their lives.[22]

These earlier models of heroism have faded. Some were perhaps less worthy than we once thought, as were some of those we honored for embodying them. Because American culture is dynamic and pluralistic it has always had difficulty agreeing on the model and image of the heroic. This difficulty was compounded in the nineteenth century when the ethos and the routines of industrial society transformed American society. A new model was added based on the heroic entrepreneur and the ethos of commerce and consumption. John Ruskin saw the principal weakness of this heroics of the industrial age and its "Goddess of Getting-On." What great buildings, he ask, will house the new heroes and the new faith, and more importantly, what great scenes or symbols will be sculpted or painted on its portals? He answered—

> And hitherto it has been a received opinion among the nations of the world that the only right subjects... were heroisms of some sort. Even on his pots and his flagons, the Greek put Hercules slaying the lions, or an Apollo slaying serpents, or Bacchus slaying melancholy giants....On his temples, the Greeks put contests of great warriors...the Christian put

carvings of angels conquering devils; or the hero-martyrs exchanging this world for another....

But what will we put on our public and sacred objects?

> I could carve something for you on your [merchant] exchange worth looking at. But I can only at present suggest decorating its friezes with pendant purses; and making its pillars broad at the base, for the sticking of bills. And in the innermost chambers of it there might be a statue of Britannia of the Market, who may have, perhaps, advisably, a partridge for her crest, typical at once of her courage in fighting noble ideas, and of her interest in game; and round its neck, the inscription in golden letters, "Perdix fovit quae non peperit." Then, for her spear, she might have a weaver's beam; and on her shield, instead of St. George's Cross, the Milanese boar, semi-fleeced, with the town of Gennesaret proper, in the field; and the, "In the best market," and her corset, of leather, folded over her heart in the shape of a purse, with thirty slits in it, for a piece of money to go in at, on each day of the month. And I doubt not but that people would come to see your exchange, and its goddess, with applause.[23]

A hollow heroic enshrined in a building dedicated to a false goddess!

Our current system of heroics fails to offer us, both young and old, anything better than this. By any standard of heroics, ours today are banal and without the general public commitment and confidence necessary to make them the living faith of the society and culture. When the young, in search of the resources to build a worthy and acceptable conception of life and how it should be lived find themselves without a strong hero system or with one they find essentially ignoble, they will reject the culture, as they did in the 1960s, or find a substitute to which to devote their lives, as they do today in the pursuit of money, consumer goods, pleasure, and long life. Modern popular and youth culture, and the trappings of mass, consumer culture, fashion a mock heroic to fill the void left by the failure of the culture to define a richer and grander heroic and meaning for their lives, one able to allow them to "feel heroic in the plan for action that their culture has set up."[24] This is what has happened to them: they have the mock heroics of the cinema and television, popular music, youth culture, and sports, all of which exist because of the vacuity and the ignobility at the heart of the adult world.[25]

The effects of these failures—of belief and the heroic—are that individuals and the society are without a clear, worthy, and solid system of beliefs and heroics. Jackson Lears, in his book about the birth of modern American culture between 1880 and 1920, sees us as modern mariners adrift on a tenebrous sea, without moorings or ballast to hold us down, weightless and unreal. The sea surrounding us is shrouded in fog, our bearings are unclear, and the light has failed us. We mariners are uncertain and confused. Our grip on the world has been loosened and we have fallen into a torpor; cut off from an ordered and purposeful world and life, our lives have become meaningless and we feel helpless and impotent. In such a state, we are ruled by the most elemental desires for comfort and security, our everyday lives are consumed by banalities, and our interests and concerns are without range or depth or intensity. In Lears' view, we have become incapable of "real living."[26]

Chapter Two
A Modern Condition

Humans at all times and places have sought to know who they are, where they came from, and why they are here. It is the common human enterprise and has preoccupied us since we emerged from the obscurity of our origins. Equipped with whatever means the times made available, human groups have striven to envision a world and create a society commensurate with their images of themselves as human beings. Throughout most of human existence, our means being pitifully inadequate to the task, we have filled in the vast empty spaces of our ignorance with products of our extraordinary powers of imagination; we made up what we were too poor to ascertain by other means. Life being brutish and short much of the time, there was consolation in our ability to imagine a world capable of meeting our basic needs, of giving us hope, and of providing security amid the aleatory and meaningless vicissitudes of everyday existence.

Today we are these same human beings struggling to achieve the same understanding. But now we are armed with means powerful enough, or so we think, to enable us to arrive at a comprehensive and definitive answers to these perennial questions. Driven by this often overweening confidence and a Faustian ambition, we imagine we possess necessary means of answering all our questions and controlling our destiny. Reason and science are the means. With them, a final and full understanding of ourselves and of the world is possible. The dark corners of consciousness and the vast dark continents stretching beyond it, once beyond our understanding, may now be opened and explored and understood. The illusions we spun to assuage our ancient fears out of the inexhaustible resources of our ignorance, and all the satisfactions they granted us, now can be replaced by the hard facts of modern thought. With this new knowledge will come liberation, human fulfillment, and a human existence in which we are rational, secular, and free from the manifold oppressions of the past.

But it hasn't been as simple and good for us as we imagined and hoped it would be during the long aspiring millennia. Two things in particular have unsettled us. As we saw in chapter two, in the effort to achieve a modern understanding we first discredited previous understandings, overturned the old orders, and in consequence thoroughly disillusioned ourselves. As preliminary work, this clearing of ground was necessary and good, but in itself and without some new growth, it was merely destructive. The great gift of our ages has been its ability to unmask and discredit all of our mistakes, wishful thinking, and pretensions, and, having done so, to show the "naked shingles of the world" and the "foul rag-and-bone shop of the heart."[27] These dislocations are tolerable if there is hope of a resettling and reordering on a new, more secure foundation. If this doesn't occur, the unsettlement becomes endemic and pathological. Modern society suffers from this condition, the result of a too thorough and continuous disillusionment and from an inability to find a way forward and beyond this condition to a new life.[28]

We have, however, in the face of the dissolution of the old world views and the weakening and fragmentation of earlier systems of belief. Ironically, this new definition has become a second source of unsettlement for us. While bemoaning the loss of a unified world, we did what we could to reconstitute it because to do nothing was impossible for us, to live at all requires some order and some understanding. Like weeds into a garden, a conception has grown up around us. And what is the new conception? It is of a human being who, being rational and desirous of freedom, is without illusions, a doubter by disposition, suspicious of all claims to truth except those meeting the most rigorous requirements of rationality and science, skeptical that even claims meeting these requirements can bring us to certainty about ourselves or the world, convinced that the works of the imagination in the past had conjured worlds that do not exist, determined to free us from bondage to all the forces within culture, and confident that a better world is possible through the emancipation and extension of the dominion of reason and freedom. It is a grand vision of both the limits and the possibilities of life. At its heart is the transformation of what in most cultures and at most times in human history would have been considered vices into the cardinal and dominant virtues of the culture. The transition has become the destination, the process the content, growth and change the entelechy. We have affirmed, formalized, and institutionalized our disorder.[29]

This solution runs against the grain of our human nature. We require more than a never-ending nomadic existence. What we need is "an integrated world conception into which we fit ourselves with pure belief and trust," one that will allow us to be at home in a universe commensurate with our yearnings for truth, certainty, and salvation from the very transitory existence the modern age wants to extol as both necessary and good.[30] Such a solution guarantees us only a nagging uneasiness, a feeling of being unmoored, a splintering of the basic structures of belief, a debilitating uncertainty, and a sense of being lost in the society, world, and cosmos.

I

The modern experience of homelessness has been used to describe our condition. It is a powerful metaphor that touches a primal chord, something elemental in us, and that sounds the depths of our humanness. It is difficult to define it. Loren Eiseley, in his naturalistic and metaphysical way, suggests that it is part of our human nature. In his essay "The Brown Wasps" he describes the practice of brown wasps sticking faithfully to their hives, to the midwinter end clinging to their old nest, "the spring hive still resounding faintly in their sodden tissues" until they drop into the oblivion of the snow. What is it the wasps want? They want their place in the hive, a place at the heart of a life and a world abuzz with an activity that once resonated through the whole of their organism. He believes "this feeling runs deep in life; it brings stray cats running over endless miles, and birds homing from the ends of the earth. It is as though all living creatures, and particularly the more intelligent, can survive only by fixing or transforming a bit of time into space or by securing a bit of space with its objects immortalized and made permanent in time." He goes on to tell of a displaced field mouse that strove mightily to recreate its home in a flower pot in his apartment after being evicted from his field by a housing development, and to describe pigeons displaced by the demolition of the old barn-like El stations in Philadelphia. He ends with a story of his own youth and the tree he planted with his father. As an old man he longed to return home to see the tree. The tree was no longer there and hadn't been for years. He ends the story like this:

So I had come home at last, driven by a memory in the brain as surely as

the field mouse who had delved long ago into my flower pot or the pigeons flying forever amidst the rattle of nut-vending machines. These... were all part of an elusive world that existed nowhere and yet everywhere.... In sixty years the house and street had rotted out of my mind. But the tree, the tree that no longer was, that had perished in its first season, bloomed on in my individual mind, unblemished as my father's words. 'We'll plant a tree here, son, and we're not going to move any more. And when you're an old, old man you can sit under it and think how we planted it here, you and me, together.'
'Do you live here, Mister?' he [neighborhood boy] shouted after me suspiciously. I took a firm grasp on airy nothing—to be precise, on the bole of a great tree. 'I do,' I said.[31]

For Eiseley this is part of the process of living and its echoes the themes of poets throughout history: the passage of time, the struggle with impermanence, the never-ending human struggle to find a place for itself in an often foreign and indifferent world, the sense of loss, and the eternal sadness of the cycle of life. It is also testimony to the urge of humans to build a home for themselves out of the stuff of their lives and to inhabit it even if they do so only in the recesses of their souls. Such a home orients them, gives them bearings, and weaves them into a full tapestry of human relationships and emotions that enrich their lives and make them fully human and fully at home.

But this home, so natural in Eiseley's view, isn't the natural product of all human social arrangements. What most animals receive as a gift of their nature, as a part of the order of things, humans achieve only through great effort, a part of an eternal human struggle that is engaged age by age, generation by generation, individual by individual. Some ages and cultures are more successful than others in making themselves at home in the world. Our modern age has not been.

The sociologist Peter Berger, in **The Homeless Mind**, claims this sense of homelessness is a characteristic of our age. He conceives this homelessness in two forms: a narrower, everyday sense and a grander, cosmic sense:

Modern man has suffered from a deepening condition of "homelessness". The correlate of the migratory character of his experience of society and self has been what might be called a metaphysical loss of 'home.' It goes without saying that this condition is hard to bear.[32]

Modern humans are lost souls in a culture which has lost its center of gravity. We are orphans lost in the cosmos, to use Walker Percy's phrase and to capture Pascal's sense of our modern forlornness. We are insecure, displaced, without a calling to gives us direction and purpose.

We lack the vital connections engendered and nurtured by having a clearly defined and stable place in a social order, an ordered and loving family that also has a role and place in a larger social order, a sense of the historic continuity of personal, familial, and social life, and a participation in something which endures in the face of the whirl of time. This is compounded by Berger's metaphysical loss: of a comprehensible universe, of fixed and authoritative moral principles, of a transcendent dimension in which we participate, and of a feeling of belonging to a larger and more important existence which fills our lives and our societies with purpose. The yearning and the need of Eiseley's wasps are those unsatisfied and unmet in Berger's modern world. It is here that the human heart breaks upon the exigencies of modern life.

The essayist Joan Didion provides a second example. She describes the same human and modern problem in "On Going Home." She has returned to her childhood home with her young daughter to celebrate the daughter's birthday. Immediately she is engulfed in the way of life of her family, of its particular people, the talk and the histories, the land and the river and the graveyard, and the old stories and personal lives in which all have a part, and the old cups, and the feeling of an old, old connection that runs in the blood or shows itself in some ghostly way in the contours of a face or an inflection of the voice. For a time she is re-absorbed into the home she once had but has left behind. She ends with a poignant affirmation of her own home and, at the same, a wistful and ambivalent reflection on what she has to bequeath to her daughter:

> In the evening, after she has gone to sleep, I kneel beside the crib and touch her face, where it is pressed against the slats, with mine. She is an open and trusting child, unprepared for and unaccustomed to the ambushes of family life, and perhaps it is just as well that I can offer her little of that life. I would like to give her more. I would like to promise her that she will grow up with a sense of her cousins and of rivers and of her great-grandmother's teacups, would like to pledge her a picnic on a river with fried chicken and her hair uncombed, would like to give her home for her birthday, but we live differently now and I can promise her nothing like that. I give her a xylophone and a sundress from Madeira, and promise to tell her a funny story.[33]

Like Eiseley, she is held to this home by the iron filaments of time, place, experience, and affection. There is something here that abides and draws one back. But Didion has a child of her own and her little girl's life is very different. She won't have a home of the sort either Eiseley or Didion are talking about, for we live differently now. Instead she will have an abstract, disembodied, cosmopolitan, rootless existence--- a xylophone, a sundress from Madeira, and a funny story. She will not, that is, have the attachment of spirit to a time and place and a morality that grows, like the bole of the tree, out of the soil of a particular people, time, and place.

Home, then, is more than a place to stay, eat, and sleep, where one keeps the many threads of her life organized and safe. It is more than the many and extraordinary places humans have made habitable, from the holes in the ground of anchorite monks to the igloos of Eskimos, the vast empty spaces of the aborigines, or the concrete and glass of a modern city. We all have a world to live in, a time and a place of a particular type that defines the parameters of our life. It goes deeper than these and touches a fundamental dimension of our humanness. Whether a habitation becomes a home depends on the qualities it possesses, its specific and special shape and substance, the way it holds together, and the degree to which it provides the breadth and richness of experience and meets the basic needs of those who inhabit it.

This sense of our modern homelessness, of being lost and cut-off, of being stray atoms out of any orbit, birds without a place to perch, is a common feature of modern thought, particularly that part called antimodernism. Jackson Lears' study of antimodernism in America describes a whole tradition of thought informed by this sense of our modern condition. His book, **No Place of Grace**, while directing most of its energy to the thesis that antimodernist thinking was co-opted and absorbed into the modern commercial and consumer culture it passionately and habitually condemned, is also a portrait of the dislocation of modern life and thought. Like the wasps of Eiseley or Joan Didion and her daughter, we find all that we have grown accustomed to, have built a life around, is gone and we fly aimlessly around our new world, disliking that it is not the same and that its new furnishings are too few and tawdry to meet our needs. The new house is not a home, and something, some fundamental part of our humanness, is harmed as a result.[34]

William James argued that the single most important thing about a person was the vision of the world he carried around within himself and that gave a shape and hue to all that he believed, thought, and did. It was the specific inclinations of the individual mind and spirit that made the world in which he lived intelligible and meaningful; it unified the welter of the world and the buzzing confusion of experience by fitting it together in a sensible and orderly whole. When conscious and systematic it may take the form of a world view or a personal philosophy of life. A person's vision is the thread that weaves together the manifoldness of each personality and gives it an integration and integrity. When the vision is vital, whole, and healthy it illuminates all elements of life, giving each a particular meaning and place in the schemes of individual, social, and cosmic life. This is what too many do not have today. It is the critical and crippling shortcoming of our age.[35]

But vision in James' sense does more than hold together experience. It holds it together in a specific way. The command a vision exerts on an individual arises from more than the ordering and understanding it brings to the everyday experiences and world of its possessor. If this is all that is required, then the theories of science or history could be called visions, as could the emotional states of the young, the calculations of adulthood or the musings of the old. They all, in their own ways, fashion or define a world in which they think and live. But these definitions are not enough. They are closer to the "knowledge" that enables birds to order their worlds with the precision required to migrate year after year the same thousand mile airway or the mechanisms that propel ants to organize themselves like Egyptians building pyramids or the vast assemblage of cells that make the extraordinary complexity of living organism work so effortlessly and well or even of a competent teacher who masters technique to create an orderly and efficient classroom. While all of these order their worlds they do so without the qualities that make human vision distinctive: a moral imperative, an ideal, and a passionate commitment to them. It is these that make humans more than another mechanical contrivance of a material universe that has wired him into a closed system of instinct and environment. These make men more than cells, ants, birds, or technicians and they make vision in the human domain more than mere order or unity. In human hands it becomes order and unity with some moral purpose, driven by a passion, and directed toward an ideal. We are homeless, in part, because in the twentieth century West we are without these.

From the eighteenth century forward we have struggled to conceive and affirm a coherent, comprehensive view of the natural, social, and human world that would tie the manifold experiences of humans into a unifying and satisfying whole and create rich and fulfilling human communities. From the prophecies of Marx about the preparatory role of capitalism on the road to socialism and communism, through John Dewey's claims that the integration of thought might not come in his lifetime but would certainly come if we pursued the path of science and democracy, to Martin Buber's and Alisdair MacIntyre's call for a return to the catacombs to sit out the darkness and confusion of our disordered age and wait for the return of order and light, modern thought has been aware of the inadequacies of its age, the transitional nature of its particular world, and its struggle to create a common vision and stable order for the age.

One important consequence has been a dislocation of earlier forms of community. We have failed to create forms of community strong enough to contain the energies of modern life and channel them into rich and humanly satisfying conventions of community life. Our age is not unique in this. It has happened before. Disruptions of social and personal relationships, rips in the social fabric and in personal lives, have occurred throughout history. One example is the Hellenistic period that followed the decline of classical age of Greek civilization. Ken Benne, an educational philosopher, used **The Golden Ass** of Apuleius to depict the dislocations of an age moving from the "rootedness in a rich community life to some unknown and unpredictable form of life." Lucius, its main character, wandered in an expanded world over which he had little control and which he found difficult to comprehend. It was strange and foreign; he felt alienated, disconnected—homeless.[36]

Didion's daughter is then a modern Lucius. But she is different from him in one important respect: her chances of seeing the time of transition through to a new unity and community are not good. There is something distinctive in our modern dislocations. We may not simply wander and wait for the reconstitution of a settled and established social order, one possessing a rich and nurturing community. Why? Because we suffer from more than the inescapable transformations visited on temporal life by birth, growth, decay, and death—from the long, slow, climb up and the short slide down, and by the vicissitudes visited on most lives and societies in the course of time. We are different in that the changes confronting the modern world have been, from the beginning, world shattering and revolutionary in their nature and impact. Since the fall of Rome the world has not seen such a monumental reordering of its ideas and institutions. The old laws and rules no longer work. Traditions and folkways have been replaced by enlightened modern practices, old knowledge has fallen before the gleaming engine of modern thought, change has become continuous, faster and faster, relentlessly moving us into an exploding future, and established relationships no longer bind or obligate one person to another. All seems ready to fall apart even in a new world with monstrous powers of organization and control. These are more than the everyday tribulations of earthly life. They are the effects of a cataclysm that has torn up roots and cut moorings and dissolved the center that held together an entire civilization. That center is always the set of beliefs, the body of information that supports the beliefs, the intellectual framework that embodies and justifies the world view constructed from the beliefs, the institutional and social system that give a body and everyday existence to the beliefs, the moral principles and ethical maxims that give a face and personality to the society. When all of these are integrated and the disparate threads braided into a working synthesis, then the center is strong. When strong it can give direction and meaning to the lives of its members, tell them what is possible and good for humans, give them a sense of their place in the order of society and the universe, and provide them a variety and richness of meaning in their lives and in the life of the society. In doing all of these, it provides individuals and groups with an understanding of the world and human life, of its cardinal and guiding beliefs, and the singular and enlivening faith that fortifies them against the doubts and troubles that accompany human existence. It is a paideia upon which community can be built and the young can be educated. It is a vision in James' sense, and a home for the lost souls of Eiseley and Didion.

Bruce Catton, in his autobiography **Waiting for the Morning Train**, describes the Michigan of his youth in the early twentieth century. He captures the pervasiveness of the sense of the passing of one world and the struggle of an inchoate yet undeveloped new one to be born. The lumberjacks came and went, as did the farmers, then came the train, and cars, and the world of his childhood disappeared forever. He and his generation were caught in the middle of it, in both its excitement and its insecurity:

> So we live as the Indians of Lewis Cass's time lived, between cultures, compelled to readjust ourselves to forces that will not wait for us. There is no twentieth century; the twentieth century is simply a time of transition, and the noise of things collapsing is so loud that we are taking the prodigious step from the nineteenth century to the twenty-first without a moment of calm in which we can see where we are going. Between the nineteenth century and the twenty-first there is a gulf as vast as the one the stone-age Indians had to cross. What's our problem? We're Indians.[37]

Indians or not, we wrestle with the destructive consequences of this condition. Such a state unsettles humans, throws them out of balance, disturbs some elemental demand of our nature for ordered and unified experience and a settled, harmonious existence; we wish to be in one stable, consistent, and safe world, not hanging between two or bumping aimlessly around in a lost or confused one. We can begin with the fact of transition, but we cannot end there. Humans won't tolerate it; something there is that doesn't love such a condition and wells up in us the desire to be rid of it. Out of this condition arises the struggle to create a new unity, a new, modern world view, an integrated system of thought. And it is a struggle fired by our human rage to order and understand the world and ourselves, and by a belief that the order and understanding possessed by our ancestors has slipped away from us, been somehow misplaced or forgotten or destroyed—lost. We too, still, are Indians.

Our problem is a social as well as an individual concern, and probably first of all a social one. James' concern with vision as the defining characteristic of an individual can be expanded, and has been in the discussion above, into the larger context of the role of vision in the life of a group or formal society or, larger still, of a culture or civilization. It does for the group what it does for individuals—orders experience, gives a unity of meaning and an integration of thought, provides a moral framework and an understanding that shapes and informs all aspects of social life. These are good for individuals, indispensable to a whole and healthy existence. They are also good for and indispensable to societies and cultures. It is this social and cultural context that is central in the discussions to follow. What is the vision that defines who we are and the world we create? What community is possible with such a vision? These are the central questions. If a person without a vision is a pitiful and incomplete thing, less than human, so is a culture without a unified vision of itself.

Judged by this standard, our modern age would seem to be pitiful and incomplete. Few things are certain for us in the twilight of the twentieth century. The very idea of certainty itself has been dismissed by many as beyond our reach. Like skeptics who know only that they cannot know, we are certain only of our uncertainty. Such a state leaves us homeless, without a vision to guide us out of our current darkness, and the pawn of all the extraordinary powers we hoped would liberate and fulfill us.[38]

Chapter Three
The Search for a Science of Man

Somewhere there has occurred a fatal misplacement of the real.[39]

Walker Percy

Every age has its consuming passion. The Middle Ages was consumed by a passion for the kingdom of God. The road to follow was the one to grace, faith, and salvation in a world filled with the will and grandeur of God. The modern age is consumed by a passion for knowledge, wealth, and progress. Its road travels across a secular landscape in an age of prosperity and enlightenment. One sought the ancient and holy city of Jerusalem, the other the modern and secular city of New York or Moscow. These different passions require different authorities and sources of knowledge and certainty. For the Middle Ages it was the church, Christian scriptures and theology, and the belief that both the church and the scriptures had authority granted and vouchsafed by God. For the modern age the source and authority have been modern science.

Mark Twain claimed that too much of a good thing is bad (with the exception of liquor, when it is just right). In the case of cultures or civilizations this is only partially true. They often gain their power and success through carrying their defining idea or vision, with passion, confidence, and nerve, as far as it will take them. Whatever greatness they achieve is often tied to the pertinacity with which they pursue their peculiar beliefs and abilities. It is also, and this is the wisdom in Twain's witticism, their downfall; the virtue of their single-minded belief and devotion becomes too narrow and dogmatic to understand and control a world that is dynamic, heterogeneous, and complex.

Science has been our particular modern genius. The greatness of our age is the result of our wholehearted faith in it and its ability to provide us with truth, power, control, and wealth. Science has repeatedly proven itself deserving of this confidence and devotion. In two hundred and fifty years it has transformed the world and our lives. The knowledge and power it has made possible are undeniable. Regardless of whether you like or dislike the new world it has created, or think it good or bad, and regardless of whether in the long run this world will become a Frankenstein monster that turns on its creators and destroys them, it has bestowed upon us many benefits. It has been, and remains, our consuming passion and the singular talent. It has defined our civilization and created most of what is distinctive and great in our age. It has instructed and habituated us to see its ways of thinking and doing things as good; it has induced in the general public a great faith and trust in its power and truth.

All philosophies, works of art, and cultures are inspired by a single overriding impulse or intuition which stains their work and lives and leave them with "some simple residual pattern of insight."[40] Science is this pattern for us and is at the heart of our insight into ourselves and the social and natural worlds in which we live. It has infiltrated the way we see and think about everything. We have become so accustomed to it that it is by definition the standard by which all else is measured: the normal and healthy are in agreement with the normal impulses and insights of the culture, the abnormal and sick are out of touch with or in disagreement with these impulses and insights. For us, this has meant becoming accustomed to thinking it the only good and reasonable way to be and to live. And, as such singled-minded devotion has in the past, it has blinded us to important dimensions of ourselves, our society, and the world around us. Too much of our good thing, science, has indeed become a bad thing for us.

With the Enlightenment we undertook to employ all the powers of the new sciences to understand ourselves. The aim was to create a science of man capable of giving us a true understanding of our human nature. With such a science we could know, once and for all, "what was behind all of man's peculiar urges, what was he trying to do as a vehicle of the life force..., what were the possibilities of life on the level of human existence; and conversely, what was there about the human condition that was hopeless?"[41] This has been the great hope of the modern era. This new science would free us from the superstitions and illusions of past human efforts to answer these questions. With such knowledge the ordering of human life would become as rational and orderly and progressive as those worlds being fashioned by the natural and applied sciences.

Through this science the human longing for a better world would be possible for us. We stood before this new human prospect like "some watcher of the skies/When a new planet swims into his ken;/Or like stout Cortez when with eagle eyes/He stared at the Pacific...."—riveted by the wonder and the possibilities of a vast new world.[42] This has been an abiding faith. Even in the gloaming of the second half of our century, chastened but not vanquished, we affirmed it: "Let me just say that if I have changed my views on many things, this change leaves intact, I believe, the basic premise of the Enlightenment which I feel we cannot abandon and continue to be working scientists—namely, that there is nothing in man or nature which would prevent us from taking some control of our destiny and making the world a saner place for our children."[43]

Lured by the often overweening confidence of science and a Faustian ambition, we imagined we possessed the necessary means of achieving a final and full image of ourselves and an understanding of the world. The dark corners of consciousness and the vast dark continents beyond it, previously beyond our understanding, may now be opened, explored, and understood. Imagination and intuition are no longer necessary except as they serve reason and science. The illusions we formerly spun out of the inexhaustible resources of our ignorance to assuage our ancient fears are to be replaced by the hard facts of our modern thought.

The triumph of science, however, has not been so easy or decisive. We have struggled from the beginning with the question of what role to grant the new sciences in our attempts to understand ourself and society. We have been aware that where we look to find answers determines what we will find and that the kind of thinking we use to arrive at these answers determines the kinds of answers that are possible, and that the answers, whatever they are, shape the world we inhabit. We are aware, too, that science might not by itself, or as defined by the natural sciences, be the way to a satisfactory and complete answer.

We have also worried about the consequences of letting this new science loose in the wider human world beyond natural science. We were aware of its power to unsettle us. In the effort to achieve a modern understanding it could discredited our previous understandings, overturn the old orders, and in consequence thoroughly disillusion us. One of its gifts has been its ability to unmask and discredit all of our mistakes, wishful thinking, and pretensions. The philosophers relish this demolition and engaged in it with pleasure. These dislocations are tolerable if there is hope of a resettling and reordering on a new, more secure and better foundation. If this doesn't occur, the unsettlement becomes endemic and pathological, and we moderns become a people living in a waste land, amid the wreckage of beliefs—we become Catton's Indians.

There has been little agreement on what this new understanding of humans should be, and particularly on the critical issue of the acceptable parameters and contents of this modern science of man. From the beginning, there have been very different approaches. Soren Kierkegaard, for example, looked within himself and through self-analysis arrived at his truths. In an 1835 journal entry he wrote that "one must know oneself before knowing anything else" and concluded that "it is only after a man has thus understood himself inwardly and has thus seen his way, that life acquires peace and significance...."[44] His means were philosophy and psychology guided by a thoroughly religious sensibility, his world one where individuals search for truth and God by sounding their souls. John Dewey, in contrast, looked to the natural sciences and philosophy for his method and to human experience for his subject matter. His views were mostly exterior vistas filled with the cleaner, harder lines of a human life and society built upon democracy and science. While for Kierkegaard it was introspection and the singular self and individual, for Dewey it was intelligence and the social self. The twentieth century social scientist Ernest Becker, whose science of man will be considered later in this chapter, sought to combine the strengths of both Kierkegaard and Dewey: an introspection in the service of science, a science that merges with religion in its pursuit of a full theory of human nature. His science of man continues and completes Kierkegaard's work. It attempts to answer one basic question: what is it that humans want and need to be healthy, happy, and whole? Armed with an answer to this question he could turn to the task of constructing a society and a world that would meet these human wants and needs. Science was the indispensable instrument in achieving his objective but it was the innermost self or soul of humans where he sought his answers.

We have learned from these attempts that the answers to our questions will not come quickly or easily, or with the certainty we had hoped for. Instead of a straightforward project supported by a consensus among those directly involved, we have experienced a protracted struggle over its methods and content. Most important, and most divisive, have been the disagreements about human nature: the realm of its possibilities, the definition of the necessary and the good for human beings. Through a long struggle we have learned that the methods of modern science are not so easily applied to realities beyond the natural sciences. The modern efforts to know ourselves, that began in the Enlightenment, slowly discovered the difficulties of transmuting a science of earth and stars into a science of man and society. What the Enlightenment began the nineteenth and twentieth centuries strove to complete. We are still struggling with it today.

It is this modern struggle to define a method with which we can finally understand ourselves that I consider in this chapter. I will range freely from Isaac Newton to the contemporary views of Ernest Becker and Colin Turnbull. The aim is to develop the theme of the first three chapters, which in sum is this. Human beings always reach beyond themselves. They aspire to a higher self and more meaningful existence. Human history and destiny are shaped by the longing and striving of humans to transcend themselves and overcome the natural limits of their human condition and the commonness of their everyday lives. There is something in us that insists upon more than materialism and secularism as the meaning of things, something that compels us to find deeper understandings and foundations of ourselves and the world, something that requires we believe that we have some significance beyond the regular running of organic and mechanical forces. Perhaps this insistence reflects the root of our problem. We are in the world but not satisfied with it: homo duplex, man and god at once, in and of this world yet of another different one at the same time. Our greatness may arise from this bifurcation in our nature, but so may our baseness and brutality. It may be a symptom of a native human pathology that condemns us to be both out of joint with the world and driven to bend the world and each other to satisfy the needs of our souls. And it is the source of all that makes humans great, of all human achievement, of all that elevates humans above the level of all natural life, of all that brings beauty, dignity, goodness, and nobility to human life. Whether we rise in glory or fall through folly, it is a single motive that drives us there. We seek more than the getting and spending of our natural energies and wealth. We seek a purpose and meaning for our lives that are richer, deeper, and more expansive than enlightened, secular society has offered us. We seek to participate in the life of a universe that acknowledges our place and purpose and that affirms that which is distinctive in our nature. We seek to stand in a special relationship to creation and God, and to find in ourselves some spark or fragment, some common element, of the glory and grandeur of that God.

These things above all else we have lost or forgotten, and left out of our calculations of human fulfillment. With the coming of the modern era, we felt that for the first time in history the limits of knowledge and power that had stunted and distorted the human prospects for happiness and fulfillment could be overcome. But we miscalculated. We misunderstood the nature of the forces stunting and distorting human life. Religion and the spiritual aspirations of human beings, and particularly their institutional and intellectual embodiments, became the **bete noire** of the new thought and were slowly ostracized from the mainstream of enlightened thinking. The two-sidedness of humans was reduced to one. The claims of religion and the spirit were reclassified as pernicious delusions. Natural man triumphed. The sweeping naturalistic reduction made humans one whole self-contained thing, but not a human being. It is this miscalculation, and the great reduction of the image of a human being that is at its center, which is the source of our modern dilemma and the subject of this chapter.

I

Alfred North Whitehead in **Science and the Modern World** describes the unsettling effects of modern science. In the seventeenth and eighteenth centuries the implications of the new science slowly became clear to some. Whitehead uses the "romantic reaction" to the new science as an example of this dawning awareness. The Romantics came to understand that the new science, in knowing and mastering the world, had lost touch with the common intuitions of human beings. The most important of these intuitions was that if life is taken as a whole, then it is more than a mechanical process and more than mere matter. Wordsworth expresses this point in his famous "We murder to dissect," and Whitehead picks it up with another line from Wordsworth's poetry: "witness the discord between the aesthetic intuitions of mankind and the mechanism of science."[45] The mechanistic view defines a universe that our intuitions resist, one where "The stars... blindly run" and the very scientists themselves have no place.[46] Whitehead concludes "that the standardized concepts of science are only valid within narrow limitations" and "that the important facts of nature elude the scientific method."[47] Whitehead concludes that modern science achieves two things: it systematically destroys that which it wishes to understand with its reductionist view of nature—Wordsworth's murdering—and it conceives a vision that is partial and inhuman in its violation of our concrete experiences and intuitions. Whitehead argues there is an alternative: a broader conception of nature as an organism rather than a machine, one in which the experiences and intuitions excluded by mechanistic science play the prominent part they do in the larger reality of our lives and the processes of nature.

This something that is left out has been, for those who accept the contention that it does indeed exist, a subject of interest in the modern age. There have been various ways of describing it, but all, I think, are variations on Whitehead's theme. Blaise Pascal, for example, a creator and master of the forms of modern rationality, expressed his reservations in words that have hung in the air for three centuries: "the eternal silence of these infinite spaces frightens me." These infinite spaces are the same ones that "run blindly." They represent an astronomical, scientific cosmos that is limitless, empty, lifeless, a giant machine, a dead universe that is both inhuman and Godless. What of us in such a cosmos? We humans are so pitiful and frail, stranded here as on an endless and empty plain, without signs to succor or save us or show us the way, without God's outstretched hand or any visible sign of redemption from this cold, inhuman reality. We cannot survive in so deadly a cosmos that denies in its nature our humanness. D. H. Lawrence says directly what Pascal does poetically: "In astronomical space, one can only move, one cannot be." He prefers "the astrological heavens,...the ancient zodiacal heavens, where the whole man, bodily and spiritual, walks in the magnificent fields of the stars, and the stars have names, and the feet tread splendidly upon—we know not what, but the heavens, instead of untreadable space." Part of Pascal would die in the new modern heavens, or would be removed from the natural order and driven so deep within him as to be all but dead to the world. But not in Lawrence's ancient heavens, where this part of him could come forth as the "prisoned self in us coming forth to live in this world.[48]

What frightened Pascal and Lawrence was Newton's universe. In it they found only silence and endless, lifeless space, a disenchanted universe. They were not alone, then or now. It even unsettled Isaac Newton, a lion of the modern kingdom. Morris Berman, in his **The Reechantment of the World**, portrays Newton as an example of the consequences of this process of disenchantment. Through a tableau of portraits of Newton, Berman shows the transformation of a young Newton who is a lively, gentle, sensitive, open, and happy soul into the dead-eyes, cold countenance, and forbidding attitude toward life of his later years. Perhaps the change reflects the natural course of aging: the toll of the years that takes the vitality and vibrancy of youth, in all its beauty and grace, away, that wears each individual down with the sufferings and sorrows of life, that tries and disillusions even the stoutest soul, and leads us to death, sometimes even before our bodies die.

But as Pascal's fright is caused by more than our natural human fate, so too Newton's transformation concerns more than the natural cycle of our lives. Berman sees in Newton's face "the tragedy of modern man." The tragedy is simply that the young Newton, the course of whose life Berman inflates to contain the essence of a whole civilization and its way of thinking, was consumed by the wonder of the life and world around him; he was convinced, as Goethe was later, that through watching and waiting he could win from nature its true nature and discover "God's presence in each element." This Newton, whose mind was mystical, hermetic and Christian, saw, with the eyes and the words of William Blake, a nature that is "God's censorium": the "world in a grain of sand,/ And a heaven in a Wild Flower," where you could "Hold Infinity in the palm of your hand,/ And Eternity in an hour glass." Blake never died to this view; he raged all his life against Newton's science and the modern age it was creating. Berman's Newton did. Nature, once alive for him, became dead matter, a machine, and God , once present, departed for a trans-natural world, leaving the laws of nature to keep the cosmos on its straight trajectories and blind running. Newton's laws, the great clockwork universe, all the beautiful precision, power, and cold calculations of his calculus, were his gifts to the age. Together they closed the doors and windows of his perceptions and transfigured the world he defined for himself and his age. In doing this, he became the everyman of our age, the archetypal modern man, the hero of our time.

Newton's struggle is that of our age. He strove to create an ordered and secure world upon a foundation which would insure what all humans and societies require: stability and certainty. He was a man for whom the elemental needs of human beings—to know, to believe, to have faith, to fit into a meaningful world, to have a purpose beyond physical survival and longevity, and to live within a cosmic order capable of containing the human soul—were the driving forces in his life and work. Unfortunately, the fruits of his struggle, still bearing today, have been bitter: the old man of Berman's portraits, the de-spirited, inhuman nature of modern science, the rational, mechanical, materialistic universe that conquered our age. So long as he was driven by the desire to discover the certainties and unities of the world and that world remained a living, human, spiritual realm, the fruit was succulent and sweet. When this drive was transmuted into, in William Blake's words, the science of the "single vision," he became the paragon of modern science, seeing with the inhuman gaze depicted in Blake's painting "Newton".[49]

But why did this happen to Newton? He seems an unlikely candidate. Deeply religious all his life, to the end aware of the limits of all his discoveries, he could as easily have devoted himself to the task of discovering the precise contours and measurements of his living God. For him to have been an architect of the scientific materialism which has become the dominant mentality of Western culture, which was built upon the conception of the universe he formulated, seems odd and paradoxical. There are two ways to explain the paradox. One is the more traditional picture of the devout scholar and scientist who spent his life studying both nature and God. He and other scientists created a mechanical model of the universe, unaware of its implications and repercussions. Newton the religious man did not imagine and would not have countenanced the extension of his model to all of reality, including human beings. There was no division in his (and in his fellow scientists') work, thought, or lives. They were not modern men as we are but men of the intensely religious seventeenth century. They sought God's design, will, and presence in the natural world. Unwittingly, they created a conception of reality and a method for discovering it that would, like Frankenstein's monster, turn upon its creators.

The conception and method were built upon this premise: "The lines of explanation that would be clear and valid for nature itself must be those that they could see clearly in the working of machines they might construct. Mechanics thus became the basic part of physics, and physics the basis of the whole science. Nature, when we came ultimately to know it, would be construed as a single vast and interlocking machine—the machine of machines."[50] They would find in nature what they presumed in their choice of method and model: a mechanical, lifeless, and highly abstract universe. Their descendants would follow its logic to its conclusion: a modern science that would deny much that is distinctively human in the universe and turn us too into nothing more than highly sophisticated machines. The irony of its birth and development is that the very forces that created it, the soul's quest for God and the mind's search for the truths of nature and nature's God were later banished from their system of the world. The authority for the banishment was the new science itself. This was the fatal turn and Newton as much as any single person steered us toward it. The world enthusiastically accepted his great work; his successors carried it to its logical conclusions.

But Berman thinks Newton's story is more complex than this. He envisions a different Newton from the one of science and legend. This is the Newton of the hermetic tradition who was more a magician than a scientist. His aim was to discover the answer to the riddle God had set before us in the natural world, a riddle which could be solved by pure thought applied to "certain evidence, certain mystic clues which God had laid about the world to allow a sort of philosopher's treasure hunt....He regarded the universe as a cryptogram set by the Almighty." The alchemical tradition, stretching back into antiquity, had devoted itself to penetrating this mysterious universe. Newton's early work is in this tradition. He saw himself as the servant of God, God's chosen one who would bring this hermetic/scientific tradition to its consummation by solving the riddle. He was God's prophet, a new lawgiver, a second messiah, bearing the new knowledge of the universe and leading the way to true and final knowledge of God's design.[51]

This Newton was caught, as well, in the social and political life characterized by the struggle to define the new society and determine the distribution and repository of power. It was primarily a political and economic struggle but it was also a battle between religious groups with different conceptions of God, church, and nature. The English historian Christopher Hill contends one of these groups, a diverse and splintered one, consisted of a collection of mystical sects committed, in their own ways, to the hermeticism Newton affirmed in his early life but later gave up. These radical sects believed in forms of social and economic organization anathema to the middle class and in a religion of "enthusiasm"—direct knowledge of God, possession by God, religious frenzy, and mystical experience—heretical to the established churches. Their view of nature was different from that emerging in the new science. The social, political, and intellectual (doctrinal) struggles went against these groups and they were suppressed. Many who had been sympathetic to the alchemical tradition converted, as least publicly, to the new society and science. Newton was caught in the middle of this struggle and the position he finally took was that of the winners—the middle classes and the victorious churches, who suppressed the whole range of dangerous irrationalities of these groups in the name of social order, true religion, and reason. They found solace in the "sober antidote" of the mechanical philosophy of the new science. For Newton such a conversion demanded he repress his interest in the occult and mask its continuing influence on his thought. As the new science gained strength he became its champion. It became necessary, as a consequence of his apostasy, to clean up his past by blotting out or obscuring his debt to and sympathy with the occult sciences. He became, at least publicly, the Newton of Blake's painting—the disembodied, de-spirited Newton of modern science, of a rational, mechanical, materialistic science that triumphed, in part, even over Newton himself. Then he became the true patron saint of modern science and put on the inhuman gaze of Blake's painting and the lifeless visage of Berman's later portraits. Ironically, it was at that point that he was proclaimed our guiding light. In reality, ironically, it was then that he became, as Blake knew and Berman argues, our great problem. When he could no longer find his answers—his order, certainty, unity, and truth—in a world that had a living, human, and spiritual reality, something happened to him and to all of us, something William Barrett called the "death of the soul" and Berman the "disenchantment of the world."[52]

In Newton's life we see the beginnings of the transformation of science. We can see in the growth of the aggressive and positivistic science of the nineteenth century the gradual loss of an element of our existence and a great hope in the possibilities of science and human life. What it did to Newton it has done in some way to all of us. We once experienced in science what the Dutch sailors of F. Scott Fitzgerald's magnificent final page of The Great Gatsby experienced as they stood before Long Island and the New World for the first time: "for a transitory enchanted moment man must have held his breath in the presence of this continent, compelled into an aesthetic contemplation he neither understood nor desired, face to face for the last time in history with something commensurate to his capacity for wonder." The conquest of the continent broke the spell for the Dutch and Americans, the triumph of science would turn the wonder into the disenchantment of an entire age.

The thinkers of the Enlightenment who followed Newton were devoted to his new science and to the hard-headed, empirical, and critical methods it employed. They were convinced that all efforts to disabuse credulous humans of their illusions, of their enchantments, were necessary and salutary. Their greatest achievement was in doing just this. They created an alternative way of knowing capable of providing humans with a better understanding of themselves, of the world, and of the meaning of human life. The result was, according to the historian Carl Becker, the replacement of the heavenly city of the Middle Ages with a modern one of their own. In the same way that there is more Christianity and God in Newton's thought than we moderns normally admit, there is, in Becker's words, "more of Christian philosophy in the writings of the Philosophes than has yet been dreamt of in our histories."[53] They, too, were of two minds: they furthered the development of science, worshipped facts and a reason harnessed to them, battered apart all first premises, and used their new light to burn away the dim and shadowy perspectives that had limited human understanding. There was liberation and progress in their new methods. There was also great danger. They proclaimed the progress, only partially understood the danger, and held them firmly together with their passionate faith in an enlightened and benign future. The genie of the new science was under their control, would do only good, and could be placed back in the bottle by the humans who had conjured it in the first place.

Like Newton, they were naive about this new method. It had its own assumptions. Carl Becker described them in this way:

> Since Whirl is king, we must start with the whirl, the mess of things as presented in experience. We start with the irreducible fact, and we must take it as we find it, since it is no longer permitted to coax or cajole it, hoping to fit it into some or other category of thought on the assumption that the pattern of the world is a logical one. Accepting the fact as given, we observe it, experiment with it, verify it, classify it, measure it if possible, and reason about it as little as may be. The questions we ask are "What?" and "How?" What are the facts and how are they related? If sometimes, in a moment of absent-mindedness or idle diversion, we ask the question "Why?" the answer escapes us. Our supreme object is to measure and master the world rather than to understand it.[54]

The faith of Newton and the Enlightenment was that this method would augment and enrich the meanings available to humans and culture, meanings which would resound to the glory of God (for the former) and of man (for the latter). In fact, it has done the opposite. The science of man that developed after the Enlightenment has diminished the "reservoir of meaning upon which the individual can draw" and, contrary to the great hope of the men involved, made personal and cultural life less rich and less meaningful.[55] Instead of amassing a great inheritance for later generations, it disinherited us. Man has become "but a foundling in the cosmos abandoned by the forces that created him. Unparented, unassisted and undirected by omniscient or benevolent authority, he must fend for himself, and with the aid of his own limited intelligence find his way about in an indifferent universe."[56] It has brought us to the cold and inhuman cosmos of Pascal and Lawrence.

Once the new science liberated itself from Newton's God and the Philosophes grand vision of Man and an earthly paradise, the new science implacably followed its logic. The genie was out of the bottle and on its own. Along with knowledge that gave the mastery and control it had promised, it bequeathed to later generations, in Erich Heller's epithet for nineteenth century German thought, a "disinherited mind." When released from the constraints of a broader vision of human existence and the cosmos, it exiled us to a place where

> the boundless faith in truth...will in the end dislodge every possible belief in the truth of any faith....Psychology will denigrate the creations of beauty, laying bare the tangle of unworthy desires of which they are 'mere' sublimations. History will undermine the accumulated reputations of the human race by exhuming from beneath the splendid monuments the dead body of the past, revealing everywhere the spuriousness of motives, the human, all-too-human. And science itself will rejoice in exposing this long-suspected world as a mechanical contraption of calculable pulls and pushes, as a self-sufficient agglomeration of senseless energy, until finally, in a surfeit of knowledge, the scientific mind will perform the somersault of self-annihilation.[57]

Slowly the potential of the new way of thinking, for harm as well as good, became clear. With increasing concern and urgency, we in the West have attempted to restrain it. Because of its great accomplishments it has had the power and prestige to withstand such efforts. But in its triumphs it has undermined itself. Even science, when subjected to its own standards, has found itself without a foundation: its great leap forward has turned it around on itself in Heller's somersault of annihilation. The realm of facts has been put to its own tests. When held up to the critical, analytic gaze seeking hard and sure facts, it has found its domains circumscribed and impoverished.[58] Wordsworth's murderous science has become C. S. Lewis' "analytical understanding" that "must always be a basilist which kills what it sees and only sees by killing."[59]

Newton and the scientists of his age were, in their way, such killers. So were the Philosophes of the century after them. But neither group were the free thinking, rootless skeptics of later ages, or the pure scientists and thoroughgoing materialists or naturalists to come later. They were, as was Pascal, caught between two worlds. The disenchantment had not descended upon them as it would on later generations. They had yet to lose a richer and more humanly satisfying vision of human reality.

The disinheritance to come involved more than the infinite cosmic spaces. It touched, too, the infinite inner spaces of the human heart and soul. They too might become cold and silent if they succumbed to the single vision of the new science. For Newton, who was deeply and thoroughly imbued with the language of the heart and the soul, there could not be silence, only a division of a self forced to live in two worlds. As Frank Manuel stresses in his biography of Newton, the mature Newton, the great man of science, was a man who silenced the heavens while the inner voice remained private and strong, a realm separated from the logic he imposed upon, invented for, the external natural order. The repressions involved in both his Puritanism and the requirements of his public and professional life as the man of science slowly sapped the vital energies that drove his work. But he resisted the intrusion of the new science into his interior spaces.[60]

The early modern thinkers were the first to struggle with this. The heart might have been silenced as easily as the heavens, but it was not. The reasons of greatest importance were those of the heart and they were not yet subject to the same laws that turned the cosmos above us into a collection of inert bodies obeying eternal physical laws. Newton affirmed what Pascal had affirmed before him, and affirmed it in the face of the new cosmos of science; he would safeguard this precious terrain from encroachment by an increasingly aggressive and arrogant scientific rationality.

Even in what seemed the toughest, least hospitable times, this other universe has survived in our experiences, intuitions and hearts. It is the human universe of Pascal's famous lines:

> The heart has its reasons, which reason does not know. We feel it in a thousand things....We know truth, not only by the reason, but also by the heart, and it is in this last way that we know first principles; and reason, which has no part in it, tries in vain to impugn them.[61]

The champions of the Enlightenment, thinkers of a different background and time from Pascal, acknowledged these reasons and understood this other universe. In words almost identical to Pascal's, they granted it a place in the order of things. Even Diderot declared that "the great thoughts come from the heart" and "Reason does not know the interests of the heart" and "Reason misleads us more often than nature."[62] They, too, never entirely dispense with a conception of the world which has survived, often in the catacombs, since then. It has remained the secret source of much of our thinking, clinging to our modern consciousness, above or below the surface of public and private discourse and consciousness, throughout the Age of Science with its limitless ambition and hubris and all its triumphs. They, too, were closer to the problems and torments of Pascal than to those later thinkers whose self assurance and confidence in the new science has required neither God nor Man as part of their hypotheses. And closer, too, to the dilemmas of an age impaled upon the competing enticements of two dramatically different universes.

II

It was during the nineteenth century that scientific rationality and its understanding of human beings reached its zenith. But during its time of greatest power and domination there were intimations of the challenges to come. Both within and without science, some were beginning to question the foundations and claims of modern thought and science. Reason was discovering its own limits. The awareness of the diversity of cultures in the world made Western science pause to consider its own presumptions. The clockwork universe of Newton seemed less a machine than an organism and the Cartesian demand for certainty and truth was increasingly difficult to achieve.

But more importantly, we were wondering about our modern image of ourselves. D. H. Lawrence, in his **Studies in Classic American Literature**, indicted Americans for their confidence in the power of light to drive out darkness and their faith that reason and light will triumph in the end; darkness, like sin, was merely an absence of the fundamental reality of things, not a countervailing or independent reality. In discussing the writings of Hector De Crevecoeur, Lawrence found a grand lie or evasion, a lie born of a refusal to look deeper into the human heart, a naive faith that light will triumph and vanquish all else, a refusal to plunge into the darkness to understand it, and a blindness to the intractable and irreconcilable nature of the world he sought to know and domesticate.

Lawrence made Crevecoeur the prototypical European of the Enlightenment facing a vast and savage wilderness. He was the new American engaged in the creation of an ideal world out of the wildness of the new world. He was Joseph Conrad's Kurtz played in a heroic and triumphant key. The problem, in Lawrence's view, and Conrad's, was that the new world was really very old: the new American man had to be created both from the light of the Europe he left behind and the dark savage forces of the new world he intended to civilize. But Lawrence's Crevecoeur sought no such confrontation. He sought new knowledge and a fuller understanding of humans. He wanted to use this knowledge to construct a new order and an ideal state. But he wanted to achieve this without soiling his lab coat or getting his hands dirty. He wanted, that is, to put into practice his pure Enlightenment faith in the goodness and rationality of humans.

In Lawrence's view, Crevecouer failed to pull it off. Why? Because he refused to, or lacked the capacity to, step beyond the bounds of his safe and self-contained white, western, rational, modern, civilized world, beyond the parlor, drawing room, or study. "Crevecouer wanted this kind of knowledge. But comfortably, in his head, along with his other ideas and ideals." He wouldn't go too near the wigwam or the woods, and instead stayed powdered and high-heeled in Europe. Yet he was determined to know, to penetrate the recesses of the human self, and to do so to "his own mind's satisfaction." Here was the rub, for his satisfaction rested in an ideal world of "pure sweet goodness," of reason, fraternity, equality and democracy—a nice, tame world. No, this wouldn't work and Lawrence caught him up for it:

> He wanted his ideal state. At the same time he wanted to know the other state, the dark, savage mind. He wanted both.
> Can't be done, Hector. The one is the death of the other.
> Best turn to commerce, where you may get things your own way.
> He hates the dark, pre-mental life, really. He hates the true sensual mystery. But he wants to "know". TO KNOW. Oh, insatiable American curiosity!
> He's a liar.
> But if he won't risk knowing in flesh and blood, he'll risk all the imagination you like.[63]

Lawrence was right about us, I think. We want "TO KNOW". We expend enormous wealth and energy on the production of vast bodies of knowledge that tell us what things are and how we may engineer the world to our needs. In pursuit of a better world, of our ideals of prosperity and progress, we have striven to exploit the powers given us by the genius of the modern age. We have had great success in this enterprise, we have prospered and transformed the world. But it is built upon a lie. It is the great lie of the modern age. It is the lie of modern science and its myth of the one method, one engine of truth, one reality susceptible to the one best and reliable method of science. We have been convinced by the extraordinary feats of modern science that it has the power to uncover all ancient mysteries, the laws of human behavior and life, and the secrets of the soul, including Lawrence's "savage mind,...dark, pre-mental life,...sensual mysteries,..."[64] And when it can't explain these things, it either reconceives them so it can or declares them non-existent.

The opposition ran deeper than a few voices in the wilderness like

Lawrence or William Blake and the Romantics. Albert Levi, in his study of modern philosophy, argued that of the two major problems of modern thought "the problem of rationality and the irrational" has been the most critical (the other being the fragmentation of thought). H. Stuart Hughes makes the same point central in his studies of late nineteenth and twentieth century social thinkers. Some of these thinkers came to the conclusion that "man as an actor in society...was seldom decisively influenced by logical considerations: supra- or infra-rational values of one sort or another usually guided his conduct" and the greatest of these thinkers came slowly to a "new definition of man as something more (or less) than a logically calculating animal." Modern thought came to these conclusions as an unanticipated side-effect of its effort to develop "theories of man's purpose—the definition of human nature..." and attempts to understand how humans achieve knowledge of themselves and society at all. It grew, that is, out of our modern methods and the pursuit of a science of man. By the end of the nineteenth century it was evident that such a science would challenge the primacy of reason in human life and even in the new science itself.[65]

There is a paradox in this attack on the primacy of reason. It was reason and science that discovered the irrational elements in our nature. In their enthusiasm to discredit and replace earlier forms of thought, particularly Christianity, and to create in their own image a new rational understanding and order, they created a weapon that could be turned on them. By the nineteenth century their new world, as thoroughly conceived and monolithic as the Christianity it challenged, was itself to be challenged at its archimedean point—the primacy it gave to human reason—first by the Romantics in the name of feeling, intuition, and imagination, and later, in Levi's estimation, by "the two great critical minds of the nineteenth century, those of Nietzsche and Kierkegaard," who for different reasons, denied this primacy: "Nietzsche denied the intellect to make way for instinct: Kierkegaard denied the intellect to make way for faith." Both opposed the dominant rationality of the seventeenth and eighteenth centuries, Nietzsche denying it in favor of the more elemental demands of the will and power, Kierkegaard for the subjective self and what Levi calls "the way of faith." I will discuss Nietzsche here, fitting as he does into my theme of the rational and skeptical mind cut from its moorings, seeking a new and safe harbor while carried by the current of his thought in the direction of nihilism.[66]

To understand Nietzsche's views on reason we must first consider their foundation. His work was based upon the idea that the traditional foundations of Western culture had passed away with the receding Christian cosmology. The new age had shipwrecked us: God had died, the old explanations had lost their force, the foundations of our beliefs and the moral order had fissured and could no longer support the system. From these we were liberated, without them we were confronted with the prospect of nihilism. This was the great theme of Nietzsche's work. The desperate passion of all his writings is to confront and resolve the shattering or revolutionary consequences of this fact of modern life. Walter Kaufmann, in his biography of Nietzsche, considers this the starting point of Nietzsche's thought and work, as does Erich Heller in his writing on nineteenth century German thought. Nietzsche's was the prototypical disinherited mind. He knew, despite the apparent pleasure he took in the demise of the old order and its God, this situation to be a disaster for humans and modern culture: "What did we do when we unchained this earth from its sun? Whither is it moving now? Whither are we moving now? Away from all suns? Are we not plunging continually? Backward, sideward, forward, in all directions? Is there any up or down left? Are we not straying as through an infinite nothing? Do we not feel the breath of empty space? Has it not become colder? Is not night and more night coming on all the while... God is dead."[67] Pascal's foreboding had come to life in Nietzsche's despair.

Nietszche, as Newton had been for earlier centuries, was to become a model and hero for an aging, less confident, and increasingly disillusioned modern age. He thought it his task to find what salvation was possible for us in such a modern condition. His affirmation of human will and power, the conception and apotheosis of the overman, was conceived as a way out of the crisis of modern culture, as the best, perhaps the only, avenue open to humans faced with such a world. The way out was to overcome ourselves and our condition: humans had to create themselves out of the void, to become more and better than human. It was no longer bearable or permissible to be merely "human all-too-human."

His new human, the man who would of necessity rise above Man, would be the heroic individual, the new man of the will to power who, out of the vital energies and the genius of his self, would make a world **ex nihilo**. Nietszche insisted we all walk this road alone and strive to achieve perfection in our individual ways through our will to exercise our powers to create our own lives. It is a road that winds through a country isolated from the contaminations—of politics, society, and common thought—of the modern Western world. Nietzsche attempted this in his own life. Out of his tormented soul and isolation, and through his work, he became Zarathustra, and then he became insane. Stripped of all the safeguards—of religion, of aristocracy, of settled and secure bourgeois sentiments and life styles, of the new bounding faith of the Enlightenment and reason, he played Lear to the age:

> Poor naked wretches, wheresoe'er you are,
> That bide the pelting of this pitiless storm,
> How shall your houseless heads and unfed sides,
> Your looped and windowed raggedness, defend you
> From seasons such as these?[68]

Nietzsche had no illusions about the power of reason. It is the "will to power", not reason, that defines humans and is the instrument of their triumph over themselves and their condition. Dionysus, not Apollo, provides the vital energies, the elemental, instinctual powers, that create the **ubermenschen** and the new order. Nietzsche wants a way beyond reason, particularly the reason of Apollo: the divine order, a harmony of restraint and moderation, a cool and serene symmetry in all things. He forces philosophy to confront the basic human material with which it works. He insists we push beyond the rational man of liberal, scientific, bourgeois, Christian society to understand ourselves. The modern age has destroyed all of our supports and illusions, all the old ideas and authorities. We are left only with ourselves. Out of our selves we can build a new world, but only if we understand ourselves first.

What Nietzsche did for philosophy, Sigmund Freud did for science. Using scientific rationality, he discovered a less rational and orderly human nature. Reason discovered the irrational and the Enlightenment's **novus ordo seclorum** trembled. The result was a more pessimistic view of humans, one different from, yet as deep as Calvin's, derived from an understanding of the non-rational roots of much human behavior, that challenged the entire Enlightenment and liberal conception of human beings. The hope for a Newtonian science of human beings was widespread in the eighteenth and nineteenth centuries. It carried with it the assumption that just as Newton's universe was orderly and lawful so must be the human world. It turned out that, as had been argued from the beginning by the challengers to the dominant science, that the reality from which Newton spun his precise and elegant theories was different from the human reality.

What Freud found in his lifelong scientific study of humans was a vastly different one from the clockwork of Newton's universe. It was one where reason played an insignificant rather than a decisive role, where clear and quantifiable facts couldn't be neatly ordered into systems of knowledge, and where, in Freud's view, a completely secular, highly complex, often pathological animal struggled to maintain itself amid the dangers—natural, social, and psychological—of its condition. In the face of such a reality, reason could not claim the reality it studied was governed by the laws of reason. It could continue to study it, confident that this reality, essentially irrational in nature, could be better understood, albeit incompletely, through the normal means of science and critical, rational inquiry.

But Freud didn't understand the implications of his findings as we have come to understand them. Both his work and his life went on as before. He lived in his rational, scientific, secular, and skeptical way, staunchly bourgeois, enlightened, and Stoic until the end. For him the world became thoroughly disenchanted. Freud became the model of scientific man. He lived the life of reason and science, accepted the shortcomings of both, and resigned himself to the folly of his fellow humans. The validity and lure of religion was rejected. It was replaced by open hostility to its panderings to the basest inclinations of humans. In understanding the basic drives or impulses of humans, those that ran in a torrent around his sedentary and fastidiously maintained bourgeois scholarly intellectual world, Freud came to see with the eyes of science what science in its enthusiasm for the purity of its new method had ruled out.

What becomes of the champion of reason and science when the world no longer seems rational, orderly, lawful, and when the evidence of science won't support Hegel's wishful thinking that the real is rational and the rational real? Having cracked asunder the shells of all our complacencies, does he go mad like Nietszche, or act as though nothing has happened like Freud? Most, simple saints of science, in their holy cells, carry on; they can live for the continuous pursuit of more understanding and bear the inevitable shortfalls and grim findings because they are sustained by the noble enterprise of their holy war against ignorance and superstition—the true and inspiring object of their lives. But can the rest of us? For us, such a stance is not possible. It unsettles us too much and leaves us cold, dissatisfied, afraid, and neither clear nor certain about who we are and what we should do.[69]

III

We have remained impaled upon these dilemmas. There is no escaping modern reason and science and no living with them. Convinced that they are the necessary means to greater understanding and a better future, we hold tightly to them; equally convinced that they somehow blind us and impoverish our experience, we push them away. As in a modern marriage, we want to live together and apart, welcoming the blessings and avoiding the impositions and entanglements of too consuming an intimacy. Even after the progress of the modern centuries we still struggle to satisfy ourselves about the central questions of life. Who are we? How should we live? What is the nature of this world in which we find ourselves? How can we know the truth about these and other vital matters? Ironically, the means used to answer these questions have instead created a new and fierce struggle over the answers.

At the center of this struggle has been the call to broaden and redefine science so that it could better understand and explain the subtleties of human beings and the growing evidence that the complexities and peculiarities of the universe were beyond its normal means. One response to this call has been the creation of a more humanistic, rather than positivistic, science. At the least, a humanistic science will include, rather than exclude or reduce to nothing, the distinctive elements of human life and experience; at most, it will become a full science of man. The next three sections will discuss attempts to define this new science in the work of scientist Jacob Bronowski, the philosopher Stephen Toulmin, and the social scientist Ernest Becker. In each, we will see, in their distinctive forms, the same struggle.

I will begin with Bronowski, the popular and eloquent champion of modern science. In both his popular and professional writings he argues that science, since the Renaissance,

> has been the spring within the movement of our civilization. In science and art and in self-knowledge we explore and move constantly by turning to the world of sense to ask, Is this so? This is the habit of truth, always minute yet always urgent, which for four hundred years has entered every action of ours; and has made our society and the value it sets on man, as surely as it has made the linotype machine and the scout knife and **King Lear** and the **Origin of Species** and Leonardo's "Lady and the Ermine."[70]

This science has shaped our world and it has been good. It is liberal, humanistic, and progressive. All of life falls within its scope and methods. It is a noble and monumental achievement of the our culture, magnanimous and gracious in its conquest, broad and subtle in its methods, confident and energetic in its approach, sensitive and humane in its vision.

Bronowski has a single-minded and boundless faith in this science. But it is too benign, too hortatory, too simple and one-sided a faith. It represents the early Renaissance view of science, before it took the quantitative, mathematical, positivistic turn after Descartes. The problems we face today arise from the conquest of the earlier science by the particular conception of it adopted after Descartes. Bronowski's view has too little appreciation of what science has become and is indifferent or blind to the consequences of the full application and triumph of this modern science.

When Bronowski claims that "all science is the search for unity in hidden likeness" and "science finds order and meaning in our experience" and that "it is... a hand reaching straight into experience and arranging it with new meaning" he gives us a grand vision of the great hope of science.[71] Certainly science has the power to arrange and give meaning to experience. But what is the new meaning it has given us? What is the new world of modern science? Bronowski understands science will recreate our world and the meaning it has for us; he fails to understand or acknowledge that science has not lived up to its promise. It has not given us the fuller and richer human order and meaning it promised. This failure has been the great event in the history of science. Bronowski, for all his studies of the history of science, particularly early science, doesn't appreciate the full force and effect of this failure. He doesn't seem to know what Pascal knew in his heart or Newton experienced in his life.

This oversight would be a venal sin of enthusiasm for and love of science if the problem with science weren't so central in modern life. It is not simply a tale of a good humanistic science pushed aside by a more brutish positivistic one. It is instead one whose theme is the internal, inherent flaw of the new science itself. The flaw is present in whatever form it takes. It dooms each one, no matter how benign and beautiful in conception and practice, and Bronowski's form is both, to fail in some important way. Neither humanistic nor positivistic science can provide the unity and meaning we humans demand. Of the two, the humanistic may be more vulnerable than positivism for at least the latter has in its own way attempted to conceive a unity and a meaning to existence based upon its guiding principles of certainty, systematicity, ahistoricity, and rationality—even if the world it conceives is a thoroughly blind, material, and inhuman one. Bronowski's science, in contrast, may lead, for most of us and for the culture as a whole, to an enervating indeterminacy, uncertainty, foundationlessness, and nihilism. For those who experience the dislocations and disorders of our scientific age it is reasonable to wonder where in his view we see the consequences of the liberation of human energies, the removal of the lids that have held the fertile and fractious human imagination in check since the classical age, a Pandoras box that, unlike the original and like so much that is modern, has released not only the good envisioned by Bronowski but, at the same time and from the same source, the evil. This is the intellectual dilemma of the modern age. Bronowski, thoroughly the man of science who embodied its model of a good and fulfilled human existence, did not sufficiently understand this dilemma. His model of the good scientific modern man is not a model of, or for, everyman.

Bronowski, though, was correct about the early science. Reason, the life of criticism, and the methods of science together conceived a new order. They were adopted with enthusiasm and the old was ushered out by a robust, triumphant, and supremely optimistic vision of an emerging age of reason, science, and liberty. The evil genie of this new order was still safely in the bottle. But it came out later, after the problems associated with the new vision had been, and still are being, combated. It helped us, in Percy's words, to "misplace the real," and brought us to the realization of the darker ends of the modern science: "To the degree that a man stakes everything on a goal isolated by the scientific method, to this same degree is he destined to despair."[72]

Bronowski's science is not Percy's. For him, science is the way to the real and can take us as close as we can come to truth. It would not bring us, by or of itself, to despair. It confronts us, certainly, with dilemmas. His book **Science and Human Values** begins in Nagasaki with a question: "Has science fastened upon our society a monstrous gift of destruction which we can neither undo nor master, and which, like a clockwork automaton in a nightmare, is set to break our necks?" His answer is no. The problem is not with science but in our failure to understand it and extend its good qualities to all of personal and social life. More science, not less, is the solution to our dilemmas. Scientists did not start the war or drop the bomb, thoroughly unscientific politicians and people did. Bronowski's science is heroic. It has been the force behind most that is distinctive and good in our modern world: "Men have asked for freedom, justice, and respect precisely as the scientific spirit has spread among them." Our modern problems are not the responsibility of science, but rather the consequence of not broadly applying the values inherent in the scientific enterprise, of "employing the body without the spirit." The spirit is this: "that the end for which we work exists and is judged only by the means which we use to reach it. This is the human sum of the values of science. It is the basis of a society which scrupulously seeks knowledge to match and govern its power." And the means are acceptance of the continuous nature of the search for truth, the "sanction of experienced fact," free and open inquiry, tolerance of different ideas, respect for individuals, and the "habit of simple truth to experience."[73]

Bronowski's book is an elegant statement of the scientific and pragmatic mentality at its best and ,I think, at its most dangerously shortsighted. It contains too little awareness of the potential of this science to cast humans adrift amid the ruins of established truths with only the lifeline of their habit of simple truth. If the habit of simple truth could so simply make sense of humans and our problems, and men were all healthy minded scientists and all scientists healthy minded men, then a meaningful and ordered human existence could be created like a theory in a lab, and the twists and snarls of our human condition could be cured by the clinical operations of his beautifully and broadly conceived vision of modern science. But the world and humans don't work that way.

To make a case like this against Bronowski might seem unfair and wrongheaded. He was a highly cultured and literate man who worked in both the sciences and the humanities and was seen by many as a leader in efforts to bring them together in an encompassing, unified, and humane science. His writings attempt to define the common ground of science and creative activity in other disciplines, a ground he conceived in the broadest, most ecumenical terms. He did not bruise the sensibilities of all the "softer" disciplines, as many have, by insisting on their being "hard" in the way of the natural sciences. He sought the common thread of imagination, the creation of understandings and meanings, and the pursuit of truth through disciplined inquiry and creative insight. He insisted all of these are present when humans strive to understand themselves and their world, regardless of the particular means by which they achieve them. Without them, all attempts will be flawed and a violation of the ways of true science and the honest, productive search for truth. They are equally necessary and present in what we consider, wrongly in his view, the opposing human approaches to truth: science and poetry.

It is here that Bronowski's position is most inspiring. At the heart of his thought is the idea that it is imagination and insight that are central in human life, for they offer us a vision that moves us toward truth and beauty and goodness. Both science and poetry produce such visions, are in fact the two most powerful sources of vision in human life.

Science without it is mere technology, mere doing; poetry without it is only fancy prose or pretty and moving music. The vision makes us human because it makes us the makers of ourselves and our world rather than passive objects moved by events to destinies beyond our control or understanding. Bronowski envisions a science of man built upon this understanding of science. It is a human science, moral in both its methods and ends (as he argues in **Science and Human Values**), both an ideal and a real science, intent upon understanding humans in their wholeness and building a better world for them upon the knowledge of this science. There is no narrow positivism in him and no degradation or dehumanization of human beings.

But still there is something missing. He offers a broad and human conception of science but one still limited by his roots in the traditions of modern science. The methods and contents of a more radical break from this science, one we will see shortly in Ernest Becker, were beyond the range of his science and outside the realm of his truth. If each thinker, and each individual, operates within some hidden framework of understanding and meaning, a framework that is deeper than even a common science, then they work and live in different worlds. Bronowski's world is that of natural science and his whole view and sensibility are shaped by it, no matter how much he broadens it. There are aspects of human experience that fall outside of his framework and even beyond his method and science. The challenge is to move into this territory, explore it, and bring back the fuller view of human beings that is the aim of his science. Bronowski, for all his expansiveness, would never cross the frontier into this territory because he would never grant it standing in his science. Why not? Because, at its heart, this new territory calls into question the essential assumptions and beliefs of his science and of his vision of human life.

For me the best example of this characteristic of Bronowski's thought is his book on William Blake.[74] The book is a portrait of Blake as a rebel and critic who stood against the mechanical and industrial society growing around him: against the inhumanity of the English society of his age and the brutal lives it condemns the mass of its people to endure in the name of progress, prosperity, power, and property. In Bronowski's hands, Blake becomes the Charles Dickens of his time, but a more radical and uncompromising one, without any of Dickens' humor, sentimentality, or feel for the human face amid the grim scenes. Blake's depictions are of the unvarnished blight of the new economic and social order. His attitude toward this order is unmitigated outrage at it cost in individual lives. His power of insight and verse are devoted to attacks on these conditions and on the whole order of thought and society propelling and justifying it. But Bronowski's Blake is more than a raging poet out of step with his time. He is also a saint of the new science's habit of truth, its reliance upon bare, in this case brute, facts, and its merger of imagination and reason to release and direct a creativity capable of seeing the "hidden unity" beneath the welter of everyday experience. Blake is a paragon of the new age even as he rails against the world it had built around him. There is a greater irony than this in Blake's attitude toward the new age, but Bronowski doesn't mention it. Blake's objections to the new order are fundamental. They are far more expansive and encompassing than the one developed by Bronowski. The enemy, for Blake, is not only the inhumanity of the new society with its engines and factories and cities and labor and poverty. It is, and this is always the critical fact for Blake, its whole way of thinking about human life. Where is the human spirit amid the new knowledge, where the soul, the spiritual world, the ancient voices and visions, the heavenly host and God? Blake is a prophet and his jeremiad is against the whole modern culture, including all that Bronowski considers its great achievements. He wants God to walk in the heavens again and angels to sit in trees and talk to him. The visions of the past, wrought by the extraordinary power of the human imagination, had been destroyed by new, unacceptable ones. This is what he could not tolerate. But Bronowski doesn't talk about this Blake, and in fact either avoids it or disparages this side of Blake's thought. This, though, is the heart of his thought and the source of his vision. Bronowski, instead, admires him for his insight into the social reality of his time and for his ability to clearly and incisively take it apart, analyze it, and condemn it with the force of his poetry. It is in this sense that he considers him visionary and modern. And he is correct in this. But this is secondary to his greater vision of a realm of reality beyond the means of Bronowski's science.

What separates Bronowski and Blake are their different models of the good and complete human being. Explicitly or implicitly, all thought that aspires to a systematic treatment of a reality that contains human beings has such a model. Bronowski has one. It is tied to his conception of the values of science. His model will embody these values of science. They are the democratic qualities of independence, originality of thought, free and open inquiry, dissent, tolerance, respect for the ideas and work of others, and justice. He believes in progress arising from continuous searching, discovering and thinking, a commitment to the habit of truth, to the foundation of facts and experience, to the inseparability of means and ends, and to the guidance and control of power by knowledge. This is his model of science. His ethics and his model of man come from its spirit and method. Blake would have agreed with much of this. But his searching, discovering, thinking, and his facts and experiences, were different from Bronowski's. Blake's vision of humans and the world is closer to Newton's than Bronowski's. They are men of an earlier, pre-Enlightenment age, of the Bible and the wisdom of a people that once spread its tents on the Red Sea shore. It is this difference that is critical. Bronowski's science moves toward a full science of man in admitting Blake, then pulls back from admitting the most important thing about him. He can admit only that part of him that fits his model of humans and the world. His modern science, thereby, becomes an incomplete and unacceptable science.

IV

Many others, from many disciplines, have attempted to find a suitable science for our age. Most have attempted, as Bronowski did, to broaden science and temper its excesses. Recently, the philosopher Stephen Toulmin has made an attempt in his book Cosmopolis.[75] The book is an extended argument against the Cartesian triumph in modern thought and a call for a return to the humanism of the Renaissance of Montaigne and Shakespeare and Bacon. This humanism embodies the characteristics and virtues Toulmin thinks will temper the excesses of modern thought with a renewed confidence in the reason of practical judgment, a healthy-minded skepticism, an appreciation of the limits of human knowledge and understanding, and an awareness of the diversity of human experience and the precariousness of all knowing and living in the world. He is aware of the nature of our modern science and spends considerable time discussing how we came to conceive of it as we do.

His specific argument goes like this. These last three hundred years have shown beyond much of a doubt that the program of modern science is a failure. Its effort to achieve a universal and comprehensive knowledge through an all-consuming confidence in and application of its methods has fallen short of its goal. More time will not alter this situation. Nor will a more rigorous and thorough application of the methods and ideas of science. We need a different model of science and reason, one which is more realistic about the possibilities of knowledge, that frees us from the straightjacket of modern thought, reintegrates natural science and the humanities, reintroduces the local and particular and everyday into the realm of science, elevates practical reason and philosophy to a status comparable to the theoretical, formal reason, replaces the demand for stability and uniformity with diversity and adaptability, rejects the Newtonian mechanics that has set the standard for all thought with a more supple and subtle post-Newtonian ecological science of the 20th century, and dissolves the privileged and separate domain held by technique and technology. The effect of these together will be to achieve Toulmin's goal—to "humanize modernity"—and better meet the exigencies of our present condition.

In much of this and in the general temper of his mind and ideas, he has much in common with Bronowski. Indeed, in his approach to science and his search for a more encompassing science or understanding of humans, he is much like him. Both, in their own ways, look for the same way beyond the dilemmas of modern science and thought. And like Bronowski, Toulmin does not go far enough. He stops short of a fuller, more complete view of humans and society. As we caught Bronowski's shortcoming in his treatment of Blake, we will catch Toulmin's in his apotheosis of Montaigne as his model man.

But before I describe his model man, I need to describe the modern world his man will inhabit. The two are inextricable from each other. Our model men are the champions of the world as we see it. They embody our hopes and visions. They define the way we see the world. Modern thought has produced more than one model. There are those who see the modern world as good and whose good and model men are those who master it and are at home in it; and those who find our age bad and see the ones who master it and are at home in it as cripples who are incomplete and unsatisfied, and less than fully human. Which model is Toulmin's. He tells us:

> In an age of interdependence and historical change, mere stability and permanence are not enough. Like social and political institutions, formal techniques of thought too easily lapse into stereotyped and self-protective rigidity. Like buildings on a human scale, our intellectual and social procedures will do what we need in the years ahead, only if we take care to avoid irrelevant or excessive stability, and keep them operating in ways that are adaptable to unforeseen—or even unforeseeable—situations and functions.[76]

What kind of world is this? It is our modern world: change, instability, uncertainty, and more change. It is just the world I have described and decried throughout this book. Toulmin wants us to adapt to it. I have argued that we cannot do so without giving up something essential to our well-being. As Bronowski did in his study of Blake, Toulmin misses the main points about his subject. It is a critical oversight.

He concedes, from the start, that the task of creating a unified, orderly, and stable body of knowledge and world view, upon which the everyday lives of regular people might be built and upon which the Enlightenment was based, is not possible for us, at least in any traditional sense. Such a world is ruled out as impossible in the modern age, so he gives us the best alternative: a free floating, ever changing life which we navigate with no illusions, a good practical sense, no great expectations, and a stoic aplomb and wit. His solution for the shortcomings of modern science is to give up on its efforts to create, through science, a new system of truth and unified world view for the modern age. He may be correct that science has taken the wrong road, but he is mistaken if he thinks we can dispense with the undertaking that science, however misguided, engaged in for three hundred years: to create a comprehensible, unified, and stable order in which humans can flourish and find fulfillment.

The real problem is not science, it is the struggle to replace the older world view. We need to put the world back together in a way that satisfies basic human needs for certainty, stability, firmly founded belief, and a sense of being at home in both our narrow lives and the larger scheme of nature and cosmos. It is not, as Toulmin argues, that we need to know how to handle our modern shipwreck with intelligence and poise, although these are necessary and good. Certainly, if we are all Crusoes, then the aim must be, as it is for Toulmin, to survive the wreck and get on in the new environment. But this is not enough: it must also be to rebuild the ship and get back home. Anything less than this, and Toulmin's modern Renaissance humanist, his Montaigne, is a lot less, leaves humans forlorn and unsatisfied and incomplete.

The irony in this is that Toulmin is aware of these needs and aims in his book to address them. In calling for a return to a form of reason, what he calls reasonableness, that requires us to look again at the particular, local, timely, practical, everyday contexts and activities of existence, he is placing the lived experience of humans at the center of thought. He knows that the newer human and social sciences and the established traditions of the humanities are necessary if he is to succeed in understanding this experience. A science of man begins for him with a shift in the focus and the means of modern thought. A humanized science and modernity must find a rationality and a science that can help it to deal with a complex and uncertain world, with the flesh and blood of our condition and life rather than the bloodless abstractions of the dominant science of the past two hundred years.

But Toulmin cannot quite do it. He stops short of the flesh and blood human experience he is seeking. The closer we get to his views, the more we see abstractions conjured by his humanism instead of real images of human beings. We get the vision of a new model of man but not one of real everyday men. He accepts Feyerabend's contention that "the appeal to reason [scientific rationalism] is empty, and must be replaced by a notion of science that subordinates it to the needs of citizens and communities," but is wrong about what those needs are. What he does gives us is instructions as to how we may rationally confront the general condition of our times. But what we need to know, if we are to decide, as humans, whether his prescription has salience and authority for the human lives we live in the modern age, is how to put the world back together again and what such a new world must contain if it is to satisfy us as human beings. He describes a way toward the rationality of public men and social life, and toward the reason needed to construct and operate a social order under modern conditions. The model of these public persons is the citizen of the polis or the artist of Renaissance Florence or the intellectual of the salons of 18th century Paris—of the enlightened humanist of the classical or early modern worlds who practiced and embodied a civic humanism. His prescription is a good, healthy minded one—a sane and intelligent way of dealing with our condition—which may allow us to create a better society. It is suited to those who have homes in an urbane and rational skepticism— his Montaigne and sixteenth century men who have found genuine satisfaction and contentment in this view of life. But they were not bereft in the deeper and more pervasive way the mass of lost souls are today. Bronowski envisioned the world in terms of his ideal scientist and, as a result, could not understand Blake's vision; Toulmin envisions a world in terms of enlightened humanists and can't understand the needs of the rest of us.

Perhaps better than Montaigne, the English philosopher of the Enlightenment David Hume represents the stance toward modern life and thought espoused by Toulmin. In considering him briefly we may better see the difficulty of making such a man or stance toward life the norm for modern humans. Peter Gay's depiction, from the final page of the first volume of his study **The Enlightenment**, captures Hume as the perfect pagan, the true philosopher, and, in Stuart Hampshire's words, the "perfect secular mind":

> For David Hume was both courageous and modern; he understood the implications of his philosophy and did not shrink from them. He was so

courageous that he did not have to insist on his courage; he followed his thinking where it led him, and he provided through his own life...a pagan ideal to which many aspired but which few realized. He was willing to live with uncertainty, with no supernatural justification, no complete explanations, no promise of permanent stability, with guides of merely probable validity; and what is more he lived in his world without complaining, a cheerful Stoic. Hume, therefore, more decisively than many of his brethren in the Enlightenment, stands at the threshold of modernity and exhibits its risks and its possibilities. Without melodrama but with the sober eloquence one would expect from an accomplished classicist, Hume makes plain that since God is silent, man is his own master: he must live in a disenchanted world, submit everything to criticism, and make his own way.[77]

The Hume of Gay's portrait is the Enlightenment's Montaigne, noble in character and courageous in facing a world so devoid of solace as to drive a lesser person, and most of us are, to quail before such conclusions about life. Quail and more, for we have resisted Hume's conclusions as determinedly as Toulmin resisted Descartes'. If the humanizing of science is necessary, then for most of humanity it may also be necessary to humanize Montaigne's and Hume's enlightened skepticism. Perhaps we simply lack Hume's character or courage, are too weak and insecure to walk the ancient Stoic way; perhaps we think he is wrong. Either way, there is something fundamental in this resistance, something that is within us and not in the stars, and that must be accounted for and understood. In making Montaigne or Hume the paragons of his new, superior, humanized science, Toulmin leaves out the very lived experience of the human beings he sought to restore to modern thought.

V

The twentieth century social scientist Ernest Becker was also committed to the creation of a human science for the modern age. His new science would require a more radical reorientation than Bronowski's or Toulmin's. His science, like theirs, ranged beyond the parameters set by the positivistic science of his day. His books recount his efforts to create a different, broader, and more humanistic "science of man."[78]

Becker sought a new synthesis of knowledge capable of supporting a modern world view built upon the great gains in human knowledge since the beginning of the Enlightenment. It must be a synthesis of all the relevant knowledge about human beings accumulated during the modern age. In the conclusion of his final work, edited and published posthumously, he envisioned a "most utopian fantasy...one that pictures a world-scientific body composed of the leading minds in all fields, working under an agreed general theory...."[79] The conclusions of such a scientific body would be the basis of a new synthesis of knowledge, of a modern world view, and of his science of man.

He did not see himself breaking new ground with this science of man. His task was, rather, to recover and complete what the Enlightenment began. For the thinkers of the seventeenth and eighteenth centuries the goal of the science of man was to fully understand human beings. The achievement of this goal was inseparable from the other project of the age: to define the nature of the new science. Modern science was still young then and was still seeking to define itself. The struggle generated by this search for a definitive form and identity focused on the scope and content of the emerging discipline of science and its emerging scientific world view. What would be the extent to which the new discipline would confine itself to the model and material of the natural sciences? Would it narrowly conceive the nature of its task and of reality by concentrating on the investigation on the material and mechanical forces and principles of the natural world? Or would it broaden itself to include the whole range of subject matters that encompass the human experience and life? Where and how would humans fit into modern science? How would science address these distinctive human subjects of study? The danger from the beginning was that science would follow the positivist path of its early work in the natural sciences. This path would lead to nothing but an investigation of the material and mechanical elements of human nature and social life: humans would be for such investigations merely material and mechanical objects, all else falling outside the parameters of such a science. This would effectively exclude humans, seen in anything approximating the wholeness of their existence, as subjects for science. Such a science would be incapable of a full consideration and conception of humans and would become therefore irrelevant to the critical challenges facing humanity. Since Becker believed these challenges to be the reason for pursuing a science of man, this too restricted conception of science could not be the science of his science of man.

There was an alternative path for science. It too was first conceived during the Enlightenment. Rather than a narrow science, it sought to expand it to encompass all dimensions of reality and keep it open and responsive to the fullness of human reality. Picking up on what he saw as this original intent of the Enlightenment's vision of a science of man, Becker insisted it be "centered on man," adapted to the fullness and complexity of the human reality. All inquiries "would radiate out from man to all the sciences." In this science, man would not be "woven at random, like an afterthought design, into an alien fabric" but "would be the central line on a switchboard."[80]

Becker considered his work to be in the spirit of the Enlightenment's initial attempts to understand human beings in a new, more complete, modern way. This science of man was essential if the problems of the modern age were to be met. The age had lost a unified world view and, as a result, had been experiencing a slow-burning but debilitating moral crisis. The medieval synthesis had dissolved in the flood of changes that marked the birth of the modern age. The Church could no longer hold the center. The humanism and classicism of the Renaissance had spent themselves in the process of unleashing the forces of science and modern which had dismembered the old order but failed to create a satisfactory new order. It was the science of man that would define a "sound basis for a new moral creed, an agreed, factual body of knowledge that men of good will could use to lay down laws for a new social order." This order and morality would be "a positive morality based on empirically demonstrated facts."[81]

Becker was convinced that the important work done during the nineteenth and twentieth centuries made possible the consummation of the Enlightenment's science of man. We could now attain a full understanding of human nature. With it, the science of man could forge a program for social reconstruction based upon a new unified world view. Becker's mission was to pull this science together.

Becker's new science was not to be the science of Bacon or Newton or the Royal Academy of Science. By their definitions his might not be a science at all. In its focus on humans, his science moved from the clear light and canonical body of natural science to the twilight world of social science. He compounded his problems with mainstream science by proclaiming his science not only a social but a moral science. It must be a "superordinate value science in the service of human betterment" in which idealism and materialism combine to create an "ideal-real" science which would "reconcile science with the larger designs of human life" and create a comprehensive world view based upon a unity of knowledge.[82] This would be a science that operates along the gray, uncharted marches of the larger kingdom of science. It stood outside the canons of science which insisted upon the separation of fact and value, the principles of dispassionate, disinterested, and objective inquiry, the assumption of the mechanical and material nature of the object of inquiry, and the belief that reason is a constituent component of reality, including human beings.

Judged by these standards, those essentially of the natural sciences, it is easy to see the problems with Becker's project. The dominant conception of science would dismiss his reconception as fainthearted and wrongheaded. It would argue that the genius of modern science need not be discarded in the pursuit of a new science of man but applied wholeheartedly to all dimension of human and natural life. An effort to alter science in the ways suggested by Becker would merely emasculate it and leave modern humanity no better than the thinkers of the dark, pre-modern ages. Science, in its age of triumph, fired by a consuming passion, thought all worlds would bend before its irresistible power. It was in this excessive confidence and pride, Becker argued, that the great inspiration, passion, and power of science overreached itself. Alfred North Whitehead contended that thought in the eighteenth and nineteenth centuries was "governed by the fact that it had got hold of a general idea [the materialism and mechanism of science] which it could neither live with nor live without."[83] Becker was certain we could not live with it because the progressive conquests of positivistic science had "blocked off rich areas of experience by attempting to divide sharply the world of the real and the not real."[84] Whatever wouldn't fit the measures or bow to the instruments of this science was beyond its pale and, in a society monopolized by its knowledge, was stamped invalid, irrelevant, or nonexistent. A science that so narrows itself either excludes humans or reduces them to its terms and thereby de-humanizes them.

Becker's science would avoid these problems. It would be the true Enlightenment "science of man," a moral science with the betterment of humans at its center and the creation of good communities as its chief aim. The knowledge produced by it would light the way to the creation of these communities. Most importantly, it would address all elements of human experience and make humans, in their wholeness and in the fullness of their lived experience, the inviolable subject for study. This wholeness would include the fact that humans "need a living and daily concern with ultimates, with the mystery of being, and with their role in the perpetuation of being" and it is just this that "rational, technical knowledge cannot give." Becker was convinced that positivism had "gradually emptied man, making him a manipulator of the world, but one who gained it only to lose its significance to him, and his deep significance to it." Such a sweeping expansion of the boundaries of science requires a different vision of the natural order: human life is conceived within "a cosmos of transcendent, divine meanings, and not under a microscope of disinterested scientific investigation."[85] Without these new boundaries, science could not construct a new synthesis upon which a society capable of liberating and fulfilling humans could be based, one capable of replacing the synthesis it had first undermined and then pulled down. This is the essential task of any new science and the central problem of our age:

> And we wonder why, with all this power capital drawn from so many sources, we are deeply anxious about the meaning of our lives. The reason is plain enough: none of these, nor all of them taken together, represents an integrated world conception into which we fit ourselves with pure belief and trust.[86]

Without this integrated world conception humans are alienated and fragmented, thrown back on their own insufficient resources, without redemption from hopelessness and meaninglessness; for all their science and power, all their Faustian ambition and conquest, moderns cannot establish the "roots upon which all 'higher' forms of sympathy and emotional life depend for their subsistence" or experience "a sense of participation in the universe." A science that aspires to include humans must incorporate and attempt to understand these higher forms and these needs.

Becker devoted his work to developing a science of man that could contain and explain them. To achieve this goal his science would have to focus on humans and produce a full theory of human nature. This theory would describe the "reasons of the heart" so important and perplexing to Pascal and some of the Philosophes. It would be scientifically based but would include all that modern science had left out. To the extent that his alternative, the science of man, can address these areas and do so rationally and empirically, then it is necessary and good.

His science would dramatically expand the sources and types of knowledge considered legitimate and draw from disciplines previously considered unscientific. If they rationally and rigorously sought to comprehend the nature of humans and their existence, then they were of value to the science of man. Literature, philosophy, religion, and the natural and social sciences all have insights and information to offer. The enormous advances in all of these disciplines in the modern age made possible a synthesis of knowledge and a new unified world view based upon the latest and completest understanding of humans and the world. It was to be the fruit of two hundred years of rigorous, rational, and empirical investigation that had produced, from across the disciplines, the new knowledge of humans and the world.

The differences between Becker's science and the mainstream of modern science were significant. These differences, and the obstacles they posed for his new science, surfaced most clearly in his work on the development of the discipline of sociology in the United States, **The Lost Science of Man**, and in the career of its main character, Albion Small. Small was a principal architect of the new discipline of sociology. His career spanned the period of the late nineteenth and early twentieth centuries. This was the period of the emergence of the social sciences and of their struggle for acceptance and respectability. Respectability meant to be scientific, and the battle for acceptance was to be won or lost based upon the ability of the discipline to be empirical, quantitative, objective, and value-free, without losing touch with the vital issues and subject matter of the discipline. This struggle was at the center of Small's career in sociology. It was particularly intense for him because his "moral stance, his concern about the welfare of man in society, his vision of sociology as a moral science centered on man and furthering the human spirit was the original vision of sociology itself."[87] Small's personal vision of sociology faced a world dominated by the entrenched and powerful tradition of a modern science whose vision was very different from his. He was caught, as was sociology, in a dilemma that suspended him between "the urgency of the social problem on the one hand and the quiet respectability of objective science on the other."[88]

Small's specific task, and the bind he had to work his way out of, was clear to him: "On the one hand, it [sociology] had to forge a methodology of the social problem.... On the other hand, it had to do this 'scientifically' and 'objectively'; it had to justify itself vis-à-vis those other disciplines that were scornful of its sentimentalism and ideology."[89] Small's solution, a fateful one in Becker's opinion, was to give up the broader science for a positivistic sociology. If precise and powerful in analysis, objective and value-free, it could gain the standing and prestige of science. To accomplish this he had to drastically narrow and thereby cripple sociology. For Becker, this was the critical, and tragic, turn taken by sociology and most of the other social sciences.

But why did it happen? Was there no alternative? Couldn't scientific sociology address the social problem and be human-centered? Becker's answer is no. But the answer had already been given, years earlier, by another early sociologist, Lester Frank Ward. Ward saw clearly what Small and sociology stood to lose. He saw

that psychic forces, and not mechanics, influence human association, that man is primarily a psychological being and not a physiological one. This meant that the task of sociology was to get at the meaning of human experience from within human valuations; it could not get at this meaning in an external, objective, abstractive, or mechanical way. Society is an arena for the play of these psychic forces in all their breadth and complexity. Sociology is thus the science that thinks of the human reality as a broad, interrelated whole; it aims to understand why men's efforts take the turn they do when men live in society, and it aims to understand this on the basis of man's subjective valuations.[90]

The methods of the natural sciences could not accomplish any of this, and would in fact compromise efforts to achieve these objectives. The reality sociology sought to know was simply not amenable to the treatment it would receive at the hands of a scientific method designed to know another type of reality. For Ward, what Small was sacrificing was a more complete and subtle vision of sociology as

> the science of actual control and prediction of social events. It is a science of purposive mind, not passive matter. Sociology is a 'telic' science in the service of human well-being and progressive development.... Sociology exists to get the objective facts about human association, but once it gets these facts, once it finds out what is going on in society, it must put its finding in the service of man.[91]

Here was a moral science capable of knowing the human reality and of putting it to use for the betterment of humankind.

Small wanted both but he couldn't have them. So he gave up Ward's vision of sociology. He knew that Ward's vision, once his own, was, in fact, itself the problem: "The point is, very simply, that Small had to liberate himself from Wardian sociology in order to forge a scientific discipline that would take its rightful place beside the others...."[92] So Small and sociology fell from what Becker considers the Wardian peak of the science of man. They fell because the power of modern science was so great, its promise of knowledge so compelling, and its enticement to status and respectability so alluring. While Ward's vision is grand and moral, it doesn't offer these benefits. Its method and mission would make it far more difficult to pin down the cold hard facts of the reality it sought to know. Both Ward and Small knew this. One thought the risk unavoidable in social science, the other thought science offered a way out of these limitations and risks. So Small's decision wasn't simply a moment of weakness, a cowardly apostasy, a selling of the soul for the rewards of the world. It was, rather, a hard choice where, in Becker's view, the wrong decision was made.

Small's and Ward's dilemma was Becker's and all who attempted to create a science of man. Yet this did not temper Becker's view that modern positivistic science was the wrong way. He believed modern science, on its own or in the form of the social sciences, had betrayed humans when it excluded the ideal and the subjective, and defined humans as matter and mechanisms and motion, entities without freedom or the creativity to shape their destinies. In being all of these it had lost the complete image of the human being by splintering the image of humans, discarding some of the fragments, and concentrating exclusively on the fragments it retained. It is this that drives Becker's science; it is what Nicolas Berdyaev lamented when he decried the disintegration of the human image in modern culture and C.S. Lewis condemned as the abolition of man.

The first task of Becker's science was to piece back together this human image. To this end, a marriage of idealism and materialism had to be arranged. Modern science had divorced itself from Becker's sort of idealism. In its search for method and identity in the seventeenth and eighteenth centuries it had left out of its calculations the fact that human beings live in a world of ideas, values, beliefs, and ideals. Humans are subjective, social, meaning-making animals and any science without this dimension violates the wholeness and integrity of the human image. This fuller image is the content of Becker's idealism.

Becker's idealism had to be based upon a clinical and empirical understanding of human beings. The hope of the new science of man had been, from its beginning, that the powers of the new methods of science would replace the ignorance and superstition that had constituted humanity's knowledge of itself for millennia. There could be no science of man without science, no idealism without materialism. Such a synthesis would contain the important truths of both idealism and materialism. It would be true to the reality of human experience and nature and meet the requirements of modern science: "a synthesis based on hard science... which left man at the center as a free creator...." Becker considered the synthesis the "natural union of materialism and idealism."[93]

In Becker's history of the science of man, Wilhelm Dilthey was the critical figure. He made the union possible with his "great synthetic truth,... the one that all the disciplines converged in, the one that told us what man was, and what he was striving for":

> Man is the animal in nature who, par excellence, imposes symbolic categories of thought on raw experience. In other words, with man, meaning has become conscious; his conception of life determines how he sees all its parts. Meaning, concludes Dilthey, 'is the comprehensive category through which life becomes comprehensible'.[94]

Meaning-making was the cardinal principle, the superordinate idea, of the science of man. It was discovered through a hardheaded and empirical investigation of the phenomenon of human consciousness and action. For Becker, it was as certainly a fact and a truth as the earth's rotation around the sun. It was the finest flower of the union of idealism and materialism.

The science of man would be based upon this union. The key disciplines would no longer be those in the natural sciences, but those of the social sciences and the humanities. The traditional methods of modern science would no longer be adequate for the distinctive nature of the new subject-matter: the meaning-making of human beings. The general demands of modern science for rigor and an empirical basis, though, would be retained. The new science, dealing as it does with humans and their meaning-making, would lose the rigid distinction between facts and values as well as those between the disciplines. The moral dimension of human existence would constitute a fundamental part of its subject-matter and pervade its practices.

This last point is a critical one for Becker. The new science, to fulfill its mission of understanding humans, must look at human experience from the inside. Once inside, science can't avoid a confrontation with human nature. In knowing human nature, science would more fully understand human needs and the cultural and social forms necessary for human fulfillment. Knowing these things, science will become an instrument of social criticism and reconstruction. Its pursuit of knowledge would produce a "naturalistic morality that would be under man's control...."[95] This is Becker's, and the Enlightenment's, vision of the science of man as an ideal-real science: "the ideal model serves a moral-critical purpose as well as a scientific-conceptual one."[96] Becker is convinced that such a science is the best, perhaps the only, way out of the crisis of the modern age; it can give the modern world a synthesis of knowledge and belief, a new vision and faith, and a unified ideal.

This science operates somewhat differently from our standard models of scientific method. It is, in fact, caught on Becker's version of the chicken and the egg: science needs complete knowledge to know the ideal but the ideal must be present to direct science. Therefore, it must always begin with "a willful option that is based on incomplete knowledge."[97] It has to study humans and assert an ideal and then study them some more. The process is a continual and dialectical one. For traditional science this is too uncertain and too easily compromised. It would lead, in its view, backwards to the dark ages rather than forward in enlightenment. The conflict could only be resolved if facts were central and the role of ideals neutralized or excluded. True science is possible only when these conditions are met. Becker saw it, instead, as an unavoidable paradox that could only be resolved by the assertion of the primacy of the moral in science. Science must serve some end, it always does, and ends are moral in nature. It should, therefore, choose to serve humans and to aid in the improvement of the human condition. It has no imperative greater than this. A self-conscious science will project a vision and strive to realize it through the pursuit of knowledge and social action. Any separation of science and morality is artificial, a vestige of an earlier dualistic view of reality. Becker argues that the "founding of a science is never a cognitive problem alone: it is always inseparably a moral problem, a problem of gaining broad agreement to act on the basis of a theory."[98] This is true for all sciences, natural and social. They must make choices and agree on a guiding paradigm in the face of incomplete knowledge. The choices that confront his science of man

> differ in no way from that of the other sciences except that the willful nature of the options cannot be disguised. The human sciences, just like the others, read nature in the Enlightenment tradition and vision: in order to find compelling reasons for agreed action. The reading can never be complete, hence the action must be always willful. All science... is thus a moral problem.[99]

Becker knew that few scientists, natural or social, would accept his science of man. The power of positivism had trampled opposing views; the times were so thoroughly imbued with the doctrine of modern science that its position was impregnable. Few would opt for a new science when the existing one was triumphant. Why would the modern world give up a scientific view that has given it such wealth, power, and control? And why give it up for the relativism and indeterminacy that must come with this science of man? Any age will resist the loss of its source of truth, its authoritative voice, and its sense of certainty. Modern society will resist this loss in the same way the Middle Ages clung to its God. Becker understood this:

> Of course the fusion of fact and value is very troubling; it weakens the authority of both science and traditional morality. Science becomes more human and indeterminate, and morality becomes more humanly determinate. Little wonder that so many have held on so tenaciously to the separation of fact and value. Without this separation, man is thrown back on his own decisions. But we must learn to trust man, as the early Enlightenment did. And this will mean learning to live with a tentativeness in both ethics and science.[100]

All this, though, is probably more technical than Becker's real reason for demanding a science of man that is a moral science. Science must be moral because human life is a moral enterprise. It is an effort to answer basic questions about humans and the world, about what is good and bad, and about what can be done to liberate and fulfill human beings and make a better world. This is the quintessential human motive behind all science. Any science that fragments the world and knowledge, and thereby the human image, leaves this motive unsatisfied and loses the human dimension of the pursuit of knowledge. To Becker, all the techniques, methodologies, and systems of thought are means to an end. When the human motive drives and shapes science it insists that "it is not dialectic that liberates man, and allows him to reconstruct and master the rich world of experience. It is not technique or argumentation, but passion and vision that free man."[101] Vision is achieved when the mind is able to unify the welter of its experience of the world, fit it together and make sense out of it, and grasp it in its wholeness. Becker thinks this vision is what the modern age needs most. It will provide answers to his questions. Science needs it as well, for without it "in science, as in life, all is disjointed, all is chaos; everything points in a thousand direction."[102] It is the goal of the science of man to meet this human need. It must give order to the chaotic state of modern knowledge and shape a vision out of it; and it must go about the formulation of this synthesis of knowledge directed by a passionately conceived and held vision of human life. When this is achieved the crisis of the modern age will have passed and the vision of the Enlightenment and its science of man will be a reality.

Chapter Four
An Alternative Science of Man

What should we make of Becker's ideas and his science? Can or should we take them seriously? Before developing them further, two things can be said. The first is, I hope, obvious by this point: the theme and the substance of Becker's thought are the same as those of the earlier chapters of this book. He is offered here as a friendly witness. His vision of our modern condition and of human existence is akin to mine. Bronowski and Toulmin were used as foils to demonstrate the problems of a too modern and scientific view. Becker is used as a model of one way to get beyond or around our problems, one that goes further than the intelligent, well-intentioned ones of Bronowski and Toulmin. All three understand that we must move away from too narrow a conception of science and human life. Each points a way out of the dilemmas of modern thought. But Becker, alone, I believe, points the way to where we need to go in our thinking and in the reconstruction of modern life. This section will attempt to clarify and refine the picture and understanding of this different, and seemingly unscientific, science of man.

Can we justify calling this a science at all? What of the rigor, reliability and verifiability of this new science? These are at the heart of what we mean by science. If the science of man is to be a science these must be as important to it as to other sciences. All of the social sciences have fought the criticism that they fail to meet these essential demands.

The response of the science of man is this. The aim is to understand human beings more completely than we have in the past by utilizing the extraordinary resources of modern thought. Science is the keystone of this modern thought and will be important for the science of man. The demands of method, the test of experience and fact, the use of a hard and relentless and uncompromising rationality, and the insistence on verifiability will be retained. The challenge is not to dismantle the modern age but to humanize it by applying the rigor of science to the more important and difficult challenge of understanding our moral, social, and personal lives.[103] This is the goal of the science of man. It must be done delicately, in ways appropriate to the content; it must not violate the nature of the subject matter with the assumptions and prejudices of its methods. Method must wait on the object of investigation and patiently find the way into its facts, logic and ordering principles, and finally its truths. At the same time, it must safeguard its commitment to the broadest conception of the truth.

Alfred North Whitehead thought the common ground of philosophy and religion was in each respecting the legitimate role of the other in the pursuit of truth: religion supplied the driving passion and invigorating ideas and philosophy forges these into general ideas that are rational and consistent with all else we know to be true. The rigor of science and philosophy guard these "higher intuitions from base alliances" with the transitory enthusiasms and influences bred by the exigencies of everyday life and the parochialism of particular times and places.[104] In the science of man, all of the disciplines of thought and their particular realms of experience will furnish the reservoir of ideas, intuitions, and information that philosophy and science will discipline with method, fact, and reason. This is the role and meaning of science for the science of man.

This beatific vision of a peaceful kingdom where science lies down with religion and literature with physics oversimplifies the reality. There will be more tension and conflict in this than such a vision suggests. The relationship is better conceived as a dynamic equilibrium in which the insights and intuitions of all the arts and sciences are worked into general synthetic truths through reflection and critical intelligence. The result is a reflective equilibrium that defines the knowledge of the science of man at a particular time. The equilibrium will bring the rich but scattered knowledge about human beings dispersed among the fields of inquiry into a rationally and empirically sound theoretical framework. It will accomplish this without violating or impoverishing the subject matter of the science. Its preconceptions and the assumptions implicit in its method will not determine what we find at the end of the investigation, as it often does in more positivistic approaches.

If the content is to define the nature and content of the new science, then the nature of this content is important, and its suitability for a science of man is critical. The history of thought in the modern age has been an effort to find what could be studied scientifically and what couldn't. Most disciplines of study have attempted to become more scientific and in doing so, as Becker demonstrated earlier, distorted the true aim and nature of their work. When the aim is a full understanding and theory of human beings—including the moral, social, and personal life of humans—then the potential for incompatibility and conflict is great. The reigning opinion has been that a science of the dominant type defined by the natural sciences is not possible for such subjects. The cause of this incommensurability is the tendency to violate the human subject in the scientific study. The study usually leaves something out, and it is commonly that which is least suitable to scientific investigation: the realm of values and morals and the dimension of human life captured in literature, particularly poetry, and religion. With these removed, a science is possible but not a complete and useful science of man. But the nature of modern science is expressed in its work with a world "determined by causal laws" and a lawful natural order. It does not as a matter of practice work with humans as knowers, free inquirers open to reason, evidence, and truth, as moral agents or religious beings. These simply do not fit into its lawful natural order. And because we do not fit we cannot be "subjected to 'theory', hence to control, hence to use: man-lower-than-man explained by the human sciences—man reified—can by the instruction of these sciences be controlled (even 'engineered') and thus used."[105]

Is there a way through this dilemma? There is only one way and it begins with the acknowledgment that there is more than one type of science, that there are types different from the one developed for the natural sciences, and that these other sciences can be rational, rely upon evidence, seek truth, and, through all of these, arrive at legitimate conclusions and valid theory. It also begins with the acceptance of the failure of the project of modernity based upon the new science of the seventeenth and eighteenth centuries. It is a failure of the narrow realism and materialism of science that has driven out idealism, morals, and deeper foundations of human nature and social life. With the intention of insuring a strict objectivity and value-neutrality, science broke with the traditions of philosophy and science that began in the ancient world and had been resuscitated in the Renaissance. The new modern science, as Toulmin argued, took a wrong turn and constructed out of its error a new modern ideology that was also wrong. It leaves out that which is essential and indispensable: the ideal image of humans and the moral nature of human existence and of science. Instead it pictures the world and human beings as machines within a great mechanical universe or as organisms struggling to survive in an indifferent material environment: truth resided in the laws of nature and those laws described an inhuman universe and a human existence regulated by mechanical principles and a society driven by the brute forces of selection and survival. This failure sets the task for the science of man: of defining a broader view of knowledge encompassing the deepest human concerns, practical and everyday experiences, and the irrational element of human personality and experience.

In his **Adventures of Ideas** Alfred North Whitehead argues that modern science has diminished the place of the ideal as the guiding vision of human life. Ideals by their nature are real only as possibilities, as goals to strive for, as prophecies of a better world. The power of ideals consists in this: "When we examine the general world of occurrent fact, we find that its general character, practically inescapable, is neutral in respect to the realization of intrinsic value." Ideals define the intrinsic value a society wishes to realize in its institutions, way of life, and individual members. According to Whitehead, ideals have been vital in Western culture since at least Plato. Modern science has undercut this tradition by removing ideals as one of the chief characteristics of humans and discrediting the nobler image of humans. In their place it has given us technical and instrumental information and a vision of brute forces and laws of nature that may be controlled and used by science for human purposes. What these purposes might be science does not say and does not know. Ideals, as conceived by Whitehead, give direction and purpose to individuals and society:

> The ideals cherished in the souls of men enter into the character of their actions. These interactions within society modify the social laws by modifying the occasions to which those laws apply. Impractical ideals are a program for reform. Such a program is not to be criticized by immediate possibilities. Progress consists in modifying the law of nature so that the Republic on Earth may conform to that Society to be discerned ideally by the divination of Wisdom.[106]

Whitehead's view is closer to the great tradition of thought that modern science has eclipsed. Science has tolerated his view so long as it stayed out of its way, but if its prerogatives or power were encroached upon, it would declare such ideals incomprehensible or nonsensical, destructive intrusions into process of science, an idle pastime of the outdated and soft-headed disciplines.

We moderns placed our faith in the power of this science to do and be all things to us. We have slowly and painfully discovered its limits. Science has given us great power but not wisdom. We have forgotten what the long tradition of Western civilization has known: power must be guided and enlightened by the ideal, wisdom, and virtue. It is this fact that inspires all of the thinkers discussed in this chapter to redefine the nature and aims of modern science and thought so that it may either offer us this wisdom or stand aside so that others may.

The science of man defines a framework of thought different from and larger than science, one in which wisdom and the ideal define the superordinate category. It will set the framework of thought rather than working within one set by modern science, and its will be a broader, wiser one. Ideals within the framework of modern science were nothing more than illusions, vestiges of old and erroneous systems of thought or religion; and morals were merely the embodiments of power, desire, or emotions. The nobler images of human beings, of either humanism or religion, were the hoary superstitions of the ignorant and immature childhood of the species. Shaped by such "wisdom," the gates of society swung open to welcome a new age and its secular, materialistic, hedonistic culture, shaped by the knowledge and technology of science in a commercial and capitalistic society. Without the higher meanings—the wisdom and ideals Whitehead insists must guide society—humans are, in Becker's words, "undermined from within as well as without" and become "insular mechanical things wired according to the standard program of self-seeking desire."[107] The great achievement of controlling nature which could aid us in overcoming and transcending ourselves has led instead only to a wholesale indulgence and apotheosis of the self. Even worse, ironically, the effect has been, according to Charles Taylor in **Sources of the Self**, to disperse or fragment this very modern self. William Barrett in his works argues the same thing. Like Narcissus, our preoccupation, in this case with the self, has led to its disintegration. These may be the wages of truth: through science humans may have discovered their true self. But I don't think so. What we have really discovered is that "we have lost our grip on the innate immensity of our true nature."[108]

It may not be something as grand and unscientific as ideals that we need. The philosopher Michael Polanyi contends that science before the eighteenth and nineteenth centuries was guided by a vision of a divinely ordered and rational system based upon numbers and most perfectly expressed in music. This vision was a beautifully ordered system of rational relations that moved both the mind and the soul of humans, in the same way music affects both and is, as we have known since Pythagoras, a beautifully ordered rational and mathematical system of relationships. For them, both cosmology and music moved and elevated our souls. Polanyi contends that all knowledge, systems of thought, and understanding require such visions that inspire discipleship, reverence, and an ordered and aesthetic conception of the larger reality. Nature for Polanyi can only be understood in terms of the reasons, purposes, acts of imagination, methods of discovery, and sense of beauty present in these visions. They are a precondition of knowing and understanding. They result in the "indwelling" of the knower in the known, who, in turn, is shaped by his or her culture, particularly its moral and civic virtues and the wisdom that is the basis for its conception of the order of the world. The critical question for individuals and cultures is always within which framework they will think, know, and live. To choose is to submit to a framework that is inescapably moral in nature because valuation is part of its nature and part of our act of choosing, committing, and acting. From these arise the intellectual passion that drive all inquiry, discovery, and knowing.[109]

If vision and background assumptions are inescapable, then what should they be for an alternative to modern science? The assumptions of an alternative are the following: sensations are always prejudiced, perception is theory-laden, facts and values are inseparable, subject and object are inextricable from one another, induction by itself cannot lead us to universal laws, mathematics as the source of certainty in science supports the dominant paradigm and its hypotheses and cuts science off from the natural world of phenomena, the Cartesian separation of mind and matter, inner and outer, primary and secondary qualities, subject and object is wrong. Upon these assumptions an alternative is built in which the self is involved in cognition, theory and valuation are always present in scientific investigation and make possible the qualitative dimension of science that mathematical-quantitative-deductive methods have driven out, and the perceiving mind (which is the truly theoretical mind), rather than the analytic mind, should be the basis of a true science. Knowing is participatory. We gain knowledge and understanding through a "gentle empiricism that makes itself most intimately one with the object." Intuition, insight, and imagination are the attributes of mind that permit the knower to penetrate and know the subject of investigation. What is discovered is the object itself and not a theory, for, as Goethe said, the phenomena are the theory themselves and the process of knowing is an indivisible, unified activity. This unity is what phenomenologists call "intentionality" and Goethe describes as a "point in experience where we are most intimately ourselves—the activity of our own will—and are yet most definitely the other at the same time, since the activity in which we participate is the constitutional structure of the object contemplated."[110]

Is the rigor associated with modern science possible in this alternative science? If mathematics has become the standard for science, and it has, then how can an alternative as distant from its method meet the test of rigor? The challenge is to find a way to apply the rigor of positivistic method, particularly the rigor of mathematics, to the qualitative elements and experiences of life, especially human life, without being reductive. If it is granted that all methods involve intentionality and theory, the task becomes to define a method with the rigor of modern science without its particular type of intentionality.[111]

There are various forms such a method might take. Goethe's **naturphilosophen** is one way. He begins not with numbers and quantity, not with hidden mechanism beyond the senses, but with the careful consideration of the phenomena themselves, seeing them closely and repeatedly, experimenting with them until the axiomatic system that defines them and their relationships emerges. The goal is to discover the "configurations that allow the hidden intentional relations to 'light up' within the phenomena." These configurations are the laws, what he calls the archetypes, of science. They are justified by the intensity and thoroughness of observation and the formal relationship they reveal. It is this seeing that is the key for Goethe. In it are the intentionality of his method and the justification of its discoveries. Neither the configurations nor the faculty of perceiving them are givens. They exist only in their relationship and in the intentional process of knowing and being known. The world reveals itself to us to the extent that we exercise and improve our intentional faculty through practice. Through use we both sharpen and alter our faculty of seeing and evolve through our rigorous efforts new ways of seeing. We, in Goethe's words, "awaken new organs." This science grows only when the scientist is the instrument of research, the whole scientist, not when the scientist is merely a wielder of a method. Goethe's method is "self-transformation in search of ever-greater objectivity." The model for this scientist is the artist who discovers through this same process, with this same method, the slow, painstaking attention to a piece of the world with the intention of bringing out of it a greater, more penetrating understanding of him or herself and the world.[112]

Our modern world view based upon science has failed to understand and appreciate Whitehead, Polanyi, and Goethe, and all those who espouse an alternative to the dominant assumptions, methods, and contents of modern science. The cost has been the loss of the vital organs of any framework capable of including human beings. The result has been worse than a misunderstanding or a fragmentation of the self. It has been, in Polanyi's words, the loss, amid all our knowledge and power, of the vital connections and meanings of our world and our selves:

> He is strong, noble and wonderful so long as he fears the voices of this firmament; but he dissolves their power over himself and his powers gained through obeying them, if he turns back and examines what he respects in a detached manner. Then law is no more than what the courts will decide, art but an emollient of nerves, morality but a convention, tradition but an inertia, God but a psychological necessity. Then man dominates a world in which he himself does not exist. For with his obligations [to seek truth and to know] he has lost his voice and his hope, and been left behind meaningless to himself.[113]

It is the goal of the science of man to avoid these consequences by giving humans again a fuller understanding of themselves in a world in which they, in all their fullness, richness, and meaningfulness, exist.

I

The danger of the science of man slipping into skepticism and foundationlessness is a real one. The proponents of traditional science argue it is the inevitable outcome of its ideas and methods. They contend it is with Polanyi's methods that we will lose our way. The science of man's response is that it is science itself that has undermined our sense of certainty and confidence in truth. But at the center of this irresolvable conflict is, I think, an agreement. When epistemological skepticism, either partial or complete, is advocated there arises the concomitant claim, from both sides, that the human consequences of such a view are untenable and essentially inhuman. It leads to foundationlessness, nihilism, and despair. Regardless of how successfully science or philosophy lead us to it, we resist its conclusions. The owl of Minerva may fly at dusk, in the twilight of the old idols, but the sun as surely rises again to shine on new idols. When skepticism touches the fundamental knowledge, beliefs, or values of a culture, as it did in the strain of the Enlightenment embodied by Hume and consummated in Nietzsche, the culture becomes disoriented and distressed. It, when threatened in this way, will employ all its resources to either recreate the old order or weave a new fabric of belief. A science of objects and observation, sense and things, numbers and calculations cannot by its nature grasp this fact. It cannot understand the human longing and the human voice that emerge from the subjective center of existence and are known in intimate personal experience of the self and of others. A science of technique and technology cannot understand these things except in a crude and brutish way that will violate their essence and ultimately destroy them. It is the person, the individual subjective center of each life, that is the goal of a science of man. Those who attempt to approach this goal only as impartial, impersonal, and uncommitted observers of human life will be left, like the brides without oil, waiting. It will not be seduced by such an approach. It is invisible before the gaze of such an advance and, if forced, it will be violated without having been known or touched.

There is, then, beyond the agreement about the perils of skepticism, a parting of the way. For the science of man, what is required is a different way of knowing and a different way of conceiving what it means to be human. St. Augustine came to Christianity partly as a result of a weariness with the demands and uncertainties of reason and scholarship. He found rest and a home in God: "Thou hast made us for Thyself, and our heart is restless until it rest in Thee." This may seem a craven capitulation to our human weakness, a failure of nerve and character at that decisive moment when a person defines himself and sets the course of his life, more a vice than a virtue when compared to the steadfastness and fortitude of the skeptic and humanist. Indeed, it can be all of these. It may be, as Becker will show in the next section, a cowardice and capitulation we are all born for. But it can be something more: for Augustine, the real failure of nerve is in not pushing on beyond the self imposed limits of our too human and rational categories. The restlessness and uncertainty need not be defined as the end, as our assigned portion or lot in life, but as the spur that prods us to faith and wearies us away from our narrow worldly view to the deeper relationship and knowledge of George Herbert's "The Pulley":

> Yet let them keep the rest,
> But keep them with repining restlessness:
> Let him be rich and wearie, that at least,
> If goodnesse leade him not, yet weariness
> May tosse him to my breast.

Augustine weariness, based on a loss of confidence in the ability of reason alone to understand either the world, man, or God, led him not to forsake or renounce truth in a blind, will-less surrender, an escape into obscurantism and mysticism, but to the assertion of a different method for uncovering it. **Credo ut intelligam** ("I believe so that I may understand") and **fides quaerens intellectum** ("faith in search of understanding") are the pillars of an epistemology that modern science so utterly vanquished as to make its conception seem a mostly forgotten fantasy of a credulous and ignorant age.[114]

There are several important points in this for our purpose here. One is that what wearied and drove Augustine wearies and drives us all. Another is that belief is necessary and unavoidable for humans and that it often precedes the long and uncertain and trying search for facts and proofs and justifications. We resist a thorough skepticism because we will not accept the condition it creates for us and our lives. John Dewey wrote an entire book to argue that the quest for certainty was a mistake and that its object would be forever beyond us. He may have been right about the latter but the book itself, the need to write it and the long historical overview of our history of striving for certainty, denies the key fact of the matter: humans need such certainty and are driven to seek and find it by an edict from the heart or the soul or the deepest structure of the self. Dewey may have been correct in a technical sense, as perhaps the skeptics may be correct, but he also knew that even if humans would agree to go without all fixed and absolute certainties they could not survive or function as humans without bringing order, reliability, stability, and certainties to their experience.

Even Dewey, a modern Heraclitus, understood this about humans. Fixed and final answers may be beyond us in his dynamic and evolutionary world, but the need to unify our experience so that it is ordered, stable, and steady is at the heart of our human experience. All experience, individual and social, seeks those moments of consummation when, amid the ceaseless stream of time and change, our interactions order themselves into a fine and satisfying harmony, finished and whole, a product of the highest human art and the greatest human need.[115]

William James also makes a similar argument in "The Will to Believe."[116] What will we do in a world that grants us very little certainty and no absolute truths, a world in which our intellects are unable to provide us clear and definitive answers? Shall we become skeptics and stand waiting, refusing always to run the risk of error, of getting it wrong and being made the fool by the world, of looking gullible or ignorant. Or shall we follow our inclinations, indulge our "passional nature," and will a belief that seems reasonable and true on the evidence we have? His answer is clear: we must will a belief, have faith, and hope for the truth of our intuitions and imperfect, incomplete reasonings. We have little choice in this. Our reason and knowledge can take us only part of the way. Since part way is not far enough, we trust to our will and heart to guide us. It is a gamble and the risk will prevent some from acting; it demands we commit our lives and souls in the absence of clear and certain knowledge and truth, without authority and justification before action. To live is to experience such incompletion and uncertainty, but it is also to define and order experience and act through an assertion of the will and belief. All must decide and act; their decisions will take life and have force because of beliefs which in most cases have no greater claim to truth in our modern age than did those of martyrs who stood steadfast in their belief. And most will choose, as humans have overwhelmingly for millennia, to bind themselves in faith to a belief that orders and gives meaning to their lives, to which they commit their lives and around which they mold their characters. To do so is to be fully human and to live fully. Skeptics may stand aside and prick us for ignorance, credulity, and weakness, but in doing so they are less, or perhaps more, than human. Yet they too choose, have faith, believe, and make a life for themselves. But there is one beyond the means and desires of most humans. For the mass of men, theirs is too thin a soup to nourish their souls, too rarefied an air to fill their lungs, too insubstantial a stuff with which to build a life worth living. Skeptics, oddly, are much like mystics: they find solace and fulfillment in a world that distresses the rest of us. They are Yeats' two chinamen carved in lapis lazuli:

> There on the mountain and the sky,
> On all the tragic scene they stare.
> One asks for mournful melodies;
> Accomplished fingers begin to play.
> Their eyes mid many wrinkles, their eyes,
> Their ancient, glittering eyes, are gay.[117]

James understood, as did Augustine, that speculation, philosophy, science, and rationality are not enough, most of the time, for most humans. They lead to only two results: simplicity and unity of conception or complexity and multiplicity. The first may result in the barrenness of simple and clean conceptions in a world that is neither, the second to a failure to "get us out of the empirical sand-heap world"; neither solves the central problem of thought which is to bring order and understanding to experience, give us something solid and reliable to believe in, to invest our lives with meaning and a sense of purpose. They too often fail to do any of these and in the process of failing squeeze the life out of our experience. By their nature and mission, they seek for simplicity and order. To achieve these, they classify, categorize, define, and systematize, which produces "the best theoretic philosophy" but at the same time is a "monstrous abridgment of life, which, like all abridgments, is got by the absolute loss and casting out of real matter.... The entire man, who feels all needs by turns, will take nothing as an equivalent for life but the fullness of living itself."[118]

The final point, though, is the most important. The vital subject for Augustine was God, the monstrous abridgment was of the relationship to God, and the fullness of living was to be found in the unity of existence in faith. All of these are possible for him to the extent that he thought about and conceived a world beyond the one defined and permitted by modern science. Science arose as a rejection of his way of thinking. It discredited, either through omission or commission, the reality Augustine came to know through his faith. To the extent that a science of man leaves Augustine's world, experience, and way of knowing out of its investigations, it cannot be a complete science.

The philosopher William Barrett takes the same position in his work. He describes our age as one mesmerized by the power of technique and technological rationality. Together they have dominated our consciousness and shaped our lives. Technique, however, has failed to understand the world as completely and well as it has claimed it could. And worse, it has imprisoned us in a palace of illusions inflated by the extravagant claims and arrogance of promoters of this rationality and technique. And amid the material progress and all the illusions of our technique and the great successes made possible by its triumph, our souls have been ignored or denied, until finally they have died. But for Barrett this death is the death of that element of our humanness that is most distinctive and important. The palace of modern illusions has no place or need for soul. Barrett is certain that human beings cannot be defined or understood without it. The triumph of technique leaves little room for the claims of the soul, in the form of Miquel de Unamuno's man of flesh and blood moved by reasons which technical rationality does not and cannot know, or for the irrational man of the existentialists and Kierkegaard's knight of faith. The clockwork, mechanical, computer man of technological society can no longer see or understand these men. They are dead to them. The soul's way of conceiving and knowing human beings and human life is also dead to them. Barrett's reality is different and is captured in the titles of his books: **Irrational Man, The Illusion of Technique,** and **Death of the Soul.**[119]

Like Augustine, Barrett sought an alternative to the dominant philosophy of his day, which in his time was a product of the reign of science, analytic philosophy. He found, as had Augustine, a different way of knowing. It required more than mere adjustments to modern thought. His solution, again with Augustine, was to "let prayer re-enter the world." It is a solution that arises from the depths of our being, from our human condition, and from a need that

> has the ferocity of hunger. Even if my life is the monotonous playing out of the end game in which checkmate is already certain, the more I realize that my position is lost, and the more impossible it becomes at each step, the more this voice cries out in me. I am obliged to pray. I shall never be silent. Never....Even if there were no ear to hear them but the void, our prayers would be the only things that sanctify our existence.[120]

Barrett here steps beyond the boundaries of technique and science into a different realm of discourse and thought. In spirit and content he experiences the paradox of philosophizing about things that cannot be philosophized about, and being rational about that which is not itself rational, or, with Becker, creating a science of things that are not amenable to traditional scientific investigation.

Barrett's call, though, is more radical than this makes it sound. He is asking of us what William James describes as a religious conversion and the Hasidic communities required of those who wished to become truly pious: to experience **teshuvah**, a turning from the everyday world and a breaking-through the armor in which this everyday world encases us. When they do this they enter into a new and different relationship with the world and others humans, and through trust, openness and being truly present they know the world in a new and truer way. We must turn away from the everyday modern world in order to truly know it and ourselves. Through such knowledge, we can transform and renew the modern world: this world, not some other, is the destination, and prayer is the way.

Barrett's prayer demands this same turning, break-through, and new relationship. It insists on a transformation of the soul that carries the person through a mystical relationship with the world to a new knowledge of the world. The world is thereby reenchanted and human experience, so fragmented in modern life, is reunited; the disinherited modern mind, like the prodigal son, is welcomed back home. Prayer is the language of the human will when it insists on deeper answers and resists the idea that we are mechanical contrivances wired into a deterministic and amoral universe. Only fatalism and nihilism can come from such a self conception. Barrett finds prayer at work most powerfully in our yearnings for freedom and morality, when we enter into a moral struggle that "must reach out toward some religious aspiration or faith to sustain itself."[121] To sustain this faith is an uncertain enterprise, as uncertain as the search for truth has been for modern thought. But it must be ventured and asserted for only in that which is beyond us, in the mystery of creation and being, do we see our human image and find confirmation. This realm of faith is not ruled by the language and method of science or philosophy or any indicative mood. It may be known, instead, when "uttered as a prayer." Barrett offers a new first principle for the modern age. It is this: "in the beginning was the prayer."[122]

The issue is, in part, whether thinking alone is ever enough. The criticism of the modern age by Barrett and others is, in part, an expression of a hatred for the rational, calculative side of modern thought and life, and particularly of the effects this life has had on any truly spiritual and poetic experience. For Barrett this loss is a loss of being. He wonders, with Heidegger, about the effects of the triumph of technique, and "whether we shall shortly be able to see around it or through it to grasp any other mode of Being."[123] If we are to get around or through this modern framework of thinking and being it will not be by means of a modern way of thinking but through some alternative: through love or Eros, according to Heidegger and Plato, through prayer according to Barrett, in the relationship of I-Thou for Martin Buber, or through participation, intuition, and transcendence for Huston Smith. All of these require that we permit the world to open before us as we stand open before it. To batter what we wish to know with our modern means of knowing is to drive it out of our sight. Instead, we need to open ourselves with a "wise passiveness" which allows us to learn to let be, free ourselves from the willfulness of the daily efforts to control and master the world so that we can experience the wonder and rapture of the world—the God's presence in all things sought by Goethe. Through these, we may achieve a full communion with the world and our true selves. Barrett, drawing on Heidegger, argues that the degree to which we have achieved this communion may be gauged by our response to poetry. When it "does not touch the daily round of our existence somewhere or other, then we ourselves have become homeless on this earth." When it does we experience the fullness of "Being and Truth."[124]

Barrett asks us to reconceive the modern view of human beings. This reconceptualization must include those indispensable elements of the soul: something to believe in, a moral content for both the self and the world, an authority beyond the confusions and uncertainties we experience in modern life, a sense of wonder and mystery, and a universe in which we play some meaningful part. The modern world discounts or rejects most of these and thereby violates that which is truly human in us, leaving us paralyzed and in despair, bare ruined choirs where the soul once sang. Barrett ends his book **The Death of the Soul** with Jesus' question to his followers: "What shall it profit a man if he gain the whole world, and lose his own soul?" He then translates it into the dilemma of our age: "What shall it profit a whole civilization, or culture, if it gains knowledge and power over the material world, but loses any adequate idea of the conscious mind, the human self, at the center of all that power?" Barrett, with all those seeking a true science of man, would respond: nothing, nothing at all.

II

I will end this chapter with brief descriptions of two twentieth century thinkers, Ernest Becker and the anthropologist Colin Turnbull, who, in distinctive ways, agree with Barrett's contention that our modern problems arise from the shortsightedness of modern thought. I present them as examples of two men who have attempted to define this alternative science of man and have come, through their efforts, to a fuller and truer understand of the nature and condition of humans beings.

I will begin with Becker. He began, in the early 1960s, by conceiving of humans as meaning-makers, as creators and bearers of the torch of culture. His work was built upon the image of man as poet—of homo poeta. His early world was filled with light and hope. These were the halcyon years, filled with an inextinguishable faith in the goodness and great possibilities of an unfettered humanity. What has prevented us in the past from realizing these possibilities? Becker was confident of the answer: the fetters of ignorance and superstition, tradition and archaic institutions, culture and society. This is an old argument, a Rousseauan vision and maxim of the Enlightenment. Becker believed it in the beginning. But from the first he sensed something was left out of this view, that some intractable element of the problem of human fulfillment would not bend to this prevailing modern view. Were the evils that plagued humans so easily and summarily dismissed by blaming them all on society and culture? Should the humans who trampled through history be seen in so soft a light? If his work had ended with this, he would have offered us only a platitude of modern humanistic psychology acquired in his novitiate in cultural anthropology and shaped by the great faith and hope of the

Enlightenment. But it didn't, and all that is insightful and provocative in his work, all that is critical to this discussion, arose from his pushing the science of man further.

What was he seeking? What was not completely understood or explained by his early view? It was human nature and the human condition he wished to understand. If he could understand these then he would know what is possible for human beings, what prevents their achieving personal fulfillment and social betterment, and what causes the evils that blight so many human prospects. His inquiry led him to study post-Freudian psychotherapy, particularly the work of Otto Rank, to the cultural anthropology of A.M. Hocart, and to the religious thought of Paul Tillich and Soren Kierkegaard. They introduced him to a darker view of humans, one to which he was, as a child of the Enlightenment, unaccustomed—its optimism and light, its often unbridled humanism and apotheosis of man, were dimmed or lost entirely. The consummation of his science offered him few consolations.

The images that dominated his later view were of a crepuscular realm inhabited by "an impoverished, weak, and frightened organism...." overwhelmed by "the utter anxiety of its finitude, its lifelong urge to drown our feelings of helplessness and inadequacy...." These human beings were lost in a universe that dwarfs them, were insignificant in the scheme of the cosmos, Crusoes shipwrecked on "an overwhelmingly miraculous and incomprehensible world, a world so full of beauty, majesty, and terror that if animals perceived it at all they would be paralyzed to act." Humans have no inherent or instinctual mechanism or structure to build them into the world. Unlike most animals, they don't mesh into the intricate fabric of the natural order, don't resonate to the rhythms of the blood or body or the earth and seasons or any of the other forces regulating nature. This is the rub for humans. They are inextricably in nature and hopelessly outside its order. The part within nature Becker called our creatureliness and the part outside our symbolic self. Impaled upon this two-sidedness, they were homo duplex, paradoxical men.[125]

Humans must resist this condition or go mad. It is too much for an overly sensitive, two-sided creature to bear. So they don't bear it; using all their resources, which are extraordinary, they produce a world that is shaped in the image of their fundamental need to escape their creatureliness, finitude, weakness, and insignificance. This is their grandest work of art, the flower of the human genius for meaning-making. It is a massive and often grand attempt to create a world according to our nobler images of ourselves. It is, also, an illusion, albeit an absolutely necessary one. This illusion blunts our consciousness and blinds us, while, at the same time, it releases the prodigious energies with which we construct a way of living and thinking that affirms and fulfills the needs of the symbolic self. The most important and powerful need of all is of a transcendent source of power and authority, a God, a ground of being, a source of life and meaningfulness. This is the grandest and most essential illusion of all, for it becomes the support for all others. This is how humans escape the limitations and terrors of their condition: the meaning-making animal transcends itself and thereby escapes the crippling consciousness of its true condition.

Humans are still meaning-making in his later thought. He still conceives them as homo poeta. But the meaning-making and the poetry arise from different sources within humans and in response to the demands of a different human condition and prospect. Cultures are no longer the source of evil in human life, humans are. Humans, unable and unwilling to face either the facts of impotence and death or to openly and consciously confront the challenge that life demands of them, construct cultures to protect themselves from the truth. Humans use culture to construct the everyday heroics that sustain them. These constructions are the source of the greatest achievements of humans and of much of the evil in the world. The lies of culture are "vital lies"; and the most vital lie of all is the character lie, the lie of self-fashioned identity, of being somebody, of rising above the bestial floor. Through them each individual seeks a sense of ultimate significance and a place within an eternal and infinite scheme of things.

Individuals cannot create the character and the culture they require by themselves. They do so always in the company of others. Humans are too weak and lost to stand alone with their meaning, to support the significance they give to human existence. They must have the legitimation of the group, the society, the culture, and the transcendent. They can have these only by transferring their hopes, loves, courage, and faith to other persons; we see our meanings as real, potent, and good when we see them in the faces of others. The grandest human projection is through our fellow humans to culture and finally onto the cosmos and God.

Our nature and condition compel us to create, as part of culture, hero systems and immortality ideologies. These arise from the need to transfer the unbearable truth of the human condition to something beyond the individual self, something capable of containing and carrying forward the heroic image. This may only be accomplished if individuals turn to their fellow humans and the cultural world they have collectively created. The culture must also turn to some higher and indisputable source of power to legitimate its beliefs. Community and religion are necessary because, in Rank's words, "man cannot live closed upon himself and for himself. He must project the meaning of his life outward, the reason for it, even the blame for it."[126]

Humans, however, do not give themselves up to culture without reservations and resistance. They are torn by contradictory urges. They wish to stand out, be special, assert their distinctiveness and rise above all others, while, at the same time, needing to submerge themselves in the group, the culture, or the majesty and power of God. They shun the herd and seek the infinite inflation of the individual self, yet are impelled, just as strongly, to identify with forces beyond and greater than themselves. There is no reconciliation of these two, only the unrelieved tension. They must turn to each other and attach their destinies to each other while wishing to stand out and shine with their unique powers.

Becker's science of man moved his thinking from homo poeta to Otto Rank's notion of humans as "theological beings," and from a science of man fired by a progressive and utopian spirit and a hope for earthly salvation to one darkened by a tragic vision of the limits of human life. It brought him to believe that it is in culture that we catch the nature of humans, and that only in and through culture can humans achieve the solace and salvation they require. By absorbing and transforming our creature consciousness, culture allows us to transcend it and deny the dilemmas of our humanness. All cultures are fictional systems that embody the intellectual, spiritual, social and economic beliefs and practices of the group. All but the very few, who through self-generation make their own meanings without a source of authority beyond their own genius, are molded by cultures. Cultures are built upon systems of illusions called ideologies. Individuals succumb to this enculturation with ambivalence; they are eager to give up the responsibility for their lives yet struggle against the anonymity of the masses. Freedom is gladly given up yet longed for; individuality is sacrificed to peace of mind but sorely missed. All of this is normal and necessary; it is also a mass neurosis—the normal neurosis of humankind; and it is all the result of human need and the nature of humans and their condition in the world. Culture doesn't repress humans; rather, humans use culture to repress themselves. Cultures work because they create the communities through which humans forge the most encompassing, enriching, and liberating meanings possible to humans—those of religion or ritual-myth systems.

Cultures, therefore, are inescapably ambiguous in their gift. They allow humans a life free from the crippling confrontation with the reality of their condition, and at the same time they deaden us to life, close it out in order to offer a life we can tolerate. They are necessary and good, yet a threat to the nobler images of humanity based upon freedom, creativity, and truth. At the least, such a conception of humans and cultures calls into question the primacy of freedom and individuality in liberal thought and the prospects for modern secular cultures; at most, it questions the ability of modern cultures to meet the most basic needs of humans.

Becker was convinced that modern culture could not meet these needs. He believed, as John Dewey did, that the modern world had lost the unity of knowledge and world view necessary to achieve these ends. Dewey envisioned our age, and his philosophy, as working itself through a wilderness created by the dramatic transformations and dislocations that brought the modern world into existence. He was confident it would bring us to a clearing where a new integration of thought, human life, and society could be created. Our pressing problem was the disruption of personal experience and community life, a disturbance in the flow of interaction, that accompanied this process of reconstructing experience and from which would come a new order or equilibrium in experience. Becker's metaphor was grimmer. The frontier and the endless forest of Dewey was a vast wasteland for Becker. Since the dissolution of the Christian world view of the Middle Ages Western Civilization had "been diminishing the reservoir of meanings upon which the individual can draw." Enlightenment and progress, heralded as engines of human betterment, had not made life richer and broader, but narrower; "both in range of objects and in richness of shared performance, modern man had been increasingly narrowed down."[127] For all its prospects the modern age had failed to produce a new synthesis, a modern unification of knowledge and moral vision upon which to built individual and community life. This, in Becker's mind, is the crippling crisis of our time and its greatest failure.

Without such a synthesis the bonds that tie individuals to one another are attenuated, humans lose a sense of place in the natural order of our planet and the cosmos, the myths and rituals that once breathed life into culture wither away, and the ideals that once sustained human actions ossify and scatter in "an epoch that has almost wholly abandoned the quest for the ideal."[128] The centerpiece of medieval society and thought, a transcendent realm of being and value, had either ossified into institutional religions with dominion over Sundays or succumbed altogether to the panderings of a secular society that had "completely eclipsed the tensions between the invisible-visible dichotomy by simply denying the invisible world." Either way, Becker thinks "we have become completely secular."[129] This secular society offers little possibility for the intensive creation of meaning in a community. It has narrowed and emptied of meaning its everyday activities and rituals. Instead, it has created bureaucratic organizations filled with isolated and alienated individuals competing for the rewards of consumer society. Such organizations are the building blocks of a rational society, beautiful in their precision and abstraction, but in essence one dimensional, incapable of fulfilling fundamental human needs, and inhuman. Human life, in Max Scheler's words, had become "an aggregation of movable quantities," within which humans wander, this time in Becker's words, "disconnected, mechanical, limited, servile, determined." Such a creature is condemned to live walled in a small, controlled, and finite world, one in which he had become meaningless to himself and "could never transcend himself, could never hope for the larger identification with the life of the universe."[130]

We cannot live with this view of ourselves or in such a world. Both ignore or deny something fundamental and irrefragable in humans, some "ultimate root" of human nature and its relation to the universe. They miss the central point about humans—that "meaning, conviction, sense of intimacy with the cosmic process" are central to human experience and fulfillment.[131] Humans are not human when they are stripped of these; indeed they become inhuman when reduced to the trivial pursuits of modern life. Becker's condemnations of modern life and culture are fiercest when fired by this belief that a violation of our humanness is involved, when our souls and humanity are being bartered for the trade goods of modern culture. What is given away in these exchanges is, in Becker's words, "the rich participation in a broad panorama of life experiences,...an expansive present" that draws upon the full range of human energies and capacities and enables humans to "live the dream of creation" in which the individual is tied firmly to the community and, through self-transcending beliefs, to the universe.[132]

This is the decisive finding of Becker's science: each individual needs "a living and daily concern with ultimates, with the mystery of being, and with his role in the perpetuation of being. And rational, technical knowledge cannot give this." Positivism has "gradually emptied man, making him a manipulator of the world, but one who gained it only to lose its significance to him, and his deep significance to it." To conceive of human wholeness requires a broadening of our field of vision to include human life within "a cosmos of transcendent, divine meanings, and not under a microscope of disinterested scientific investigation."[133] Without this expanded horizon science cannot create a unified and inclusive understanding of humans and their prospects, cannot construct "an integrated world conception into which we fit ourselves with pure belief and trust," and cannot build a society capable of both liberating and fulfilling humans.[134] Without this broader vision, humans are alienated and fragmented, thrown back on their own insufficient resources, outsiders in the scheme of creation, and without a means of redemption from hopelessness and meaninglessness; for all their science and power, all their Faustian ambition and conquest, they are bereft, having lost "a sense of unity and participation in the universe," the loss of which "cuts away the ultimate roots upon which all 'higher' forms of sympathy and emotional life depend for their subsistence."[135]

III

Beneath much of the criticism of modern life there is a vision of what is necessary, good, and possible for humans. However long the odds and however often the realization of the vision eludes us, there is the pertinacious faith and enduring hope that we can make a better world. The critique of modern society is framed by such a vision of human life and society. The vision offers an alternative to the present and acts as a device for revealing the nature of our age and the outline of a better future. This is certainly the case with Becker and his criticisms. It is also the faith and inspiration of the work of the anthropologist Colin Turnbull.

Turnbull's book **The Human Cycle** is an interesting example of the use of comparisons to both criticize modern society and show a way beyond it to a better world.[136] The book describes a cycle of human life he has found in all of the cultures he has studied. He uses his descriptions of this cycle, as it operates in three different cultures, to reflect on modern culture and the world it has created for us. With the Mbuti tribe of Africa he shows us the qualities of a small-scale communal society: mutual responsibility, interdependence, the integration of individual and social life, a community of belief, the centrality of religion, the art of living fully, and the unity and richness of individual experience. In his experiences in India he finds a way of life in which spirit guides and gives meaning to reason and knowledge, the greater "Self" breaks the shell of a too narrow and exclusive concern for the smaller, secular, everyday self, and the sacred is a necessary and natural part of life. By holding these two up to his own experiences of growing up in pre-World War II England, he shows us the weaknesses of our own modern way of life.

In each of these cultures he observed the different degrees to which their members were educated by and lived within organized systems of belief and webs of relationships and responsibilities that gave meaning to their lives. When a culture fails to deliberately and effectively provide its members with such an ordered world of meanings, as Britain failed to do for him, it fails to meet a fundamental need of humans. That need is the one I described earlier: meaning and purpose commensurate with our highest aspirations, a community of belief embodying these meanings and purposes, and a common faith based upon a sense of the sacred or religious. It is just such a world that Turnbull didn't find in the Britain of his youth and in the modern societies in which he lived most of his life.

Let me begin with a general description of the three cultures he describes. The Mbuti dominate his discussions of childhood and adolescence. They are hunter-gatherers who live in the Ituri Forest of Zaire. The forest defines their world and, at least until recently, has isolated and protected them from threats to their way of life. Isolation has allowed them to carry-on, as they have for generations, the seemingly eternal rhythms of their lives in the sacred domain of the forest. The forest is the source of all that is necessary to them—food, shelter, clothing, warmth, and affection. It is the source of all power and fruitfulness—a sacred mother, father, and lover. They live in it as a womb that nurtures and protects them. All life is sacred to them and they trespass on it whenever they, of necessity, exploit it to meet their needs. Their lives are circumscribed by and integrated around the sacred circles of womb, family, community, forest, and universe. These lives are characterized by non-violence, interdependence, a spontaneous generosity, orderliness without law, cooperation, a spirit of wonder and exploration, and an awareness of the Spirit that pervades all things and ties them together in an indivisible whole. This wholeness is found in the natural world, in the tribe and its culture, and within each individual.[137]

Turnbull's discussion of India is confined to specific aspects of Indian life. The overall picture of the culture, so powerfully presented for the Mbuti, is not present. The focus is on youth (after adolescence) and the passage into adulthood. His portrayal is drawn from his experiences in Indian schools, the traditional **gurukula** or forest university, the more modern Banaras Hindu University, and his experiences in ashrams. The theme in his discussions of all of these is the beauty and truth of the sacred or spiritual life at the heart of education and life in India. It is the spiritual and religious life of traditional Indian society which interests him most. The sense of wonder and the joy of living, so characteristic of the Indians he portrays, are possible for Indians because their life, both at home and in public life, is ordered around the symbols and rituals of their religious and cultural beliefs. It offers a life shaped by a vision of the greater potentials of human existence. At the center of such a life is a "quality of being both in the world and beyond it...."[138] This quality is achieved only through a discipline that prepares the young for an adulthood of work, marriage, and social life guided by the broader vision of spiritual life. Whether this adulthood follows the "spiritual path" (removed from the world), the "religious" (within the world), or the secular, the source of its strength is the spiritual life. Its discipline, and the devotion it engenders, lead to a liberation and enlightenment different from those sought by the modern western world. Turnbull thinks they offer a kind of human fulfillment the West does not offer its young.

What of Turnbull's own culture, our modern Western culture, and his own life within it? He holds his life, from infancy to adulthood, up for inspection and comparison. The comparisons are usually at the expense of his own culture and his experiences of infancy, childhood, and adolescence. The son of upper class parents, his early life was with nannies and without his parents. His life was privileged, but lonely and empty. His adolescent years, spent at an established and prestigious public school, were brutish and ugly. The contrast with both the Mbuti or the Indians is stark. But in his twenties, after his good years at Oxford and the perfunctory performance of his duties during W.W.II, he went to India to study and his life changed. In the **gurukula**, the **ashram**, and the university he went through a "second adolescence, properly this time." It was here that he learned the art of learning, the art of being ecstatic, and the art of reason. Through these he achieved the goal of all the stages before adulthood: "learning what to do with your life rather than your mind."[139] From this time forward, his life, the inner life of his mind and spirit, was no longer strictly Western or modern. Regardless of his work, as researcher, museum curator, or professor in the U.S., he was, at heart, a member and product of the tribe and the **ashram**.

What is the vision of life he learned in India and Africa? It is, in both what he praises and criticizes, an essentially anti-modern vision. Its essence is a criticism of much of modern Western life. This life denies us rich areas of human experience by closing or deadening our perceptions of the reality around us. Turnbull found in them a different world and richer experience, one in which

> all around us, at every moment in our lives, reaching out and touching us, there is a world of excitement and fascination. Its riches are denied to none, for beauty and wonder lie at every stage of the life cycle, from childhood to old age, transforming poverty into wealth, squalor into magnificence, tedium into sport, fear into recognition, hatred and bigotry into understanding. Access to this world does not require any great feat of intellect, nor does it demand a lifetime dedicated to the quest. All that it needs is a mind and a soul, the soul being that which opens the mind, breathing life into it, making it infinitely curious. The senses that are common to all of us, regardless of who or what we are, provide us with all the tools we need.[140]

We moderns have closed ourselves into too small a world and come to believe it the only world there is. We see too little of the potential of human existence because we have convinced ourselves that our modern world is all there is to see. Our modern mind killed our souls through indifference and neglect and then found itself permanently closed to the wonders of a world it can no longer hear, touch, or communicate with. We have lost the capacity to see that "there is so much potential for beauty and goodness at every stage of life, in any culture; so much potential for living life (and enjoying it) better by living it for others as well as for ourselves," but instead "find so much of life to be unsatisfactory, somehow not quite what it should have been, filled with little disappointments."[141]

But Turnbull offers more than a repeat of what has been said already. He shows us the specific ways in which this modern condition has harmed us and how we can change it. If he is correct about the potentialities of life, then we must rethink the way we live both in the light of these potentialities and of our feeling that something is wrong with the modern way of living.[142] Our modern mistake, in Turnbull's view, is our conceptions of self and society that over-value the individual at the expense of the social, allow for the creation of society but not of community, permit big and bureaucratic social organizations to dominate our lives, ignore or misunderstand our largest, social self, and forget that the aim of group living is to order "interpersonal and intergroup relationships into a comprehensible system that achieves the maximum advantages for the society as a whole while allowing the maximum possible freedom for each individual to develop his own way and make his own unique contribution to society."[143] We have disregarded the immediate and intimate relationships that are constitutive of genuine and good community, preferring instead to focus on the more formal and legal social arrangements of society. We have thereby created structures that too often isolate and fragment individuals and groups. We have prized freedom at the cost of both this isolation and fragmentation and of the benefits attached to community. Religion has been removed from its integral and integrative role. The collective ritual and symbolism upon which a community of belief rests have been discredited or discarded. All of these failures, taken together, have made it difficult for us to "inculcate the habit of mutual interdependence, the habit of sharing and caring in a manner that is both consistent and effective in daily life."[144]

It is these characteristics and qualities Turnbull discovered in the Mbuti tribe and in India. In every case, they existed because of a systematic process of education that inculcated them throughout the different stages of life. At the center of this process is one foundational belief: "life itself is seen as a constant process of socialization, and binding the various stages of life together, just as it binds individuals into communities and communities into societies, is the integrative force of religious belief and practice."[145] If we in modern society are to achieve the richness and fulfillment he found in these small, closely knit, pre-modern cultures, then we must change our basic values and way of living. These changes will not occur unless we begin in childhood and carry them forward in our educational system. We must educate and socialize our young into them. But, more importantly, they will not occur because most of our modern societies, particularly American and British, have the wrong values and way of life. This is evident to Turnbull in their inabilities, in their educational and social systems, to create communities of belief inspired and enlivened by the higher human qualities he labels "Spirit" and "soul." They do not offer their young an explicit and comprehensive moral education, do not help them create social selves through a single-minded preparation for social life, and fail to make central the goal of becoming an individual who is a "fully integrated whole, using his whole being in all that he does... mind, body, heart, and soul, or Spirit."[146] With these, modern society could become "a human society instead of a mechanical state."[147] In such a state we can attain both a truer and fuller individuality than the one we so ardently pursue today and a richer social and communal life.

The power of Turnbull's case, both against modern culture and for his alternative, is in its wealth of specific descriptions, examples, and stories. Through them you gain a sense of the life behind the abstractions; through them we feel the words: the ideas breathe, we can feel their pulse, see their eyes and the expression on their faces, and hear their voices. Here are some examples from his experiences.

Turnbull tells a Hindu parable about God. It goes like this.

> God...got bored with being God...so he manifested himself as a pig. That was much more fun but after a while he became rather lonely. So he divided himself and made manifest a sow. That was more fun still, and before long there were lots of little piglets. The parents told the piglets that it was all a sort of divine comedy, a game of make-believe, that really they were all one and the same God, manifestations of the one eternal truth....The first piglets told their children what the parents had told them, but after several generations the minds of pigs and piglets were so engrossed with other things that the story lost its interest and eventually parents never bothered to tell the story at all. Which is why we no longer recognize our own divinity; we are too busy thinking that we are pigs and enjoying it.[148]

This is an idea found in most cultures. Humans fall from God, or grace, or Eden, or the golden age, or virtue, or ideals, or innocence. One of the ways to fall is to forget. This happens because we have poor memories, or become old, or can't stand the comparison, or become preoccupied with something else. Forgetting is, seemingly, as natural as falling. We pride ourselves on our knowledge, take our lack of knowledge as a challenge, commend ourselves for how much more we know than previous eras, and discount what we have forgotten as unimportant, superstitious, or no longer relevant or true. We are misguided in all this, as Turnbull's parable shows us. He makes the connection clear in the last sentences of the book:

> We are like the piglets who like it that way and have quite forgotten the ecstasy of divinity. Like them, for us the human cycle has become bogged down in the muddy business of survival rather than being a soaring flight of rich fulfillment.[149]

Turnbull also tells a lovely Bushman story that expresses something else the piglets have lost. The story is about a child who one day sees a reflection of a beautiful bird as he drinks from the waterhole. The boy decides he must see the bird again, for it has flown away. His quest lasts all of his life. In the end it takes him, an old man now, to Mount Kilimanjaro. At its summit, exhausted, he prepares to die,

> content with a life well spent, for he had been lucky enough to find beauty once, and in his heart he had never lost it. As he closed his eyes

for the last time on an empty sky, he called on the name of his mother, who had given him such a wonderful and joyous life. And as he stretched out his arms in a final gesture, his open hands upturned, down from the sky came a solitary feather and settled in one hand. The hand closed slowly, then held it as tightly in death as the vision of beauty had been held during life.[150]

Here is the Mbuti's and Turnbull's idea of a life worth living, one filled with the highest ambition and the grandest purpose, one fired by a vision of beauty and goodness, one that calls out of each individual the special abilities necessary to aspire to live in the fullness of his own powers and the wonders of the world. This Bushman's life and his vision embody more than the self-infinitizing idiosyncrasy of one man, but a sign that tells us something about our selves and about the life of the Bushman's people.

Our modern quest is different from the poor Bushman's. So is our idea of the heroic pursuit of some noble end. We have those who seek fame and power through business, sports or politics. We have our heroes and our idea of the good life. But they are mock heroes and offer us a sordid boon. We have laid waste our powers even as we gained great power over the whole world; we have exiled our hearts and muted our memories so as to silence their admonitions. And for what? A sordid trade in money and a politics of narrow and mean self-interest. It is this ethos we transmit to our young. If they are listless or surly, refusing too often our good advice and guidance, it may be that we have not enough of the Bushman in us. We have not given them a vision of what a life should be in its fullness, and of the heroic, the beautiful, and the ideal. The crisis of modern culture "is precisely that the youth no longer feel heroic in the plan for action that their culture has set up."[151] We have reduced man to a fraction of his being, dismembered him and severed him from sources both within himself and beyond himself that give the richness and depth to his life; in such a world, living such a life, man is no longer human.

Much of what we associate with religion is present in these two examples. Religion, the divine, Spirit (which Turnbull prefers), and God can be a safeguard against the urge to submerge ourselves in the comings and goings of everyday life, of getting and spending, of eating, working, copulating, and sleeping. It carries us, both as individuals and as groups, beyond our inclinations to lose the fullness of our lives in the struggles and satisfactions of our temporal existence. Religion makes us look up or within or around us to see a different world, one suffused with a second sight or an alternative way of knowing that arises from sources in humans as powerful and inherent in our constitutions as our practical arts of living. In its way of seeing and knowing and being, Turnbull's alternative way is ancient and common to, in one form or another, virtually all humans and groups throughout history. Without it, or with it hedged and subordinated to our other interests, as it is often with established religions, we become crippled and incomplete.

Religious beliefs and practices are also important, as has been said earlier, because they are powerfully integrative social forces. This is true for the Mbuti. Their world is filled with spirits. The forest that supplies all their needs is their God. All of their lives are filled with the power and beauty of the Spirit that pervades their forest world. In their world all life is sacred, all actions sacred rituals and "acts of consecration."[152] The lives of the orthodox Hindus of India, also, are ordered by a spiritual entity that "is the vital part of the hustle and bustle of the active, adult world of doing just as much as it is a part of the contemplative life of the monks, or the academic life of the monastic students."[153]

Turnbull tells a story about the Abbot of a Tibetan monastery. He was a jolly, chubby old man, not inclined to extreme forms of asceticism. He had a lively sense of humor and saw little sense in a too rigid application of the rules. His monastery was a serious, disciplined, and happy place because of him. As a leader and head teacher he would not command or teach: "Like the Buddha, the Abbot did not teach; he barely even advised; he just was.... Those who chose to listen had to find the way for themselves...."[154] But in Turnbull's eyes he was a saint and a master teacher.

Why? Because he "radiated energy and love, not as two distinct things but as one."[155] While his influence was great, it was particularly powerful on the adolescents. They would come to the monastery on the verge of the transformations into youth and adulthood. The Abbot would guide and advise them but not teach in any formal way. He would listen, lead, and indicate the way.

I tell about the Abbot because of the following incident. One day he walked with two boys up a mountain near the monastery. Along the way they chattered about flowers and plants. At the top they found no flowers just snow and a deep depression with snow down to the bottom where a black pool of still water stood. It was a place of inexpressible beauty and grandeur. Turnbull learned later the walk was the result of the boys having been caught playing with each other's genitals. The Abbott's response, in Turnbull's view, was

far more than a lecture about birds and bees, and the mountain climb was far more than a lesson in the necessity of conserving energy, the mechanical tricks of which the boys learned in their classes. The Abbot gave them something worth conserving energy for, the wonder for the great beauty that always lies a few steps higher, denied us if we rest content with the lesser beauty we found below.[156]

Again, Turnbull stresses that it is the higher rather than the lower things with which humans need to be concerned. It is the "wonder of the great beauty" that should guide our lives. It also shows us a form of sex education different from what we see in our modern schools and from Turnbull's experiences in school.

One final story is from Turnbull's education at Westminister, an English public school. It is one of the few healthy and productive experiences of his time there and highlights one of his central themes: the importance of ritual and sacred places. The sacred place was the ancient school hall of Westminister, the hall of the ancestors. Each day after classes the whole school assembled for Latin prayers which became for Turnbull the most sacred time of the day. An atmosphere of sanctity was created by the exclusiveness and specialness of the old hall and by the intimacy and immediacy of prayer and finally by the use of a Latin that seemed to contain the whole grandeur and mystery of God and Spirit and all higher things.

It was here, too, that the old ritual of "handing" was administered. Again, the attraction for Turnbull was the sanctity of the place and in the ritual. Handing was a punishment for the severest offenses. The entire school was assembled in the hall and the offender was called to the raised dais at the far end. On the dais was a table with an open drawer with two sacred birches sticking out. The offense was proclaimed and "the headmaster then lightly touched him on each hand with one of the birches, and that was that. The effect was powerful; the boy was never again regarded in quite the same way, and the handing carried with it unmistakable ostracism."[157] Here for Turnbull was the world, sacred and profane, moral order and everyday life, pulled together in an indivisible unity, a world capable of touching and forming the heart and the soul and the mind of the young.

What Turnbull finds so essential in all of these experiences and descriptions is that which makes possible a rich and whole life: a community of belief and the socialization of the young into this belief; an awareness of the "Spirit" and the religious dimension of life; a sense of mutual interdependence, responsibility, obligation; an appreciate of the whole range of human needs; and conceptions of self and society that makes all these necessary and good. In celebrating the cultures that possess these attributes he also criticizes those that do not, modern society most of all. We are without a community of belief due to the structures of modern society, the fragmentation and specialization of our economic and social systems, our beliefs in individualism and the isolation it produces, the preoccupation with freedom and individual development at the expense of a commitment to and obligation to the community, and the pervasive secularism of public life that denies or ignores an important part of our self. Ours is a world built on a "mechanics of fragmentation and isolation" in which individuals achieve success either outside of social life or in opposition to it. We have lost the idea that humans become fully human as social selves who achieve individuality through society, who live in a world that is both secular and spiritual, who can have free and full lives through the obligations and responsibilities imposed by the community, who find the greatest fulfillments in life in experiencing the richness and the miracle of human existence.

As an alternative, Turnbull offers an insight into a different way of looking at the world around him and of understanding the needs of its human inhabitants. It is this insight and understanding that is the integrating force holding all his particular examples, ideas, and beliefs together. It both expresses his vision of things and describes the essential attributes any vision must possess which hopes to successfully integrate or unify human existence. In the Bushman's life, for all its primitiveness, we see these attributes. He seeks something beyond the concerns of ordinary routine or everyday life that, when affirmed and followed, transforms that life and fills it with the higher purposes of life: the pursuit of beauty and truth, an awareness of the transcendent and spiritual nature of human existence, a devotion to an ideal, and a dedication to a vision more encompassing than one defined by our modern getting and spending, individualism, and freedom.

Chapter Five
Paideia Agonistes

This book has attempted to work toward a critique of contemporary education. While education has been the topic in only one chapter so far, all the rest has been a foundation for this undertaking. The foundation is, though, the key to the discussion of education. Since much is built upon it, much time has been spent upon securing its footings. In the end, we will hopefully proclaim, as I imagine ancient mariners did, that the short stay ashore was worth the endless hours of tacking across the sea.

To understand education in late twentieth century America, both in and out of school, it is necessary to understand the society and culture in which it occurs. This is the central assumption of this work. Education, as considered here, is always within a context and that context is the culture of the society that creates the formal and informal educational system. The quotation of Margaret Mead in chapter one makes clear this assumption and its implication for our current educational and cultural condition. It is worth repeating it here:

> Not until we realize that a poor culture will never become rich, though it be filtered through the expert methods of unnumbered pedagogues and that a rich culture with no system of education at all will leave its children better off than a poor culture with the best system in the world, will we begin to solve our educational problems.[158]

The quality and kind of culture, therefore, is critical in the quality and kind of education a culture possesses and is, in important ways, the single most important factor in the education of the young. Poor, sick, or crisis-ridden cultures, those that have lost their richness and unity, will do a poor job of educating their young; they can do little more than pass on the empty spaces of their culture. Rich cultures make available to the coming generations the abundance that flows from their creative energies.

An axiom of Mead's idea, articulated by Joseph Hart in **Education in the Humane Community** is that good education can exist only in a good community. Community is the living body of a culture: rich or poor, cultures array themselves in the specific forms of community life. Schools should reflect the wholeness and integration—the life—of their communities. They also must be integrated into that community life. The boundaries between the life of the community and the life of school must be a door, not a wall; the life of the community should fill the schools, set its spirit and subject-matter, define its goals and values, and stand as the model for living and learning. The whole community must be the school and the school must be a miniature community. Those essential ingredients of a good community, of a life lived so that individuals are fully human, are the indispensable elements of a good education. The specific task of Part Two is to examine and affirm this view through an examination of the qualities of a good community and a good education.[159]

A second central assumption, developed in the first chapters, is that there is something wrong with our modern culture and world. There are many arguments as to the causes and the nature of our troubles and many different estimations of the relative effects of its virtues and vices. There is more agreement as to one fact about it: modern culture is without something that is of vital importance for human beings. It does not possess, in Mead's terms, the richness necessary to educate and fulfill human beings. The weakness of community in modern society is both an effect of this condition—for it is the richness of culture that makes healthy and strong communities—and a cause of it—without community culture lacks a vessel to hold it and give it life. The modern age has been effective at undermining the bases of existing community and ineffective, even indifferent, in its efforts to create new modern community. These effects have been impervious to the particular forms of social or political life, for community has been harmed by both exaggerated individualism on the one side and the various forms of modern collectivism on the other. This loss is of vital importance to human beings because it has crippled their capacity to be fully human. Similarly, education is crippled by this situation: a crippled culture can offer no more than a crippled education to its young.

Both assumptions insist upon the broadest definition of education. It can not stop at the school door or be assigned to one specially designed and designated institution. It is an affair of the whole culture and the entire experience of the young; whether in school or on the street, education is always of, by, and for the community. Parents teaching children the simplest skills, schools teaching the narrowest vocational or technical subjects, churches instilling the doctrines and morals of their faiths, or television teaching whatever it teaches are each part of this larger definition and configuration of education. It is the life of the culture that occupies the central place in the many institutions and relationships that educate members of society. Parents, teachers, ministers, employers, and friends may not separate themselves and their teachings from the life and educational process of the society.

This is true when education is broad and liberal in its aims and practices. It is also true when educational institutions are narrowly technical in their nature and function. In modern societies there is a powerful tendency to make education narrow, technical, and functional. This type of education reflects the larger realities of the society and culture, not a peripheral, insignificant, or anomalous element. It tells us something important about the nature of our culture. When the major educational institutions so conceive themselves that the narrow and technical functions drive out the broad and liberal ones, and slowly turn themselves into training centers rather than educational institutions, education and culture suffer primarily from the impoverishment of the culture, not the shortcomings of the educational system.

This tendency toward narrowing down the functions of schools parallels the tendency in modern societies to narrow or reduce the rich variety of educational forces and institutions of the society. As non-school educational institutions have weakened the schools have been asked to pick up those responsibilities abnegated by the larger society. Schools have, in effect, been asked to both narrow and broaden themselves at the same time. As a result, they have become unclear as to their precise identity and role. As the principal educational institution in society they have assumed responsibility for the care, education, and general well-being of the young while, at the same time, they have been pushed to narrow their conception of what the schools are for, teach basics, and stay out of students' lives. Expected both to compensate for the shortcomings of the society and to not overstep their proper place by intruding into those sensitive areas of belief, morality, and value, schools are pulled in opposing directions, which both strengthens and attenuates the bonds between school, community and culture.

This has been our route to educational confusion. At the center of this confusion is the loss of a clear conception of and commitment to the essential connections of education and community. Education becomes predominantly a matter of schooling, not of the whole community and schools. Turnbull's case for our failures, discussed in chapter four, is built upon just these narrowings of our view and practice of education. Yet this is occurring at the same time we define schools as feeders, doctors, parents, counselors, baby sitters, moral educators, and instruments of commerce and competitiveness.

The issue of community in modern society has been present throughout this book. The whole argument is based upon the importance and problem of community. The social scientist and activist Harry Boyte wrote a book in the 1980's, entitled **Community is Possible**, that articulated this concern for community.[160] The book, as its title suggested, was a plea presented to an often skeptical and indifferent audience, a cry in the wilderness, a shout over a tide of doubt about or indifference toward the idea of community. He was speaking to most of us as inhabitants of modern societies. As a group we experience the dislocations of modern life, the atomization of associations and everyday life, the difficulties of finding groups that bind us together and shape the world in which we live. Having experienced them for a long time, we have come to think them natural and unavoidable parts of our modern life. But he is addressing all those who feel this modern world has gotten beyond them and is now controlled by institutions too large and far away to express their will or permit them any meaningful participation in the conduct of affairs fundamental to the life of a citizen in a democratic society. It is, most importantly, addressed to those who feel that these developments have undermined the primary institutions that should give meaning and purpose to their lives, afford it the richness of tradition and shared values and beliefs, a sense of belonging and roots. Boyte assumed that this audience is enormous for a simple reason: the power and the nature of modern society create a world where community, the kind of community that provides individuals with all of these things, is difficult to create and sustain. Such difficulties breed many things, but for many today they have bred, too often, the feeling of helplessness and the experience of defeat in the face of seemingly irresistible forces of modern society. His book exhorts each of us to rise up and try again, to affirm the value of community and the possibility that it can be created here and now in our modern world.

I am a part of his audience, believing as I do that community is important but doubtful about its possibilities in our time. I have known there is an issue or problem with community in our time. I discovered it as I grew into adulthood, in the course of navigating the progressively shallower stream of my modern life. And I saw it in the problems people faced in searching for associations that offered the prospect of participation in the life of their group, organization, town, or government. What I found was that groups and organizations exist and individuals join them, but without finding or creating community. Instead they found companionship and friendship, fellow enthusiasts for one hobby or recreation or another, lonely or isolated individuals reaching for human fellowship. Perhaps this is why so many go to all the group events listed each week on the radio for classes, meetings, performances, help sessions. All of these meet a need and are one element of the urge to create community. But by themselves they are not sufficient to create or maintain the qualities of community. They reflect the deep need and the superficial and insubstantial solutions modern life has concocted as a way out of the problem. These are the trappings of our troubles, the often pitiful attempts of people to fashion some semblance of a rich life within the steel structures and the cold logic of modern life.

Another book, this one from the 1950's, Robert Nisbet's **The Quest for Community**, describes and regrets the state of community in modern society.[161] His quest for community, like most quests, is after something we no longer have, perhaps never had, but wish for and need. It calls us to an important and compelling undertaking, one in which all of our higher aspirations and noblest virtues would be required and fulfilled. The community Nisbet describes demands a commitment and a binding belief, one capable of defining and sustaining each of its members lives. This is the community that is important in this work. It is the one we do not have in modern society and the one we need badly enough to quest for.

Books like these two arise from the prophetic urge to turn people in a new direction by awakening them to the shortcomings and the possibilities of their lives. They are often and easily discounted as atavistic, nostalgic, romantic, quixotic--- out of step with our times and the way things work in the modern age. And indeed they may well be. But maybe, instead, they are correct and it is the times that are out of joint. I believe they are. They are out of joint in a way that goads us to reconsider and reorder our modern world so that it better meets are most powerful and fundamental needs. The issue of community tells us, at least in part, both where we have gone astray and what it is we need to find our way.

I start, then, from this problem with community, one which must be remedied if we are to achieve the kind and level of human fulfillment we proclaim as our cardinal ideal. There is something fundamental and necessary to humans in community. The qualities of community are those defined in the works on community of the great early sociologists, Weber, Tonnies, Durkheim, and MacIver, and by the thinkers discussed earlier in this work. In all of them, community means the ideals that hold a culture together, the unity of knowledge and belief that undergird those ideals, the social forms that give shape and a hue to the essential and binding beliefs that unify individual members of a group and constitute the heart of a society. It is a name for the bonds—intellectual, moral, and spiritual—that hold a people together, a name for all that gives them their deep and lasting commonalties, a name for the collective experiences of belonging, of having a place, of being at home. It is a name for all that a good culture provides it members.[162]

Community is a quality of the life we live together. It is always characterized by the intimacy and immediacy of a small and closely knit group that produces a sense of belonging, rootedness, identity, and meaning for the individual. At its center is a social intercourse which partakes, and is filled with, fellowship and communion. Where individual human beings are tied to their neighbors by bonds of shared values, commitments, beliefs, and the intangible ties of affection and a common life, community exists. Community, in this broad sense, may be either good or bad. An exhibition of the bad is Nazi communal ideology and behavior; of the good is the Christian brotherhood of the Amish or Mennonites. This capacity for both good and bad doesn't dilute or taint the central point here—the importance of community to human beings and to the modern age. Rather, it makes more urgent the need for a conception of a good community, one that meets the human need for community without enslaving or brutalizing its members or its neighbors, one which observes the complexities and contradictions of human beings and their human condition, particularly those dilemmas surrounding the web of relationships that connect community, pluralism, individualism, and freedom to one another.[163]

Community is at once a grand vision of the possibilities and fulfillments of human life and a grim reminder of the limitations of the human prospect. It describes more than a world moved by the confluence of interests of rational, rights-bearing individuals sharing associations and collective ends; more too than the democratic process of free and equal persons engaged in dialogue. Good communities may be founded upon some or all of these, but only when they participate in and satisfy the deeper foundations of community. When community builds on such a foundation, it is another name, a modern one, for the paideia of the Greeks.

The concept of paideia is valuable here because it connects qualities of community, culture, and the process of education. Like community, it is a difficult word to define. It too is protean, changing shapes with each use and defying attempts to definitively fix its meaning. This hasn't stopped its being used by many, particularly lately when it has been made more commonplace and popular by Mortimer Adler's **Paideia Proposal**. Adler defines it on the dedication pages as follows: "**PAIDEIA** from the Greek pais, paidos: the upbringing of the young.... In an extended sense, the equivalent of the Latin humanitas signifying the general learning that should be the possession of all human beings." Both elements of his definition are present in his "educational manifesto": the young are educated into full membership in our democratic society while, at the same time, they are educated into their full humanity through general learning. He develops a plan for curriculum that furthers and realizes the ideals of democracy, particularly the demand for equality of opportunity, through a common curriculum of traditional study with a heavy emphasis on classical and humanistic approaches to learning and education. His paideia describes the ideals of education in a modern democratic society. These ideals arise from our heritage of classical culture and its humanism. The emphasis is on a naturalistic and individualistic view of humans and the world. The outcome of education is a specific type of human being. His plan details a course of study leading to a democratic society and a model of a good human being and citizen.[164]

J. Chambliss also uses the concept of paideia in his recent book **Education Theory as Theory of Conduct**. He too sees two elements to paideia: "In one sense paideia stands for an ideal: what kind of human being the educated person will be. In another sense, paideia stands for educational practice, which aims to achieve the ideal by a curriculum consisting of the classical poets in its early stages, and oratorical and philosophical studies in its advanced stages."[165] For Chambliss, paideia stands for both the ideals of the culture as it defines the aim and the outcome of education or for the educational practice which works to realize these ideals through educating the young. He goes on to discuss the "Christian paideia" of the early church for which the beliefs and ideals of Christianity were paramount in education. All educational practices were shaped by the writings and teachings of the church toward the goal of producing a virtuous and faithful Christian. While Adler's definition, when compared to Chambliss' description of a Christian commonwealth, seems broader, vaguer, more generic and universalistic, and more modern, their paideias both agree children must be raised and educated within a body of common knowledge and the ideals of the culture.

The historian Lawrence Cremin, too, uses the concept. He describes the formulation of a "republican paideia" of the nineteenth century common school movement. In the second volume of his history of education in the United States, **American Education**, Cremin describes the efforts of the new republic to define itself and to create an educational system capable of building and sustaining its experiment in democracy. Filled with a revolutionary's faith in the power to make a new world, and faced with the task of defining the character and institutions of a new nation, the leaders agreed education was essential to the health and survival of their social and political system. Education was to be the instrument with which they could fashion the new American man and the true democratic citizen. They needed a new man for a new form of government and society. The new man was to be created by a new type of education—"a paideia appropriate to the aspirations of the new nation." This paideia would produce "a new republican individual, of virtuous character, abiding patriotism, and prudent wisdom, fashioned by education into an independent yet loyal citizen." This goal for education was based upon the belief that "the republic could not thrive in the absence of public virtue,....piety, civility, and learning in the populous at large...." The system of education they wished to create would be founded upon a commitment to these ideals and to the use of education to realize them in the lives of individuals and the daily life of the society. To achieve these ends they would use all the resources of the society, for it was the "full panoply of institutions that had a part in shaping human character."[166]

Cremin's use of paideia reflects both Adler's and Chambliss' idea of education shaping human beings using the ideals of the society. They all see paideia as the educational process that realizes these ends in individuals and the life of society. Adler's paideia, however, is different. He aims to educate individuals for citizenship and for 'living well." He wishes to equip them with the knowledge and thinking skills necessary to both earn a living and live a full and rich life. The content and ends of his education are influenced by preoccupations with individual development and the autonomous, deliberate creation of the individual self by and for that self. The process of liberal education is based upon reason and on the great tradition, the classical, humanistic tradition and writings of the West. While there is the sense of upbringing as socialization and education as an induction into the ideas and issues of the tradition, it is not clear that his conception of education and paideia intend the deliberate shaping of individuals in accordance with an ideal, the development of character after a model, or the inculcation of a culturally specific conception of virtue and the good life. All of these are required by Cremin's and Chambliss' paideia. Adler, I think, holds back from their more expansive conception of paideia. His paideia is more modern, whereas theirs are descriptions of paideias of the past. The difference is about the ideals themselves and their views of human beings. These differences are those between Hume and Barrett, Freud and Newton. They are important and will be discussed shortly.

These differences are part of a more general distinction in the way we think about paideia. There are stronger and weaker senses in which we might use the concept. The weaker defines it as the upbringing of the young, their education and induction into the adult society of their culture. This happens, to one degree or another, in all cultures. The goal is the preparation of each new generation to function in adult society and to meeting its needs for workers and citizens. This socialization achieves two essential, related, tasks: to maintain and perpetuate society and to provide the young with the knowledge, skills, beliefs, and behaviors required to function and prosper in the worlds of work, politics, and social life. The stronger sense accepts the basic contentions of the weaker but adds some leaven to it. W. Jaeger, the German classicist, argues in his three volume **Paideia: The Ideals of Greek Culture** that the essence of education, of paideia, is the crafting of human beings in the way the "potter moulds clay and the sculptor carves stone into preconceived form—this was the bold creative idea which could have been developed only by that nation of artists and philosophers. The greatest work of art they had to create was Man. They were the first to realize that education means deliberately moulding human character in accordance with an ideal."[167] Paideia in this stronger sense conflates education and the ideals of a culture. Education becomes the ideal of culture and the culture defines itself in the continuous process of recreating its ideals and itself in the young. Education is the highest ambition of a good society. This ambition is realized only in a society that has a unified and vital set of ideals and a commitment to the creation of individuals in the crucible formed by culture, community, and education. Another metaphor can be substituted for Jaeger's potter: the finest flower of education and culture is the individual cultivated and nourished by the richness and depth of the aspirations, beliefs, and ideals of the community.

Regardless of the metaphor, a critical relationship for paideia, as for a conception of community, particularly when considered from a modern perspective, is that between the individual and the group. The differences between Adler, Chambliss, and Cremin arise over this issue. Conscious of this fact, Jaeger, using Plato, addresses it in his definition of paideia: "the essence of all true culture, or paideia, is the education in arete [virtue, excellence] from youth onwards, which makes men passionately desire to become perfect citizens...."[168] This is socialization in the grand style, where the development of the full powers of the individual of classical and humanistic thought is in harmony with an education whose chief aim is the energetic and systematic inculcation of the ideals of the culture. It is a precarious and delicate balance. In our age with its heightened awareness of individual autonomy and freedom and with its difficulties in defining a shared and compelling body of ideals of culture, it may offer too little protection of the individual from the imposition of the ideals of others. It is always a volatile and unstable compound. Adler, more representative of this modern reality than Jaeger, less inspired by a Platonic and Hegelian temperament, conceives a modern paideia more sensitive to the dilemmas of such a view in our modern age.

There is, amid these differences, an agreement that paideia includes both culture and education. There is not, however, agreement as to the exact content of the concept when it is present in a particular culture. This is due, in part, to the fact that it is a formal concept that describes a relationship between education and culture but not the specific character or content of the culture or the education. Differences in the use of the word may therefore reflect the type of culture being described rather than a disagreement over the meaning of the word itself. The differences between Adler, Chambliss, and Cremin are perhaps best understood in this way. This is not to minimize the importance of these differences because they may be critical. To accept, for example, either Adler's or Jaeger's view is to envision and advocate a distinctive culture and education, one different from the others regardless of their common commitment to the close connections of culture, community, and education.

This close connection is the paideia of the chapter title. What of the agonistes? Must the concepts of community and paideia be tied to a grim and pessimistic view of the modern world? Who says our world is so grim or troubled? In some ways this is the hardest issue to address, for the question contains an important element of truth about our age— it has brought many blessings. The world may be a far better world than it has been before and it may continue to get better if we address our problems. The talk of lost community gives a distorted view of our current condition and too often degenerates into gloomy defeatist predictions about our future or nostalgic portrayals of the past and its idyllic communities of village life or medieval society. We may have lost some community but this loss is relatively small in comparison to the great progress of modern life. We know more now, we have and can do more, our health is better and our lives longer, we are freer and our opportunities are greater, and all of these are more widely distributed throughout the population than at any other time in history.

Even the loss or change of community isn't all bad because community isn't all good. We can do without the blessings of community, for its history has been one of oppression and bloodshed. Communities throughout history haven't liberated as often as they have enslaved and exploited the bodies and the minds of the human beings who inhabited them. The golden age of the past was rather a grim place. The call for community may bring all this back, this time through the use of the enormous power of the modern state. Such community is often at the expense of the individual and our modern liberal ideals. It threatens to impose a uniformity on the diversity and the latitudinarian inclinations of modern society. Community is seen as a threat rather than a salvation.

Those holding these views see those who denounce our age and call for community as hysterical dreamers, mystics, insatiable malcontents. The maledictions of these malcontents are a refuge, harboring those with a nearly pathological distaste for and despair about the modern condition, who escape depression or madness through a sentimental, romantic, idyllic, often pastoral vision of a once vital but now ruined communal life. In their dark vision, the modern world is the asp's bite and community the doctor's antidote; the problem of community is more than one consequence of the coming of modern life, it is the mark of all our woes, a cause of all our discontents and a weapon with which to flail this evil age.

It is true that too dark-sided a view of our condition, a congenital disposition of many calling for community, suffers its own sort of blindness. The modern age is in many and important ways a blessing. Science and technology have brought many benefits, the ideals of the Enlightenment have been a boon, and modern secular society has opened and enriched our horizons. All this is true. The forces and ideas that have made it possible may not be put aside. But it is also true that they, in taking their particular modern form, have also harmed us. It is this harm that is the ineradicable core of my understanding of our time. It is the challenge of our time to redress it while holding onto all of our gains. We need, more than anything else, some way to negotiate the good and bad in all this and to find a pathway through the dilemmas.

Regardless of this appreciation of arguments to the contrary, my guiding or informing vision is that of the critics of our age. We have become dulled to what it means to be fully human, to the range and richness of human experience. The modern world is without a vision of human existence capable of encompassing these experiences and fulfilling human beings, and has instead denied their importance or existence which has resulted in the narrowing and fragmenting of human existence and experience. One of the fragments, a shard from the broken image of a unified vision, is the spiritual urge of the human heart: the demand for an orderly and meaningful existence, a sense of belonging to a place and being in communion with a group, and for a home in a universe calibrated to the rhythms and the reasons of our human hearts. The failure of our age to conceive such a vision is the critical and crippling deficiency of modern society. This failure becomes tangible, and all of these concerns coalesce around, the failure of society to produce genuine and good community.

We have created instead a world blind to the need for such a unifying vision and community, and at least partially blind to the nature and needs of human beings. The calculations of modern life and thought have found the reasons of the heart too subtle, elusive, and insubstantial. Amid the bounty bestowed upon us by the genius of the age—a horn of plenty unimaginable to all earlier ages—we moderns are uneasy and troubled, we experience the dull and debilitating ache of hunger, some elusive yearning for a solid and deep foundation for our lives, for a certainty upon which to prepare the banquet made possible by our bounty. We are like Tolstoy confessing in his mid-life that for all the successes and great works there remains the sense of emptiness and meaninglessness, or like Pascal who stepped in his lifetime from communion in an enchanted garden to the cold solitude of a mechanical universe and who, with Wordsworth, saw the dream and the clouds of glory scatter and the "shades of the prison-house begin to close...." This grimness may be lightened by arguments proclaiming modern progress and its virtues, but there is too much that abides for an easy escape from the gloaming.

This is the paideia agonistes of the title. It is born out of the decay of cultural coherence in our age, the fracturing of meanings, the loss or degradation of the ideals of culture; for us, paideia is no more than the gleam in an antiquarian's eyes, the sweet but fantastic dream of an age that has gone to sleep and forgotten much of what the past knew—but still knows it in its longings, in the sense of an emptiness and incompleteness at the center of things, in the desires and needs its world cannot satisfy. The agonistes arises at the intersection of these longings and the possibilities of the modern age. The modern age is an impotent lover standing before these unsatisfied passions of modern men. From this arises our unsettled state of mind—the agonistes—and the struggle to find some way beyond our present condition. But there is no way around this condition. We may move forward only through the deep divisions within our modern world and within our desires: an age of individualism and liberty rears back from the scent of restraint, dependency, and control in paideia; an age that lives and dies by a science it has made the arbiter of truth and the engine of its everyday existence is incapable of answering the most important and pressing questions about how to live and what to do, and about our true and essential needs and nature. We are impaled on a set of dilemmas from which we cannot lift ourselves, and the more we struggle the more deeply we impale ourselves.

We are like Samson whose strength and passion made him great, the hero of his people; but these also led him to enslavement by the Philistines, blindness, and menial labor. Samson agonized over his loss, his fall from grace, his betrayal by Delilah, and his doom. He is a tragic figure. Perhaps we too, we moderns, are victims of our own great strengths and passions, we too have become captives of the Philistines, are blind and condemned to menial labors, are eyeless and lost, paideia-less in our brave modern world. Perhaps, too, our salvation will be found in pulling the temple down on our heads as Samson did. But perhaps not, for the better way may be to enlarge, redesign, and renew the temple we already have. By working through our dilemmas, and forging the new community out of the old, community and education may become one, as do John Donne's lovers in "A Valediction Forbidding Mourning":

If they be two, they are two so
As stiff twin compasses are two:
Thy soul, the fixed foot, makes no show
To move, but doth, if the other do.

And though it in the center sit,
Yet when the other far doth roam,
It leans and harkens after it,
And grows erect as that comes homes.

I

It is necessary to define more precisely the general characteristics of this good community. I aim for as encompassing a definition as possible, one able to meet the demands of its many proponents and address the difficult issues any conception of community faces in the modern world. Eight years ago I wrote a dissertation on the concept of community in the thought of two very different philosophers, John Dewey and Martin Buber. Surprisingly, I found that their concepts, while different, had significant common ground. From their common ground I defined a set of foundational tenets of a concept of community for modern society. This section is based upon these tenets. Using them, I will describe a general model of community in society and in education. I will build this common conception on three foundational ideas: the social nature of human life, the rhythmic nature of human existence, and the central place of the individual and freedom in human life and community.[169]

Both Dewey and Buber include community in their visions of human existence. For both, attachment to and participation in a community are necessary for the well-being and fulfillment of individual humans. Regardless of their differences, they both insist on the primacy of community in human existence. In addition, in both thinkers the important role of community in human life is the result of the social nature of human existence: humans are human in and through their intimate and daily connections and communication with each other and the social experiences that constitute their lives and communities. From Dewey may be taken the case for the social nature of all human experience. The phases of human experiences are phases of the individual within some sort of social life. Also from Dewey comes the idea that human existence and community are bound to communication, the finest product of the social art. Buber offers an equally important point: there is no genuine relation and therefore no wholeness for the person without the relation "between man and man" which in turn is the basis of all community; man without man has no way to community or God or to himself. There can be no unity, completion or wholeness for humans outside of these relationships. When social life encourages and extends this process the life of individuals is whole and healthy; when it distorts or suppresses it this life is diminished, incomplete, and unhealthy. Community is the culmination of a life lived in accordance with this natural flow of human relationships and experience.

The sustenance that community affords humans comes through the inescapable need of humans to either reconstruct their experience or engage the world in dialogue. This they must do as members of a community, not as isolated individuals. But the sustenance comes also from a source within human beings and their condition in the world. That source is the fact that humans, more than anything else, desire to know the meaning of things and to assert and affirm the meaningfulness of their existence. In Dewey it is in the intercourse of community life that such meanings are wrought and confirmed; in Buber it is only in the genuine meeting with others in community that humans as humans can receive confirmation of the meaningfulness of human life. In their views the isolated individual seeking meaning stands in violation of the natural process of human life. Such individuals are separated from the primary source of the meaning they seek—another human voice and face.

There is a rhythmic pattern to human existence found in both Dewey and Buber. There is a close connection between this pattern and their concepts of community. In both, it is a two beat rhythm, one beat corresponding to the fluidity and change of life and society, the other to the need, generally overlooked or de-emphasized in our time, for a solid, secure, and stable foundation for individual and social existence. Both men attempt to restore the rhythm by balancing this modern misunderstanding of the human beings with one that more fully reflects the nature of human beings and their needs. Community is the place where the balance is struck.

It is on this point that their similarity is most striking. They agree that humans need to both move ahead, change, reform or reconstruct themselves and the world and, at the same time and with equal urgency, they need to stay put in a place that provides a secure and stable home. They both envision a world continuously moving and changing while, at the same time, continuously coalescing into some stable and orderly whole. In Dewey the model is the evolutionary process; it creates, in each era, forms that embody the consummation and culmination of its process only to crush them in the force of its slow inexorable evolving. Out of the flow of time and change, as out of the flood of human experience, emerge those finely wrought, delicate forms that give shape and sense to the world and to experience. In Buber the model is of a soul that must turn away from its ordered world to enter into relation with the world as an I to a Thou, and then return again to renew and reorder the world filled with, inspired by, the spirit of genuine relation. Both insist on the fact of the rhythm and of the necessity of both having a home and travailing the open and endless road.

Community is a name and a form of this ordered wholeness. It is possible for humans, in their existence as social beings and in the relations between person and person, to achieve a unity, a consummation and a realization, of their experience and their lives. Communities form in the intensity of this consummation and realization. The place of such moments in existence is firmly grounded; it is in Dewey a part of the natural process of experience and in Buber an inherent characteristic of the alternation of I-It and I-Thou relationships. While they will inevitably give way in the course of time and the force of circumstance to the equally powerful urge in humans to move on, and the tendency of communities to petrify and decay, they are as vital to humans as water and sun to plants.

The third general point is that the individual and freedom may not and need not be sacrificed to community. The individual human being is the building block of community. Community may not be built upon the forfeiture of individual independence or the demotion of the place and value of the individual; community is essential to humans because it is necessary to the fulfillment and completion of individual human beings. Respect for the individual and a sense of the dignity and worth of each person are presuppositions of the community Dewey and Buber advocate; their protection and promotion are the chief end of all communal existence.

The relationship of the individual and the community is key to an understanding of this model of community. The modern age is the age of the individual and, while Dewey and Buber each reject large parts of modern culture, both agree that the individual is the unit of measure for and the most precious product of human existence and the human enterprise. Their understandings of the individual are, however, different from the standard classical liberal version. Both, in fact, reject this standard version in which the individual is defined by his opposition to the group. One of the striking similarities between the two thinkers is the effort by both men to reconceptualize our modern conception of individualism. Their solutions are also similar: individuality is achieved in community. Humans live together and they may be fully human and truly individual only in community.

Their reconceptualization involves a recasting of the problem.

Instead of conceiving the individual entrapped by the group and liberation as the answer, they see the modern individual entrapped in a way of thinking that isolates him, destroys the basis of cooperative and communal society, and violates the nature of human existence. The answer is not more individualism, it is a new type of individualism in which the paramount position of the individual is maintained through and by community rather than in the rejection of and liberation from community. What Buber says about independence holds for individualism as a whole: "...independence is a foot-bridge, not a dwelling place."[170] The dwelling place is the life lived in the fullness of choice and commitment, of relation and reconstructed experience, of the growth of the unique individual in the community of his fellow humans. Without community all the rest is impossible and only in community can the individual become a whole human being.

The same type of recasting is necessary when we consider freedom, another building block of community. Traditionally, freedom and community stand against one another, the well-being of each seen as threatened by the enfranchising of the other; freedom's gain is community's loss and vice versa. This is freedom from all that restricts the individual in the pursuit of his interests and the realization of his unique aptitudes or ends. Dewey and Buber discard this as inadequate for the simple reason that humans are social beings who become what they are and achieve their fulfillment within their social setting and in relationships with their fellow humans. What kind of freedom applies to such a being, assuming, as both thinkers do, that freedom is a human good? For both, it is a freedom that permits the individual to freely and openly meet the world of experience, interact with it, reconstruct or enter into relation with it, and live in the light of the living experience or relation the meeting makes possible. All of this takes place in the company of those with whom the individual lives and within the group that is the inescapable condition of human existence. Human existence is bound by the relationships between humans; the communication that passes between individuals is the life-blood of human existence. Freedom is the ability to choose and act within this human context; it is the arms and legs of community and of individuality, but it is not their heart and soul. It is the context, the community, which is the heart and soul and which sets the boundaries and the course for these arms and legs.

Freedom must also be understood in the light of the rhythmic pattern of existence. The rhythm requires freedom; it is the force that drives the life from one perch to the next, from one cycle of relation, through the ossification into It, to the renewal of relation. Human freedom stands against the inertia of the world of It, the lure of stasis, certitude, and an end to all searching. But freedom, too, drives human lives forward within community; its greatest glory is the voluntary community of individuals bound to one another through their relations with another and the common, shared experience they jointly construct. Freedom, like independence, is a foot-bridge that carries the individual to where he chooses to live, to what he takes responsibility for, to that to which he commits himself—to community. And it is this community that defines the content and the direction of the freedom. There is a delicate balance in this. If we disturb it, too much freedom may leave us lost, empty, and homeless, and too much community make us prisoners, trapped and powerless in our own homes. Neither is satisfactory, for both make us less than human.

Democracy too is necessary in their community. I refer to the broader sense of the word, not the narrower application to political arrangements. This broader sense is of a social life characterized by the active participation of all in the decision-making of the group, the respect for the rights and needs of each person, the openness of communication and the free expression of ideas and sentiments, the freedom of individuals to choose and live in accordance with their choices, and the tolerance of diversity and disagreement. Democracy is a name for the open society and the open society is the way to the growth of experience, the encounter with the Thou, and the creation of community.

Democracy, however, is not only process. It is more than openness and freedom, more than a process for organizing and operating social life. It cannot function without the ideas and ideals inherent in the process. The means and ends, process and content, of democracy, as with Dewey's science, are inseparable. Democracy requires, at the least, respect for individuals, protections of their rights and prerogatives, freedom of thought and action, acceptance of differences between individuals and groups, open communication, equal treatment, and personal control over vital decisions of life. These are both means to the operation of democracy and some of the ends of a good life and society. But there are others ends in democratic societies. Each democratic society defines them for itself. They embody the peculiar beliefs and values of its special time, place, and people. Not all are the same, except in the basic principles and procedures required by democracy. Dewey and Buber, both champions of democracy, envision, as we will see in a moment, different communities. All of them, however different, are democratic. They offer, in their distinctive ways, both the openness, freedom, independence, and individual control of democracy and the specific ideas, beliefs, knowledge, and history with which each creates its own democratic home.

What makes it a home is its common center. Buber refers to it as the living center that binds individuals together in community. The idea of a center and of some binding force in community life, more directly than any of the qualities or characteristics mentioned so far, forces us to face a fact about the type of community being described here. In everyday usage the concept of community is defined loosely. It is where we live, with whom, the institutions and occupations that shape our lives; it is the set of connections that attach us to our social group. This use of community need not, and often does not, possess the qualities and the meaning of community that has been developed in this study. It is held together by instrumental relationships and its existence is determined by technical measures as in, for example, the communities of location (neighborhood) or the communities of occupation (scholars). The type of community central to this study is different from this technical and instrumental community. It possesses a unity beyond that created by the rational, organizational, or technical measures that define and constitute the everyday conception of community. It is interested in a quality of community that is present in the relationships of the members to one another and to the group. The qualities essential to this community arise from the fact of a common belief, a shared experience and commitment, and the fellowship and communion of a common faith. The common center is a name for these bonds that bind the individuals of a community together through their shared commitments or beliefs; it is the ordered, unified, and completed existence which adds flesh and substance to the democratic process, gives meaning to the individual within the community, and provides the community a living and sustaining faith.

The use of the word faith raises the issue of the rational nature of such a community. Faith arises from a decision and a commitment that may or may not be based on reason. When Dewey is using it, as he does in **A Common Faith**, it is reason that guides the individual to the threshold of a faith that is the unification of experience. But Dewey refuses to characterize the last step as the culmination of rational inquiry or problem solving; in the qualitative experiences of humans, in those moments when experience consummates itself, there is no calculus to decipher or describe it because it is a work of art imbued with all that is religious in human experience. For Buber no such rational prelude or participation is necessary since his way to faith is through the I-Thou relation. Both Dewey and Buber agree that, whether rational or not, such a shared or common faith is the culmination of genuine human relations and the keystone of community.

What is the place of religion, the religious, and God in this common center and community? Both Dewey and Buber would agree that religion as commonly defined and practiced obstructs all they think essential to a full and human life. Dewey would discard it altogether since it is the institutionalization of a view of the world he thinks outdated and incorrect. If anything is to be substituted for the traditional religions it might be a natural piety or a cosmic evolutionary consciousness, but more likely a secular or civil religion based upon science and democracy. Buber's objection is to the deadly consequences of the institutionalization of the primal impulse of religion. Institutionalization destroys the vital impulses that are the origin and essence of true religion. It leads to ossification of these impulses and the loss of the living relationships of the I-Thou relation and the encounter with God. When this impulse and meeting become institutionalized in religion they die. Without them religion becomes a relic, a monument to the dead and the past, and a citadel of the world of It.

But Dewey and Buber also acknowledge the existence of and grant the importance of a religious impulse or spirit institutionalized in religions. They both see it as an important and natural part of human experience and life. The religious is the culmination or consummation of their visions of human experience and existence. As a part of the common center, it binds the members of the community together and fosters the resolve and commitment that can unify and give meaning to the experiences and the lives of all its members. Whether naturalistic or idealistic, theistic or atheistic, community is conceived as a body of individuals held together by the commonly held and shared meanings of its members and those meanings must define the ideals and purposes of human existence and give order and unity to the world. To be a genuine community there must be "a common faith" that courses through the daily life and consciousness of both its members and the community as a whole. These meanings may take the form of a religion, find their authority in God, be purely secular, or be embodied in the values and life of a democratic community. So long as the fires of the experiences and the relations that breed them burn brightly, illuminating all that they do, they are true communities.

As with religion, both Dewey and Buber are ambivalent in their approach to the role of tradition in community. They both reject it when it acts as the dead hand of the past, suffocating the growth of experience and of genuine relation. Tradition is that which humans must be unshackled from in order to be fully human; it arrests human development by blocking experience and it serves the world of It more often than of the Thou. But their views of tradition are more complex than this. If tradition is a long established and authoritative body of beliefs, morals, practices, and institutions whose force and validity are tied primarily to its stability and longevity, then Dewey and Buber will have little to do with it. This is dead tradition. It contradicts their basic visions. There is another understanding of tradition that both Dewey and Buber endorse. Buber calls it a living tradition. It is tradition that is continually reborn and renewed by each generation. Dewey's process of experience is suitable to such a conception; experience grows and is reconstructed but is continuous and organic as well, building on what came before but transforming, enriching, and regenerating as it moves forward. Dewey might call it evolutionary tradition and mean essentially the same thing. Here, as many times before, the new formulation runs counter to customary usage which conceives tradition, when a component of community, as the vehicle of stability and order, of all that is unchanging and fixed in the social order, of that which is customary and conventional and therefore beyond the whim of time and circumstance; it is the unbending and unbreaking steel of community. Dewey and Buber grant this but insist that it is a steel that must be reforged repeatedly if a community is to be a living, liberating, and fulfilling one. This is the only form in which tradition may be part of Dewey and Buber's communities. It is the only way tradition and community can be a boon and a blessing to humans.

Both Dewey and Buber offer models of the communities they envision. Dewey uses two models: the scientific community and the small local democratic community. Buber also presents two: the kibbutz and the Hasidic community. Is there one model to be found in or fashioned from these four models? The answer is no. Their differences may not be overcome. They shouldn't be overcome. There is more than one way. The power of the connection between these two thinkers is in their distinctive approaches, in their differences as much as in their similarities. Yet the similarities show them to be on the same journey, seeking the same end. Each in his own way harkens back to another era and an earlier way of life: the commune and local community, the agricultural village common throughout human history, the New England small town life of the 19th century, the utopian communities of the 19th century and the religious or devotional communities of nearly all centuries. Each thinks the modern age lacks something vital to humans. But they aren't interested in going back. They are both optimistic and progressive, neither is prone to brood or despair, and both see a nearly unlimited power of renewal and growth. What they want is to create, in modern times, a way of life that provides humans with the community they need to be fully human.

Both Dewey and Buber also specify a particular condition for the communities they envision. In nearly identical statements, they grant the large corporate state its dominance and place in modern society but at the same time insist that for genuine community to survive and to thrive small local social organizations must be maintained or restored. The engine of community, all that I have been describing in the preceding paragraphs, will not run when the boundaries of the community are so large that the immediacy, intimacy, face-to-face nature of communication and human relations are so attenuated as to lose their force. The face-to-face dialogue of local community life is necessary in the democratic communities they advocate. Community may emerge within large social units only when small units are present to give shape and substance, a habitation, to the qualities and characteristics of the community Dewey and Buber envision.[171]

II

In this section I will give some body to these general and abstract ideas of community by describing the specific characteristics of the communities Buber and Dewey offer as their models. I will begin with Buber. Local and organic community is Buber's ideal. Community must be intimate to be based upon the personal relations of dialogue. It is in, and only in, local community that the inner structures of community—the center and the I-Thou relationship—can flourish. Centralization is the great nemesis for community because it invades and undermines the life of the local community. Those for community "must be decentralists, federalists, autonomists,..." They must uphold the ideal of the "village commune," the "decentralized social structure."[172] These possess the conditions necessary for the active involvement of all individuals in the life of the social organization, for openness and accessibility in the relations of individuals and the operation of the group, and for mutual, living, reciprocal relations between all members which create the living center of the community. For these reasons local communities are rich in the structures of social life that were common in the past and so absent in the modern age.

These structures are the "associative units" and "community-forms" in which individuals live and through which genuine community is created. "'The real living together of man with man can only thrive where people have the real things of their common life in common; where they experience, discuss and administer them together; where real fellowships and real work Guilds exist.'"[173] This is only possible in local communities. The collectivist and centralist practices of the modern age cannot produce community.[174]

Buber's communities are organic in nature. He agrees with Proudhon that it is not the individual that opposes, or should oppose, the State but "the individual in organic connection with his group, the group being a voluntary association of individuals."[175] What gives life to this natural group, and force to the bond that holds it together, is the organic continuity of community life. This continuity is his tradition: the heritage of social forms, the myths and meanings wrought in the past and sustained in the organic memory of the living community. It is a continuity, forged by generations and embodied in society, that binds individuals into a community. When taken as a whole it is called the communal spirit. It is the living history of the community.[176]

The organic community is the "little society" in which the individual is "embedded." When humans and groups lose this organic connection to each other, to the group, and to the world, they lose "the most valuable of all goods—the life between man and man." In the modern collective this organic and intimate connection of humans is lost:

> autonomous relationships become meaningless, personal relationships wither; and the very spirit of man hires itself out as a functionary. The personal human being ceases to be the living member of a social body and becomes a cog in the 'collective' machine. Just as his degenerate technology is causing man to lose the feel of good work and proportion, so the degrading social life he leads is causing him to lose the feel of community....[177]

Buber is convinced that this little society is to be found in "the rebirth of the commune" which declares itself primarily in the common and active management of what it has in common...."[178] There is no other road to genuine community.

The need for organic community is as old as humankind. From the banding together of primitives, through clans and tribes, to the polis and village, humans have sought the succor, safety, sense of place, and feeling of belonging that organic social units have provided. These were usually formed on the "basis of functional autonomy, mutual recognition and mutual responsibility" both within individual communities or between separate communities. Even size need not threaten this organic community if it is built of "organic, functionally organized..., communes and communities," in which "the individual human being, despite all the difficulties and conflicts, felt himself at home as once in the clan, felt himself approved and affirmed in his functional independence and responsibility."[179]

Community may be either a single celled organism or a more complex multi-celled organism. So long as the communal bond is intact and the local communal units remain healthy, the size of the organism need not threaten community. These units must be maintained for it is in them that "direct life relations between I and Thou, genuine society, genuine fellowship" exist.[180] Within these organisms both unity and diversity, stability and change, individual responsibility and communal identity exist. Such organic communities exist in both the worlds of It and Thou, but in genuine community is always lighted by the flame kindled in the relation to the center fueled by the dialogue between its members.

Buber's model for this community is the Full Co-operative of the Jewish Village Commune or Kibbutz. It is based on an eternal human need:

> the need of man to feel his own house as a room in some greater, all-embracing structure in which he is at home, to feel that the other inhabitants of it with whom he lives and works are all acknowledging and confirming his individual existence. An association based on community of views and aspirations alone cannot satisfy this need; the only thing that can do that is an association which makes for communal living.[181]

The Village Commune was forged by the needs of the particular situation of the Jewish people and by "the dictates of the hour." The ideals that forged its movement were tempered by the demands of the immediate condition and the effort to bring those ideals to life in the form and the life of the commune. Ultimately, it was the product of a twentieth century crisis that propelled the Jews to their original act of relation and creation.

From this original act sparks flew throughout the group, kindling the fire of relation and the openness of the I-Thou relationship that is necessary in real community. From the crisis arose the "common cause and common task" that binds the daily existence of individuals to the whole. Each of the communes will be distinctive according to its situation, ideals, and cause. Each commune was one cell in a larger organism: the federation of communes.

His vision of the Village Commune is a vision of a religious socialism.

> Religious socialism can only mean that religion and socialism are
> essentially directed to each other, that each of them needs the covenant
> with the other for the fulfillment of its own essence. **Religio**, that is the
> human person's binding of himself to God, can only attain its full reality
> in the will for a community of the human race, out of which alone God
> can prepare His Kingdom. **Socialitas**, that is mankind's becoming a
> fellowship, man's becoming a fellow to man, cannot develop otherwise
> than out of a common relation to the divine centre, even if this be again
> and still nameless. Unity with God and community among creatures
> belong together. Religion without socialism is disembodied spirit,
> therefore not genuine spirit; socialism without religion is body emptied of
> spirit, hence also not genuine body.[182]

This religious socialism may exist only when humans create it in the
concrete events and actions of their everyday existences and build it
from the "the immediate living with and for one another of men in the
here and now." Only through "standing and withstanding in the abyss
of the real reciprocal relation with the mystery of God" and "with the
mystery of man" will humans realize this religious socialism,
community, and genuine relation; and only through these can they
realize their wholeness as human beings. When they so stand and
withstand together in community, they live in the fullness of Buber's
vision.[183]

Dewey arrived at the same place using a very different set of ideas.
To better understand and appreciate this conception of community as
part of a modern philosophy and vision I will describe Dewey's
community in more detail. I do so with Dewey because his ideas are
often seen as more modern, relevant, and American than Buber's, and
because some of the tenets described above seem to contradict our
general and common understandings of Dewey's thought.

Dewey's idea of community develops from his ideas about
communication. Without an understanding of communication,
community can't be understood. Consider this:

> Communication is consummatory as well as instrumental. It is a means of
> establishing cooperation, domination and order. Shared experience is the
> greatest of human goods. In communication, such conjunction and
> contact as is characteristic of animals become endearments capable of
> infinite idealization; they become symbols of the very culmination of
> nature.[184]

And this:

> Communication is uniquely instrumental and uniquely final. It is

instrumental as liberating us from the otherwise overwhelming pressure of events and enabling us to live in a world of things that have meaning. It is final as a sharing in the objects and arts precious to a community, a sharing whereby meanings are enhanced, deepened and solidified in the sense of communion. Because of its characteristic agency and finality, communication and its congenial objects are objects ultimately worthy of awe, admiration, and loyal appreciation. They are worthy as means, because they are the only means that make life rich and varied in meanings. They are worthy as ends, because in such ends man is lifted from his immediate isolation and shares in a communion of meanings.

At those times when "the instrumental and final functions of communication live together in experience, there exists an intelligence which is the method and reward of the common life, and a society worthy to command affection, admiration, and loyalty."[185]

Human life for Dewey consists of human groups held together by the meanings communication makes possible and by the shared experiences that are the stuff from which such meanings are made. Communication requires shared experience which in turn, through language, creates meanings that are the mortar of a community life where each individual is bound to all by the things they hold in common. And the things they hold in common are those things that make them fully human and alive: common belief, value, purpose, action, and a binding commitment to them and the community that gives them a living and tangible form.

The discussion has slipped easily from communication to community. For Dewey such a slip covers little ground. Common, communication, communion, and community are connected to each other through a common root and a common meaning. They all come down to the things being held in common through participation and sharing. A community comes into being when a group achieves a level and kind of communication capable of creating a commonness of meaning—of belief, value, purpose, and action—that welds individuals into a unified whole. This community is a type of communion, in both its secular and sacred senses. When community exists, a social group has realized the consummatory as a fact of its social life.

The danger in Dewey's position on community, to this point, is that it is too abstract and imprecise in its description of communication and community. These concepts take on something close to a religious significance for Dewey. If they are to mean anything for this work, they must be nailed down. It is to this task that I now turn. Before I do, though, two things need to be said. First, the whole issue of community is a slippery one. As I discussed earlier, the entire topic can become, by its nature, a sinkhole or a tractless jungle and, as a result, a nightmare for the philosopher attempting to penetrate and explicate it. The subject is as difficult as it is vital, and this should be kept in mind as we work through Dewey's thought on it. Second, it is for Dewey a realm of human existence where humans push up against the barriers of their humanness, much as they do in art and religion—in all consummatory experience. The dimension that makes humans distinctive, capable of greatness beyond their material means, is involved in the discussion of community, even for a thoroughgoing naturalist like Dewey.[186]

The consummatory in communication and community is a good place to begin to nail Dewey down. The conjunction of the consummatory experience of communication and community is clear in the quotations above. The issue here is what Dewey means, in specific social contents, by this consummation. The consummatory is experience that achieves unity and wholeness. It is found most often in art and in religious experiences. It is qualitative in nature. It moves on the edges of the hardheaded gradgrinding world of quantities, instrumentalities and the quotidian; it forms the sixth sense—the mind—that defines, and therefore unites, the world of experience. When applied to human association, it performs the same function, creating and constituting the explicit and the tacit understandings and meanings upon which societies and, under felicitous circumstance, communities are founded.

The close connection between art and community is a good way to understand this. The relationship between the two is pure Dewey: community manifests its "unified collective life" in its art, and its art plays an essential part in the creation of this collective life. The degree to which the art of a group reflects the integration and inclusiveness of its communal life is the degree to which the group has achieved community. Community of this sort involves the "whole of the living creature" and, most importantly, the whole of social life. It is never mere organization, an arrangement of social forms, relations, and institutions. The whole set of meanings produced in the intercourse of social life and embodied in art is the building material of genuine community. Art is the conclusion, the consummation, of the act of social reconstruction, the "remaking of the experience of the community in the direction of greater order and unity."[187]

Order and unity are not, therefore, simply structures of social organization, but are the integuments of the spirit of the lived experience of individuals and the community. Community arises when a group creates meaning out of its shared experience and collective life.

Art, as an artifact of community, is the representation of the beliefs and values, the meanings, produced by the community of experience. "In the end, works of art are the only media of complete, unhindered communication between man and man that can occur in a world full of gulfs and walls that limit community of experience." Art is the consummation of communication, which is the life-blood of community.[188]

This still seems too vaporous or ghostly. It is visible but intangible; it melts away before your grasp, like a fog that recedes before you, everywhere but where you can touch it. The way to a more concrete conception is again through Dewey's conception of art. As well as being the paragon of communication, it is the bearer of the personal and social bonds that make a community: friendship, affection, loyalty, communion, ceremony and celebration, the drama and song of shared festivities, and religion.

> Every intense experience of friendship and affection completes itself artistically. The sense of communion generated by a work of art may take on a definitely religious quality. The union of men with one another is the source of the rites that from time of archaic man to the present have commemorated the crises of birth, death, and marriage. Art is the extension of the power of rites and ceremonies to unite men, through a shared celebration, to all incidents and scenes of life. This office is the reward and seal of art. That art weds man and nature is a familiar fact. Art also renders men aware of their union with one another in origin and destiny.[189]

In doing these things, art is the consummation of experience; in consummating experience art creates, as it is created by, community. And community, in giving humans those bonds of affection and the bearings gained by a sense of the meaningfulness of life, gives them a place in an orderly and unified world.

To those who see Dewey as the arch proponent of reason and intelligence, as the architect of instrumentalism, this view will seem strange. There may be too much of the dark and unaccountable side of humans in it for the champion of the practical application of intelligence and knowledge to practical problems and solutions. This narrower view of Dewey overlooks his concern for other dimensions of human experience, and these are most important in his work of the 1920's and 1930's. It is during this period that he realizes "that emotions and imagination are more potent in shaping public sentiments and opinions than information and reason," and that the "problem is that of effecting the union of ideas and knowledge with the non-rational factors in the human make-up." How is this union to be accomplished? Through art, which is "the name given to all agencies by which this union is effected."[190]

What does Dewey mean by the non-rational factors in human life? Two things I think. By the 20's and 30's Dewey wondered why humans hadn't used their great newfound knowledge, produced by science, to make a more rational and peaceful world. Why did the old ways persist even in the face of modern power and knowledge? Dewey questioned the Enlightenment's optimism about the future of humanity once he was armed with knowledge. What held them back? Two things. The old impulses, desires, and needs were still there and until society, using its new methods of science, reconstructed itself in light of its new knowledge, they would continue to exist and operate in accordance with their earlier forms. These forms were the habits, customs, and traditions of the past, and they were ingrained and obdurate. Dewey also realized that intelligence isn't the sole or even the primary way men order their experience. Imagination and its artistic products, particularly in the area of community, is paramount and it operates according to different codes and canons, and on different material, than does modern science.

To consider Dewey without an awareness of these points is to see him too exclusively from the vantage of the instrumental side of his thought. Such one-sidedness can never capture the deeper foundation of Dewey's thought. To the charge that Dewey missed man in his philosophy, left out the aching and aspiring human soul, I respond that the critics have missed part of Dewey in their critiques, left out the consummations that capture the lived experience of man. The Dewey who unmercifully ripped the old ways and the blindness of ancient superstitions and religions, and who gloried in the achievement and potential of modern science, could also claim that the old symbols, regardless of their inflated claims, contained "some trace of a vital and enduring reality, that of a community of life in which continuities of existence are consummated." And he could go on to finish his thought with a statement that expresses the heart of his view of human beings and community:

Consciousness of the whole has been connected with reverence, affections, and loyalties which are communal....Within the flickering inconsequential acts of separate selves dwells a sense of the whole which claims and dignifies them. In its presence we put off mortality and live in the universal. The life of the community in which we live and have our being is the fit symbol of this relationship. The acts in which we express our perception of the ties which bind us to others are its rites and ceremonies."[191]

This is the consummation in community.

So far I have used Dewey's general philosophy to define his concept of community. While this lays a foundation for community and establishes the relation of community to his thought as a whole, a connection that is indispensable for an understanding of his view of community, it fails to include Dewey's handling of community in his social philosophy, where the concept has direct application and is of central concern. A description of community in his social philosophy should also give additional weight to what has been said so far, as well as bring it further down to earth.

When we turn to Dewey's social philosophy, we turn back to where we have just been—dealing with the consummatory. The basis of his conception of community is that community is found where the group unites its experiences—its beliefs, values, the bonds and ties that hold it together, the affections and loyalties that wind through it—and stitch them into one tightly knit whole, into a total and integrated experience of the world that is made and held by each member but that is the possession of the collective life of the group. The ties that make this community are the result of the intimate and intense association of individuals participating in the construction of the world in which they live; this task is carried on through the continual interaction of all the members of the group who form the world of their collective experience in this interaction. The terms by which this interaction operate are both the method of intelligence and the imagination, and it is by the imagination that the final product is fashioned. The world that the community inhabits is, when it is truly a community, a qualitative world. It is a world that is alive with the meanings that bring the world into a living unity. The meanings it lives by are the ones that provide its members with a sense of purpose, value, significance, and a place in an orderly world. Through community humans come to participate in a universe that has meaning, one in which they have a place. It is therefore a consummation, a completion, and one wherein humans achieve the confluence of the streams of their experience, the braiding together of the separate strands of self, society, and cosmos.

All the arguments about specific political forms and social arrangements, individualism and socialism, freedom and conformity, liberalism and conservatism, industrialism and capitalism, line up behind this fact. It is primary because it establishes community as a moral concept, and makes it the means by which a group invests itself with ideals and values. Through the imaginative construction of an understanding of the world and the vivification of this understanding in the portrait it paints of a meaningful world, it creates itself into a community. This portrait is a projection of the good the group honors and seeks; it expresses the ideals dear to the community. When this experience, a consummatory experience, occurs, the group becomes more than a mere collection of individuals, it becomes a community possessing an integrity and cohesiveness, a unity of experience; it becomes a community of experience.

If community is depicted in this way, then it is clear that it contains both esthetic and religious dimensions. As consummatory, it would have difficulty avoiding some connection with these preeminent forms of consummatory experience. In fact, they both are indispensable to community. The birth of a community is an artistic act. It is the experience by a group of the unity, wholeness, and completion characteristic of a work of art. Art is the means of both expressing and creating the "coherent and integrated imaginative union" that is the heart of community.[192] A society whose art fails to achieve this union has failed to achieve community. The same is true for the religious. When a society attains a degree of unity of commitment and purpose, an integration of its will and its meanings and ideals, its experience is religious; in meeting the requirements of religious experience, it has fulfilled those of community.

This, though, is still too abstract and philosophical. Community is a practical reality of everyday life, a critical component of the lived experience of human beings. For his position to have force it must take some tangible form. Dewey gave it form with his models of the community of science and the communal life of a true democracy. Almost all of Dewey's discussions of community in the modern age center around one or the other of these two. From each he extracts the same thing: their methods of operation. Both rely upon the free and open exchange of ideas, the participation of all members in the interchange of ideas and opinions, and a method of inquiry to identify and solve problems. Both rely on communication within a group to create general meanings and ideas which bind the group together. For Dewey they represent types of social organization that possess the methods of operation and organization capable of producing genuine community.

First I will describe Dewey's idea of the community of science. It is a method more than it is a body of knowledge or a view of nature or a philosophy or a set of values. The value it has is in the way it conducts its business. When a person does science he enters into a method of operating that ties him to all other individuals doing the same thing. What binds them together is the method they use and their common participation in a common undertaking devoted to a common end. This group of scientists shares experience, communication, information and ideas, and through these they work to order and understand experience.

An added benefit of science, one not present in the past, is its commitment to experimentation and testing of results. The tendency of older forms of association and community to fall into set patterns of behavior, into habits, and for these to defy or ignore the actual conditions of the world around them is ruled out by the method of science. Science is, by its nature, self correcting, always investigating and questioning and always in the forefront of change. Science has worked out a "method of inquiry so inclusive in range and so penetrating, so pervasive and so universal, as to provide the pattern and model which permits, invites and even demands the kind of formulations that fall within the function of philosophy."[193] And the function of philosophy is to clear away the dead wood of old and established ways and pave the way to the future. Science becomes the model for human interaction with the world and the light that will shine humanity's way through the darkness. It also becomes the model for human interactions and the pathway to future community.

One of the problems in pushing science forward as a prototype of modern community is that science is closely tied to its work in discovering the nature of the physical world. Since it has been predominantly used to study and understand the natural order in its physical forms, it is seen as inappropriate to other areas of human concern.

This is part of the problem facing the modern world, according to Dewey. The failure to integrate knowledge and reunite experience in modern society is due to its unwillingness to apply science to social and moral problems. Science is a method and this method can be used in all areas of human experience. The method is the method of intelligence and is itself the heart of science. What is the method of intelligence? "It is a shorthand designation for great ever-growing methods of observation, experiment and reflective reasoning which have in a very short time revolutionized the physical and, to a considerable degree, the physiological conditions of life, but which have not as yet been worked out for application to what is itself distinctively and basically human."[194] The challenge of overcoming this rift is the challenge of the modern age and the last great dualism to be toppled. "When science is impregnated with human value,...the split between the material, the mechanical, the scientific and the moral and ideal will be destroyed."[195] Until then, science will be unable to fulfill its potential; it will be unable "to effect a working connection between old habits, customs, institutions, beliefs, and new conditions."[196] The organization, operation, and spirit of science are the ingredients necessary for any community that might come in the future. The community of science is within itself a living model of what the modern age may create on a grander scale in the future.

Science as a method of intelligence is therefore an important component of Dewey liberalism. Like science, liberalism is confronted by the loss of community in the modern age. It participated, as did science, in the destruction of the old order but has been unable to create a fitting replacement. "The instruments of analysis, of criticism, of dissolution, that were employed were effective for the work of release. But when it came to the problem of organizing the new forces and the individuals whose modes of life they radically altered into a coherent social organization, possessed of intellectual and moral directive power, liberalism was well-nigh impotent."[197] In both cases, those of science and liberalism, the failure has been one of omission, of an unwillingness to go far enough in the application of their principles. The need is for a more thorough-going application of intelligence to the problems of society. Dewey is confident that when it is extended, intelligence will cut a path out of the wilderness of modern culture, overcome alienation and insecurity, and create an integrated society. When it does, the society will be, of necessity, a liberal, that is a democratic, one.

Democracy, as the guiding principle of liberalism, is the idea that Dewey develops as the basis of liberalism and as the second way out of the modern predicament. John Herman Randall conceives Dewey's vision of democracy as religious and communal:

> The democratic life, pursued in a conscious unity of interaction with one's fellows, is the religious life. Democracy is thus for Dewey not only...a common experience in which common man can take part: it is literally a religious communion in which men find themselves at one and in unity with their fellow men and with the natural condition of human achievement.[198]

Democracy is, for Dewey, a moral imperative rather than a type of organization or form of government. It is an ideal whose form is determined by the type and quality of the interactions that take place within it at any given time. What is important is the amount and the type of communication possible in any social organization. When it is open and free a society is democratic. Participation and shared experience are its hallmarks. Without them, it isn't a democracy, regardless of the number and kind of procedures instituted to earn the label. Democracy "is toughest and strongest when it is the work of a continuously recreated voluntary consent, which in turn is the product of continual communication, conference, consultation, contact; of the free give and take of free beings."[199]

Democracy, like science, gains its value from its methods of operation. They are both means in that they create the conditions by which human beings can best interact with the world and each other. Through this interaction individuals and societies develop the meanings by which they will live. When these meanings are created under the conditions present in both science and democracy, and when science and democracy become a way of life for individuals and groups, community is possible. In the case of science, we have seen that until its scope and application are expanded it will be incapable of moving the last step to community. In the case of democracy there is no such shortcoming. Democracy, by its nature,

> is a means, the best means so far found, for realizing ends in the wide domain of human relationships and the development of human personality....It is ...a way of life, social and individual. The keynote of democracy as a way of life may be expressed as the necessity for the participation of every mature human being in formation of the values that regulate the living of men together, which is necessary from the standpoint of both the general social welfare and the full development of human beings as individuals."[200]

It is a name for a type of association of human beings in which they can communicate and interact with each other and the world and out of this communication and interaction create a world of meaning, collectively made and held, to live by. As a way of life, democracy encompasses all aspects of human concern; as a moral enterprise it defines ideals toward which the group may direct itself. It has at its disposal both the power of intelligence and imagination. When it permits all these elements their due, it becomes more than a means, but an end in itself; at these times it is capable of bringing to a stop all the restless energy of its own processes, breaking down the barriers that fragment existence, and achieving the unity and wholeness of a consummatory experience. When this occurs, democracy becomes religious and communal, capable of unifying experience—"mediating social transitions"—and creating genuine community in the modern age.[201]

Science and democracy are distinct paths to the future integration of thought and society. They do, however, have significant similarities. Their principal similarity is in their method of organizing human activity so that communication is the cement that holds it together. When communication is unfettered, intelligence can grow either through scientific inquiry into nature or social inquiry into social, political and moral life. When this occurs humans are in a position to reconstruct their experience, unify it, and produce community. The method, though, is more than the means. It contains the critical and core values. Science and democracy aren't value neutral, they are filled with "moral lessons to be learned from the attitudes, dispositions, and habits required for open experimental inquiry." These lessons could be applied to all aspects of human existence. Rationality, tolerance, freedom of thought, the value of communication of ideas and information, the rejection of fixed or final answers, patience and fortitude, discipline, interdependence, humility, a respect for others, equal treatment of individuals, the value of invention, initiative, and responsibility, are some of the attitudes, dispositions, and habits that make up the method of both science and democracy.[202]

The paths of science and democracy carry us back to the primal scene: humans in nature using the resources at their command to make a life for themselves. Science and democracy offer the best way to do this. Humans should confront the world of experience as inquirers. When inquiry is guided by correct method, then it is best able to expand and enrich human experience, and to offer the possibility of a unification and integration of experience. Inquiry is as natural to man as eating, and more fundamental. It can't exist without communication, specifically the type of communication inherent in and vital to science and democracy.[203]

Here we have come full circle, back to our original contention that there is a rhythm at the heart of human experience. Dewey's community is a consummatory experience. It unifies, orders, and stabilizes human experience. But with the introduction of science and democracy as paths to some future modern integration of experience, the issue of the instrumental or questing, restless spirit of humans enters the discussion again. And it must, because all of human experience is caught on the two horns of the pattern of experience. While some ages tend to live within one mode of existence to the exclusion or restriction of the other, the basic tension, the twin pulls or needs, remains an elemental fact of existence. The long lament of modern humanity for a restoration of integration, unity, harmony, and belonging, is the eruption of this elemental fact in a world gone destructively one-sided. The specific point in the context of science and democracy is that they are, regardless of their potential for consummation, instruments of movement and change, transformation, new horizons, progress, and ultimately must be seen as creatures of the vast spaces beyond the arch of our narrow and settled experience. Inquiry is the essence of each and it is the spirit of the frontier, of the ever new and continually receding human prospect. With science this point is indubitable, in the case of democracy it is less so; at the least, though, democracy must be seen as walking a narrow ridge between the instrumental and the consummatory. This is not a criticism of democracy, but praise. It is true to life. This is why Dewey never wanted to define democracy. He never presumed to know enough, or thought it possible for humans to know at all, what form future experience might take. Democracy is the means, the best means available, for man to realize the possibilities present in the world of experience. One of experience's possibilities, and democracy's, is the consummatory experience that is community.

Dewey's way out of the modern dilemma is democracy guided by a social inquiry modeled after the method of science. When democracy is fully realized, when it comes close to its meaning as an ideal, life will be a communion of men in a community created through that very communion. The modern age will then have become an integrated and complete whole. Steam and electricity, science and technology, will no longer dissolve the bonds that hold community together, but instead be the means of a fuller and deeper consummation:

> When the machine age has thus perfected its machinery it will be a means of life and not its despotic master. Democracy will come into its own, for democracy is a name for a life of free and enriching communion....It will have its consummation when free social inquiry is indissolubly wedded to the art of full and moving communication.[204]

Dewey argued that this democratic community would have much in common with local, face-to-face community. The local community Dewey sketches is of a particular milieu: the late 19th and early 20th century small town. Perhaps his preference is the result of his Vermont small town agricultural community background, or of his separation from this life in the big cities of Chicago and New York where he spent most of his adult life, or of the strain in American thought that sees small, rural communities as symbols of the simplicity and sweetness, the closeness, harmony, and naturalness, of such a life. Regardless of its source, it fits neatly into his thought.

It fit into the thought of many during his generation. Jean Quandt's **From the Small Town to the Great Community** makes the argument that the social thought of the intellectuals of the progressive era was concerned with the erosion of community life due to the coming of a new economic and social order in the United States, and with the loss of the older communal arrangements of local, small town America.[205] What did they see in the older form of such value that it should be retained in the new order? What did they see as the shortcomings of the new order? The answers to these questions can give us a good idea of the current of thought of Dewey's time and an entry into his understanding of local community.

The small town community of 19th century America embodied a way of life and a cultural and social unity that was disappearing in 20th century American society. It was this way of life that many social thinkers of the early 20th century wished to either maintain or restore. These communities were small size, relatively independent and self-sufficient, and democratic. Smallness bred regular contact, common interests and concerns, participation in the affairs of the town, and a sense of intimacy. Intimacy engendered a feeling of belonging, of roots in a community life that sustained and enriched the individual and the group. The individual was enmeshed in a web of personal relations and common experiences. The web itself was supported by and made from the moral and ethical life of the community, which usually had its basis in religion and the ideals of republicanism. An ethic of duty and personal responsibility, of love, loyalty, and communion grew from the social organization of the small town and from the social relations of "friendship, neighborliness, fraternity or whatever you may call the spirit of comradry that comes when men know one another well...." Life was a cooperative venture which created a communal sentiment, like-mindedness, and common ends. The spirit of community was a sense of solidarity with one another and with the group.[206]

This view of the small town carried with it a corresponding view of the big cities. The characteristics and qualities of the towns were not found in the modern city. The city by its nature couldn't have them. It undermined the basic structures and relations necessary to such a community life. Large, impersonal, and pluralistic, the city was unable to maintain or reproduce the experience of the small town. The only refuge for community was in transplanted primary groups, immigrant cultural enclaves for instance, but for the masses who migrated from the rural or small town areas to the large urban centers there was just the uprooting and the loss of a communal life. Religion and ethnic associations, clubs or societies, and the family all confronted the city as bastions of the older community. But they were all doomed to defeat, dissolution, or irrelevance. The modern world put them aside, pleasant but quaint relics of a dead way of life.

What was wrong with the new urban life? Most important, the new life fragmented experience, cut the individual off from an organic and complete relationship with his fellows, his activities, and his culture. The integrity of the lived experience was violated by a new way of life that fragmented experience and destroyed the sense of vital connection with and commitment to the group. The effect of this on the individual was isolation and alienation, rootlessness and anomie, and the loss of the unity and integration of personal and social life. The instruments of local community no longer existed. There was no common experience or end, like-mindedness or communal sentiment, solidarity or moral identification. When these existed, and some did, isolated enclaves of another age, they were cut off from a participation in the larger processes of modern social life. Faced with this reality, the individual became speechless; he lost his ability to use communication in the creation of his own and the group's experience. Life was being stripped down, layer by layer, to its mechanical and functional components: motors, steel girders, and nothing more. Community was also stripped off.

There was something in humans that didn't, couldn't, love this modern city. Dewey's sympathy with this view is captured in his view of the worker in modern urban society. The experience of work in this new society is of alienated laborers controlled by forces they are unable to understand. They stand within the urban, industrial system as "K" stood within the legal system in Kafka's **The Trial.** Here is Dewey's depiction of it:

> The problem primarily roots in the fact that the mediating science does not connect with his [the worker's] consciousness, but merely with his outward actions. He does not appreciate the significance and bearing of what he does; and he does not perform his work because of sharing in a larger scientific and social consciousness. If he did, he would be free.... he would have entered into the ethical kingdom.[207]

Dewey's awareness of this problem of community is akin to that of his contemporaries. Repeatedly he refers to the transformations of American society, of the old and the new, and of the loss experienced by the destruction of older communal forms. Complexity, specialization, standardization, the division of labor, the rise of an asocial individualism, the creation of a pecuniary culture, the fragmentation of knowledge and belief all undermined earlier forms of human association; the logical outcome was the loss of an organic, common culture with open and widespread communication, shared interests and values, and a sense of belonging to and participating in a community. The critical loss in the development of this new society is of face-to-face relations and the participation in the forms of social life characteristic of local communities. No genuine community can exist without these. Communication is crippled, being only partial, without them. The natural and organic process of human life is disrupted and the wholeness of human experience is thereby lost. Face-to-face community is necessary if individuals are to be fully human and society is to be a genuine community. And any society which either asserts or aspires to be democratic must be a genuine community, since "democracy is not an alternative to other principles of associated life. It is the idea of community life itself."[208] Dewey, along with others of his time,

> calls attention to the need for face-to-face associations, whose interactions with one another may offset if not control the dread impersonality of the sweep of present forces. There is a difference between a society, in the sense of an association, and a community. Electrons, atoms and molecules are in association with one another. Nothing exists in isolation anywhere throughout nature. Natural associations are conditions for the existence of a community, but a community adds the function of communication in which emotions and ideas are shared as well as joint undertakings engaged in. Economic forces have immensely widened the scope of associational activities. But it has done so largely at the expense of intimacy and directness of communal group interests and activities.[209]

There is a danger of romanticizing the small town and the older rural forms of life. The Whites, in **The Intellectual Versus the City**, describe the tendency of American thinkers to fall into an atavistic anthem when singing the praises of the past. Dewey, they point out, didn't fall into this trap. He is aware of the shortcomings of local communities, their narrowness, parochialism, intolerance, inflexibility—of what Marx called the idiocy of village life. In the name of a common culture and of community they have been known to strangle themselves with their traditions and customs, to resist change as a threat to established ways, to ignore the value of reflection and reconstruction, and to restrict communication to the channels made deep and safe by years of repetition. Routine and habit can and often have been the mainstay of these communities, and this is something Dewey couldn't condone. What Dewey wishes to restore is what local community has been when it lived up to it possibilities in the best, and only genuine, communities; he is after community when it lives in the light of its own ideal image, which is also, not surprisingly, Dewey's image.

Dewey could, as well, see good things in the coming of modern society. The greatest advances of the modern age were the product of modern science and technology. Together they were transforming human experience and nature. They had already transformed modern society into a corporate entity vastly different from the small scale and localized economic and social arrangements of the 19th century. It was conceivable they could produce a corporateness in society possessing the characteristics of the older local communities; community could be created on a scale unimaginable a century before, held together by communication made possible by technology, filled with the spirit and methods of the science that made such communication a reality, and infused with the common interests, aims, beliefs, and values created through open and widespread exchange of ideas, information, opinions, and beliefs. This modern community could overcome the pettiness, bigotry, and stagnation that so often afflicted local communities and stop the fragmentation of knowledge and experience in modern society. It could bring into existence a large scale scientific and technological version of the older community which would combine all the gains of the modern and all of the lasting value of the older communal forms. This was an ideal, a vision, of human experience enriched, expanded, and liberated as it had never been in all the millennia of human existence.[210]

Dewey's awareness that under modern conditions local communities as centers of social, political, or economic life were obsolete led him to conclude that any synthesis of the sort he envisioned would entail the "development of local agencies of communication and cooperation, creating stable loyal attachments, to militate against the centrifugal forces of present culture, while at the same time they are of a kind to respond flexibly to the demands of the larger unseen and indefinite public."[211] This would produce pluralistic and functional communities suffused with the old communal spirit, linked together through the extensive communications and the common enterprises of modern social life. In these communities, the vastness of the modern age could hear the timbre of the tiny individual voices talking to each other, and the prodigious power of matter and machine could create the great society of the modern age without suffocating the human soul. This is Dewey's synthesis. It is his best of all possible worlds.

Dewey's most forceful and famous statement of the necessity of local face-to-face community and its relation to modern society is at the end of **The Public and Its Problems**. Almost always the man of method, Dewey in these concluding pages is the man of vision. It is the vision of local community as the heart of the modern "Great Community." It is about the irreducible human need for the ties and bonds of community and the face-to-face associations that make these possible. The heart of it is this: "There is something deep within human nature itself which pulls toward settled relationships." And "no one knows how much of the frothy excitement of life, the mania for motion, of fretful discontent, of need for artificial stimulation, is the expression of frantic search for something to fill the void caused by the loosening of the bonds which holds persons together in immediate community of experience." The settled relations of local community aren't mere creatures of historical circumstance, they are "the ultimate universal, and as near an absolute as exists." Humans aren't human without these communities; and democracy, the instrument of human fulfillment, can't exist without them, for "democracy must begin at home, and its home is the neighborly community."[212]

But surely the ingenuity of the modern age, the most ingenious of all the ages, can find or create some substitute for the earlier, now outdated, community. It can't, for "there is no substitute for the vitality and depth of close and direct intercourse and attachment." The modern age must then recreate the spirit, structure, and substance of communal life with the means the modern age affords it if it wishes to satisfy the elemental need of its population. If it succeeds, it will create a new and a better community, one that " will manifest a fullness, variety and freedom of possession and enjoyment of meanings and goods unknown in the contiguous associations of the past. For it will be flexible as well as stable, responsive to the complex and world-wide scene in which it is enmeshed. While local, it will not be isolated. Its larger relationships will provide an exhaustible and flowing fund of meanings upon which to draw, with assurance that its drafts will be honored." The qualities of earlier communal life can be recreated; "there is nothing intrinsic in the forces which have effected uniform standardization, mobility and remote invisible relationships that is fatally obstructive to the return movement of their consequences into the local homes of mankind." The forces of the modern world can be used, so long as they are mediated or directed by the method and conclusions of intelligence and the life of community. There is no turning back in Dewey's vision, it is all out in front of human beings and if they use the resources that the slow progress of humanity has made available to them, there are no insurmountable barriers. The greatest of these resources, intelligence, can become the seminal agent in the creation of the "Great Community" when it is communicated face-to-face in "local communal life." The "systematic and continuous inquiry into all the conditions which affect association" must be "accomplished in the face-to-face relationships by means of direct give and take. Logic in its fulfillment recurs to the primitive sense of the word: dialogue. Ideas which are not communicated, shared, and reborn in expression are but soliloquy, and soliloquy is but broken and imperfect thought."[213]

Dewey's conclusion from all this is simple: humans can make a humanly habitable society and future, but only to the degree that they regain the consummations of community life. With community, Dewey consummates his vision.

III

To think about the relationship of the individual to community is to confront some of the fundamental and intractable issues of modern thought and life. The discussion of Dewey and Buber has raised some of them: the importance and nature of freedom, individuality, and independence, the relationship of social authority and tradition to individuals' efforts to achieve authenticity and autonomy, and the competing human needs for a feeling of belonging, with all its restrictions and limitations, and of being free of these limits and restrictions, with its loneliness, isolation, and estrangement. In considering these issues further, I hope to clarify and develop their relationship to the concept of community.

The desire for both individual and group independence has been one of the most powerful forces shaping the modern world. The winning of independence has been one of the greatest goods of the modern era. Whether in the form of demands for individual autonomy and liberation, human dignity, or human rights, it has shaped the modern consciousness that affects, even dictates, the way we look at ourselves and the content of both private and public discourse. Its common form is the loose set of propositions we call modern liberalism. The principal proposition of this individualism is this: to be independent is to be unconstrained and uncoerced by other individuals, by institutions, by society, and by the past. The individual is an end, not a means to social ends, and as an end, must be free to shape him or her self in ways of his or her own choosing and to pursue a future that corresponds with his or her talents, interests, beliefs, and unique identity. It requires that individuals not be told what to do by others, by social institutions, or, where preventable, by the circumstances of life. It insists individuals have the power and the ability to govern themselves: to be free to be oneself, to be the unique, authentic, and autonomous individual each of us is or can become.

The liberation of individuals, and of groups, has been the signal preoccupation of the modern era. In the beginning the concern was with the enormous task of throwing off the fetters forged over centuries—of rulers, institutions, customs, traditions, ideas—of all the ways of life and of society that yoked individuals to oppressive conditions of established orders. The villain, the great oppressor, was society and the culture it embodied. Rousseau was the great modern spokesman for this view. The aim of this liberation was simply to free people to have greater control over their own lives. The early struggles were those of the enslaved seeking first emancipation from the institutions and society that enslaved them and then the creation of a new life and society in which they could live freely and control their lives and institutions.

The struggle for independence has been the struggle for freedom. To be independent is to be free. To be free is to be free from control by others. The ideas, values, customs, traditions, and institutions of an established social organization threaten this freedom and independence of the individual to live his own life, shape his own destiny, and be his own person. Freedom is the liberation of the individual from the dependencies that have limited his potential and violated his spirit throughout human history. It can break the shackles of the past and open the cage in which societies have incarcerated the individual. Freedom makes possible the emergence of humans from the conformity, facileness, and oppressions of primitive and traditional societies, as well as, on a cosmic scale, from the anonymity and insignificance we see in the expressionless uniformities of a material universe. Freedom is the tool with which humans carve their distinctive relief on the vast background of human and cosmic existence. In it we have placed our faith and hope, from it received a sense of meaning and purpose upon which to build a modern way of life.

The converse of this apotheosis of liberation and independence is the denigration of restriction and dependence. Dependency is a form of slavery. It is to be under the control of some force that uses the individual as a pawn or a tool of its own designs. The critique of individual dependence focused, particularly in its early battles, on the social and political systems that denied basic rights and liberties to individuals as a means to control, exploit, or oppress them. The great revolutions of the modern age have been fought to break such social and political systems. Having won many of these battles, attention was directed to other forms of dependence. In the lives of most people, dependence is created by the institutions that shape daily life—family, school, church, and local community. Dependence may be created by these even when the social and political system has been changed. Each of these more intimate and immediate forms of social life may foster dependence, hamper the development of individuality, and deprive the individual of the freedoms necessary to achieve independence: of thought, of life-shaping choices, of opportunities to grow and change, and of belief. Their contents, structures, and instructions shape individuals into adults by defining the ideas, attitudes, and behaviors required of them by their particular society.

Modern liberalism has had more difficulty winning these battles. It has been less confident of its position in these areas and more ambivalent about what to do with these infringements on the independence of individuals than with those created by the larger structures and forces of culture and government. The original struggles had been devoted, in part, to the liberation of these very entities—families, churches, and localities from control by the larger community or state. Individual independence would be possible through the independence of these entities. Intrusions into the life of the individual by these entities, however, seemed more natural, unavoidable, benign, and necessary. They arose from the natural associations of life into which we are born or into which we voluntarily enter, and were by nature more intimate and altruistic than those associations created by the larger forces and institutions of society and government. For the young especially, nurturing and educating agencies were necessary. This is why societies and their governments have always either tolerated or established such agencies. However necessary and inevitable they may have seemed in the early struggles for freedom, modern liberalism has become increasingly wary of all of them. More expansive conceptions of individualism see them as threats to the independence and autonomy of the individual, and especially dangerous when they become instruments of the larger society. While liberal thought is divided on how to apply its principles to these institutions, all agree they must be opposed when their practices fail to affirm the core values of liberalism (for example, when they endanger the development and well-being of the individual) or too tightly restrict the independence of thought and action of their members.

The pursuit of independence and freedom, in its most expansive modern moments, goes further. Limitations on the individual's freedom may come in another form. The two above are inter-subjective (first state, society, culture, then family, church, and local community). A third is intra-subjective. There is no precise dividing line between the types of dependencies produced by government or families and those that lodge themselves within each person's self. We cannot escape that we are individual selves and dependent upon, even created by, selves that we did not create and cannot escape. We are at the mercy of our own peculiar personalities which are tied to the forms of dependency— culture, society, family, church, and school. In the internal conversations we have with ourselves we come up against these internal limitations to independence. The modern pursuit of independence, having triumphed over the political systems and limited the permissible restraints imposed by the family, church, and schools, now struggles with the difficult issues raised by these internal constraints on our independence and freedom. And this struggle is part of the larger debate over the source and nature of human freedom, fulfillment, happiness, and the self.

There are two major positions in this debate. One contends that the sources of these impediments are in the social arrangements of society. The evils that afflict individuals, and that have plagued humans throughout history, are the result of unenlightened and oppressive social organizations and of the types of cultures that have defined, and limited, the possibilities of human life. Rousseau is a champion of this view. So is Marx. We are born free and end in chains forged for us by society. If we could escape culture or transform it into a means of liberation and human fulfillment, then the flowering of the powers of individuals would be the common destiny of humans rather than the extraordinary and courageous achievement of the few who fight through to their individual conception and creation of their selves. Once unshackled, humans will create a better world with their many talents and the inherent goodness of their nature. Dependence, here, is an evil to be rejected, independence the guardian angel to be honored and followed. The Enlightenment's confidence in the great possibilities of human liberation are at the heart of this view.

There is a darker view of the human prospect at the heart of the opposing view. In this view, culture is not the villain, we human beings are. I described it earlier. It is the view of Ernest Becker. It has a long history in the Jewish and Christian traditions, in philosophy beginning with the Greeks, and in modern psychology, especially modern psychotherapy. Culture exists to save humans from themselves and to solve the problems of a creature that is out of joint with itself and the world. Humans are not healthy and good, they are driven and divided against themselves. The evils we experience are the result of our working our problems out on each other, both individually and collectively, and in our attempts to satisfy basic human needs and instincts. The vision of a better world through liberation and the autonomous creation of the individual self, in this view, is misguided for two reasons: humans don't really desire either liberation or autonomy and if they were to have them they would quickly escape them by repressing themselves and enslaving others. Culture, when properly conceived and adequately regulated, can contain these propensities, but it cannot get rid of them. Yet we do wish to be free individuals and be independent. We both want them and can not tolerate having them. We run both toward them and away from them at the same time. The need to submerge the self in the group and bestow on the group special status is part of our effort to overcome the brokenness, the disconnectedness of our natural existence. We are in nature but out of it, with others but not at one with them, single solitary individuals but not at one or peace with ourselves. In our compulsion to make ourselves and the world whole we create all the good and evil of culture, society, and history. Dependence is one means of salvation from a part of our human predicament. It is therefore necessary and good. But it is not a complete, easy or safe salvation. It is caught in the complexities and ambiguities of human relationships and culture. There is no salvation from our human nature and from the destiny it defines for us: crippled by doubts, trapped in the paradoxes of our human condition, we are impotent to straighten the twisted stuff of our humanness.

Dependence, in this grimmer view, has its place and its redeeming qualities. It is as necessary to humans as the struggle for freedom. It is a way for individuals to resolve the problems of their nature and human condition by building themselves into the world. Through it the individual can give an order and structure to his or her life, find a sense of boundaries and authority beyond the self, build a certain confinement that makes life manageable within the security of established bonds and affections and the comfort of an organic connection with the world. Most importantly, it grants a release from the pressure and responsibility of liberalism and individualism, and, when the state of dependency is a rich and human one, it offers a meaning and purpose to life which possesses a power and legitimacy beyond the resources of individuals acting and living independently.[214]

Freedom and independence are not unmitigated goods. With them comes also the possibility, perhaps the inevitability, of loss, and of estrangement from the social and natural orders that have protected and supported humans. This estrangement brings loneliness, isolation, insecurity, anxiety, rootlessness, and the solitary confrontation with a world that becomes more open and indeterminate as the bonds of dependence wither or break. In this perspective, "the achievement of freedom—the act of liberation—is always an estrangement, both biographically and historically. From the traumatic emancipation of birth onward—or from the traumatic emergence of the individual out of the tribe—freedom is encountered in fear and trembling."[215] The process of liberation disturbs, and can destroy, the vital web of connections and relations that are fundamental to human life and alter, often for the worse, the internal landscape of the self.

There is a limit to our capacity to expand into the vast and infinitely complex world around and within us without experiencing these side-effects. The goal cannot be to free us to explore all possible worlds and to change constantly. Freedom and independence in this expansive or absolute sense are too great a risk and may be beyond the natural limitations of our condition. Alfred North Whitehead was correct when he lamented, as one of the inescapable shortcomings of existence, that choices exclude alternative possibilities, and that we are forever in the process of opening some doors while closing others. We all live within these limits, in cages of one sort or another. They may be imposed from without or constructed from within. Either way, we are constrained in our thinking, believing, judging, and acting. It is these constraints that define us as individuals and set the parameters and the course of our lives.

Those constructed within the individual self are, regardless of their source and nature, part of these natural limits. The self requires them in order to function and remain healthy and sane. The sensory and psychological systems all filter and order the world we perceive and know. The extraordinary fact of human life is that this ordering of experience is not pre-programmed or built-in to us. We do it for and to ourselves. But we must do it. Freedom and independence are the blessing and challenge of human life, both exhilarating and terrifying us. There are opportunities for both good and bad in them. The temptation to order life either too much or too little is powerful and dangerous. Mental institutions are filled with people who crossed the limits, and so is history. Some ages and societies move toward one,

some to the other. The blessing of our age is greater freedom and
independence for more people. Its curse is that we may have carried
them, or they may have carried us, beyond the needs and natural limits
of our humanity.

The most important limitations are those set by the social nature of
human beings. The radical notions of individualism are wrong in their
view of humans, as are those of contract theorists. There is not now,
and never has been, a natural state of freedom where each individual is
a law unto himself—roaming, autonomous, independent. The reality,
then and now, is that humans are born into and nurtured by groups, and
become what they become because of their lives in groups. We are all,
to use a current word for it, "embedded" within the cultures that rear us.
What we see, think, feel, know, and believe come to us from the life of
the group. We grow in a particular soil in a particular place and time,
and are cultivated by gardeners who desire and intend to grow only
specific types of plants. The educational philosopher C.S. Bowers
argues that contemporary social philosophy too often overlooks this
natural embeddedness and, in its preoccupation with individual
freedom and autonomy, ignores not only the fact but the necessity of
this embeddedness. It is the need for this web of connections and the
wholeness of this social fabric that is important here. The world must
hold together for individuals. An asocial or anti-social individualism
can too easily dismember the social world which embeds us, and cast
us adrift in a world in which our natural relationships have been
replaced by the modern ones—the source of the great modern theme in
literature   and   philosophy—of   estrangement,   emptiness,   and
forlornness.

John Dewey and Martin Buber made these same points earlier in this
chapter. Humans are social. Efforts that pull them out of a social
context and loosen the bonds of social life will make them less than
human. Their humanness is realized in society, in the associations and
activities of group life and in the meeting of person and person. For
Buber

> the soul of man needs confirmation because man as man is in need of
> confirmation. An animal requires no confirmation, for it exists simply
> because it exists and is never disturbed by doubt. This is not the situation
> of man, however; he is sent out of nature's kingdom into the hazards of
> the single category; from birth he is encompassed by chaos, and keeps his
> lonely and fearful watch for existence to give him its sign of affirmation,
> which can only come from the soul of man to the soul of man. It is men
> who nourish one another with the mana of being.[216]

This nourishment is more than the mutual solace shared by cold, scared, and lost individuals stranded in a foreign place. It is also the communal attachment which allows them, together, to become fully human and to find a home in the world.

The problem is that humans have various needs and limitations that do not easily coexist with one another. To understand the problem, as Dewey and Buber did earlier in this chapter, and as Becker did in chapter three, we must posit twin or dual urges of human beings, one to independence and autonomy and one to integration, union, and communion. Humans need to be free, on their own and, at the same time, to be bound in community and tied to one another. These mesh in a human life in a rhythmic pattern of exist, one close to William James' view of human existence as an alternation of perching and flying. Humans love freedom and they hate it; they desire community but they flee from it, they have to have a home but they always seem to have to leave it. Contradictions, contrary urges, a thoroughly divided human heart are at the center of our human condition. We may not deny these contradictions or ignore either set of claims upon us for very long.

Is there an inherent conflict between these urges? Are we condemned to be divided against ourselves? The answer is yes. There is something inextinguishable and unaccommodating in both. We can't get rid of either of them and don't want to. They are each, in themselves, good. Rarely does one vanquish the other completely. They continuously struggle to find an acceptable basis of coexistence and mutual satisfaction. But most of the time there is an inescapable tension between them. The community may set the terms of existence, even the terms of the individual's self consciousness and conception, but there is the voice that stands apart in its separate and unique interior space and says "I" and wishes to be free. Once free, there is another voice whispering "we" and wishing to be in community.

This "I" of freedom takes different shapes and assumes different relationships in the "We" of community. Our modern "I" is independent, self-confident, and assertive, capable of being brutishly anti-social, and likely to see life as an either/or choice in which the individual must either burst the bonds of socially constructed reality and seek, alone, a new world or, failing in this, to succumb to the deadly routines and various oppressions of society. This modern "I" defines itself in opposition to things, in a battle against constraints. Its guiding principle is freedom, a freedom which also conceives itself in a war against that which stands in its way. The modern balance has tipped in favor of independence, autonomy, and the individual. This is good, but there is danger in it. It may bring enlightenment and new life. It may also, particularly in the hands of romantics and existentialists, show us a land of lost souls, anomie, rootlessness, despair--- a dark night of the soul from which we may not emerge.

What is the place of community in this age of the individual? Community still, even in our time, makes its claims on us. We have not been able to cast aside all that community provides or create through the herculean powers of the liberated individual a better world. We have instead discovered the limits of the individual without community. This discovery, however, has only defined the problem: how can we have good community and free individuals in the same society. Since the claims of both are strong, a solution may not be found by an encroachment on the basic requirements of either. Without some encroachment, however, a solution may be impossible. Most in modern society are deeply committed to freedom and the individual. They are often unyielding and difficult to conciliate, preferring the problems caused by too much freedom to those that come with not enough. We are stuck: we cannot move forward with only one of them but we cannot find the formula for having them together. We are impaled on the horns of a dilemma. There is no escape from it. All attempts to resolve it must contend with the paradoxical nature of the demands involved and the divided desires and needs of humans. It pushes up against the limitations of our humanity and human condition. In doing so it shows us the human prospect in all its possibilities and limitations, its triumphs and tragedies.

There is, however, neither triumph nor tragedy without our participation. Like tragic heroes we are accomplices in the unfolding of our lives and the history of our time. We are not pawns. It may be that the dilemma of community and the individual is too much for us and that it is a tragedy of modern life. But it is not true that we are without means to make a life for ourselves that is responsive to the need for both. Such a life might be conceived in many ways. Dewey and Buber offer two ways.

Part of the difficulty in achieving such a life is due to the way we define the key concepts. We need to be conscious of the way we define them. The definitions can determine the requirements and possibilities for progress. If, for example, freedom is understood in sweeping, absolutist terms, as we currently understand it, then any community capable of coexisting with it must be defined in narrower and weaker terms. Without this adjustment we will founder on their irreconcilable claims. Redefinition must come from an alteration in our thinking about concepts and human needs. Any accommodation will be stable and tenable only if the restrictions of one can be shown as necessary to achieve benefits in the other and, more critically, in the over-all well-being of individuals. This well-being must remain the aim and the measure of all redefinition because it holds the focus on the one factor, the key one, that can guide it: the nature and needs of human beings. This is, I believe, what both Dewey and Buber accomplished in their models.

In our modern case, freedom has muscled community aside. It has redefined community nearly out of existence and we have suffered for it. If we are to restore the balance we must redefine freedom and individualism. What would a redefinition and rethinking of the meaning of individualism and freedom be? Here is one: individualism might mean an individual within a community and freedom the power to freely assert membership in a community and to freely affirm its beliefs and way of life. Autonomous individuals would freely create communities, bind themselves to them, and live happily within the confines of their chosen community.

This redefinition demands significant changes in our current way of thinking. What rights and freedoms must be retained? Choice involves the restriction of freedoms and, in this case, of the prerogatives of a more radical individualism. The kind of commitments and values associated with a full-blooded community would generate demands those committed to individualism and freedom would find difficult to accept, even if freely chosen. Redefinitions may be merely prestidigitation, or worse, a form of the thought control used in totalitarian societies. The reality of communal constraint, obligation, self-denial, commitment—all of which entail an abrogation of the ways of individualism and freedom—is circumvented rather than confronted.

The resistance to these constraints and limitations is so powerful because of the place of freedom and individualism in modern consciousness. Our age is overwhelmed by the Enlightenment's concerns with individual autonomy and self, the private and personal, rights, individual freedom and independence, liberation from custom and tradition. Community, within this consciousness, consists of self-interested private individuals pursuing their separate ends with as little interference as possible, free of an overarching framework of authority, power, or belief. The social or communal sector exists only to regulate these private interests. There is very little of the kind of community I have been discussing in this modern consciousness.

This consciousness is the product of modern liberal thought and society. But it is also based upon principles of social organization reflecting the scientific and technological world of modern society. This consciousness reflects the bureaucratic structures of mass society: dynamism, anonymity, depersonalization, bureaucratization, mass communication, rationalization and integration of social and economic structures, the fragmentation of current and traditional patterns of social organizations, the need for predictability, and the dominance of the passive stance or the client status of the individuals who live within this modern society. It is one of the contradictions, ironies perhaps, of modern life that these two forms of thought and social organization have come to preeminence together. One consequence has been the fragmentation of human consciousness as it was being both liberated and more closely regulated. The fragmentation brought a slow separation of the public and the private realms, both within the society and within the individual self. The hold of the individual became supreme in the private world. The rational and technical order of the public world became inhospitable to the urges which drive the private. Within the private, individuals attempted to integrate and sustain meanings and give a deeper sense of meaning to their humanness and their lives. But this world is vulnerable to the forces of the public mentality, to the invasions of mass media, to the impersonality of urban life, to the materialistic ethos of the public realm, and to the dislocations of rapid change. The forces of socialization intrude into this private world, the haven of the self. When this intrusion is strong and successful enough we begin to conceive private life in the terms of public life. Our identity is then shaped by a way of life that is destructive of a private realm of individual power, control, and freedom. Such destruction may be experienced as liberation, as a new openness and tolerance, as an opportunity for personal growth and great freedom. But in fact this private self is being lost through the absorption of the individual into the routines and rules of public life and consciousness. Calls for community are less appealing when the individual is threatened in this way. Community under these circumstances may be seen as this modern public realm dressed in sheep's cloth.

The private world has been infiltrated and undermined in other ways. The escape from the public world, and from community, to the private world, prompted partly by the logic of liberal thought and partly forced by the nature of modern mass society, has forced us to depend upon a private world that itself has experienced a crisis of identity in modern and post-modern thought. As we have fortified our inner world to protect our individuality and freedom we have found it less certain, orderly, comprehensible than we had hoped: having finally liberated the individual we discovered that the individual wasn't there in the form we had envisioned, and worse, that nothing like a solid, fixed self existed at all. The inner realm proved as fluid and elusive as the outer world. Again, there has been both liberation and loss in this. It has expanded the range of freedom and self development by weakening internal constraints on the definition and development of the individual self. We can be imprisoned within our private world by a self we do not understand, did not make, and cannot control. The inner world may be a prison as well as an open frontier. The realization of the complexity and multiplicity of this inner world offers a potential liberation from the more rigid, fixed, and culturally predetermined conceptions of the self. But it creates profound insecurity and anxiety and a need to find moorings for self and life. Even more, it precipitates a crisis of identity for individuals who now have to struggle to create a private world ex nihilo and alone. As difficult as it has become to find a home in the public world, it now has become as difficult to find one within oneself.

The fragmentation of modern life, however, has affected the public realm as well. The reign of rational and technical approaches to social and economic life has brought, in addition to order and regimentation, an end of the normative and ideological domination of society by a few privileged, authoritative groups and ideologies. Amid all the order, control, and uniformity of the new technological age there exists a crisis of cultural identity and authority. Along with its vast social and economic machine it has created cultural heterogeneity and pluralism. Breaking the hold of traditional and often monolithic cultural institutions and beliefs was liberating. Living among the ruins has proven more difficult. To create a new order with enough authority and legitimacy to support personal and social commitments and belief, difficult in the best of times, is particularly difficult in a time when analytic intelligence and an individualistic ethos continually call all authority and legitimacy into doubt. The common response to both this new order and disorder is to resist through retreating to the private world.

But resistance and the retreat to a fortress of private life offers us little relief. It casts individuals out on their own, undermines the public, social nature of existence, makes each person the manager of his or her own life, and ends, as it has for us today, in a technology of private life. And this technology, even in its urge for order, leads to the fragmentation of experience and the discounting of all experience which won't fit into its way of doing things. I have argued that this will not satisfy individuals. It is incapable of providing them with an integrated and human set of meanings and institutions, a public which satisfies the human need for confirmation through fellowship with one another, the sense of organic connection within oneself, with others, with the natural world, and with the universe. It does not offer a place, a home for humans in the world.

The way beyond the dilemma of the individual and community is to conceive a reconciliation of these two competing goods so that a stable self and society may be created. Robert Kegan's recent book, **In Over Our Heads**, attempts to both understand this dilemma and find a way out of it. Kegan contends that modern life places mental demands upon its members that they are unprepared to meet. There are orders of consciousness that individuals and groups possess at different times in their individual development and history. Each is a distinctive way of understanding, ordering, and relating to the world and to one's self.

Kegan is both a developmentalist and a constructivist. As a developmentalist, he defines a progression through five orders of consciousness; being a constructivist, he defines the public and private worlds we construct with these different consciousnesses. In life, these developments and constructions are usually messy, mixed-up affairs. There may be, for example, more than one type of consciousness present in members of a society. When this occurs an individual's consciousness may be different from, and at odds with, other forms of consciousness that are present in and important for a society. One consequence is that the various worlds an individual inhabits—of home, schools, work—may require different forms of consciousness. This, in his view, is the situation today. Modern culture demands a way of thinking and consciousness most of us have not attained; we are therefore in over our heads when faced with the requirements of home, school, work, and social life.

Kegan's forms of consciousness offer us an insight into the issues I have been discussing in this chapter. He defines an ascending scheme of five orders, the third, fourth, and fifth of which are important for modern societies and individuals. These three encompass the general order of adult consciousness capable of abstract and logical thinking, an awareness of others and their distinctive points of view, roles, and separate consciousnesses, and a self conscious of the inner states and subjectivity of the self. He labels the three orders of modern consciousness the traditional, modern, and post-modern. The principal dilemmas of the modern age may be seen in the place of these three forms of consciousness in our modern times.

Most citizens of modern culture are traditional in their consciousness. They can function in the realms of abstraction (generalizations, inferences, hypothetic and propositional thinking, ideals and values) with an awareness of both others' and their own points of view. They function within a context that is concrete, with a shared and given point of view, and a conception of individual needs that are enduring and set by the "homogenous fabric of value and belief, a shared sense of how the world works and how we should live in it." Kegan uses Alice Miller's **The Drama of the Gifted Child** to describe the "communities of mind" of this order of consciousness:

> When we live in communities of mind as well as geography, the number of original decisions we have to make about how we conduct our lives is dramatically smaller. Whether such communities are literally religious in nature, they are all implicitly so, providing a common core of beliefs that are entered and reentered via a seamless fabric of ceremony, celebration, ritual, gesture, and symbol. Whether bound by explicitly religious loyalties or ethnic, regional, or civic ones, such communities are distinguished by a kind of homogeneity that makes the notion of 'role model' pandemic. Everyone older is a role model, and the elders are unrecognizably inspiring in that young men or young women, without even being aware they are doing it, 'breathe in' the way they are to conduct themselves today and tomorrow through their inescapable association with and fealty toward those who are a generation ahead of them.[217]

The problem is that it isn't very modern. It sounds and is old, pre-modern, as its name says, traditional. Specifically, modern societies usually do not have the "the community's collective consciousness that is itself the source of order, direction, vision, real-creation, limit-setting, boundary-management, and developmental facilitation." Instead, quoting Alice Miller again, "it is necessary today for the individual to find his support within himself." To do this the individual must have a new fourth order of consciousness.

Kegan defines the differences between the third and fourth orders with two analogies. The first analogy is of driving a car with an automatic versus a manual transmission. To drive the first you need less skill and are less directly involved in one of the essential functions of the vehicle. The manual transmission requires more of the driver, more responsibility for keeping the vehicle moving, more knowledge and skill in its operations. Kegan's point is that cultures and orders of consciousness are the same as transmissions. They build more or less individual responsibility, decision-making, and knowledge into their operations. Some require more than others. In a world of automatic transmissions drivers take for granted that the machine will and should run almost on its own. When for some reason the automatic transmissions are no longer available, then individuals in this world must change. This is the situation of traditionalist consciousness in a world that makes it increasingly difficult to maintain traditional consciousness. Fourth order or modern consciousness requires a driver able to use a manual transmission, one who is able, in fact, to adapt to either type of transmission and capable of assuming greater control of and responsibility for its movement. Kegan argues we need fourth order consciousness to support third order traditional consciousness and community because the conditions of modern life require it.

The difference between these two forms of consciousness is in their different conceptions of the nature and source of authority for both individual consciousness and social institutions and practices. Where the traditionalist finds fixed foundations and enduring entities and values, the modernist does not. One is foundational, the other foundationless, one dependent upon a concrete, law-abiding world and self, the other on an abstract, indeterminate world of self-generating and autonomous selves. The fourth order is based upon this priority of the self and the belief that the self exists within a system of interrelationships to which it gives order, meaning, and completeness. Kegan's fourth order modern consciousness is the consciousness that has been described in earlier chapters as a source of our modern problem. In the move from traditionalist to modern, third to fourth consciousness, we see the seed and the fruit of our crisis of culture and self.

The second analogy concerns this move from one to the other. Third order consciousness, in a world demanding fourth order consciousness, is a fish out of water. It has three options according to Kegan. It can thrash about until it finds "another pond to jump into," it can thrash about until it dies, or it can, with effort and luck, evolve into a creature capable of surviving in the new environment. We, like the fish, opt for the first or the third and naturally sort ourselves into two types of people: those who "provide a new pond to jump into and those that facilitate the evolution from life in the water."[218] Most are unprepared for this evolution in their consciousness so they escape the transition by looking for a new pond. Kegan believes most will rise to the new consciousness with time and education, but modern societies must understand the difficulties of the transition and assist their members in negotiating it.

If the fourth order is at first beyond the majority who live in the modern age, then the fifth order is beyond nearly all of us. It continues the movement toward eliminating firm or fixed foundations. In it the one firm footing left is dispensed with. Even the autonomous, single self is found to be a fiction. The fourth order's systems of relationships, anchored by the self, gives way to a fluid and polymorphous self, with multiple selves in one individual, the "interpenetration of selves" and "inter-individuation." The social systems and ideologies within which the self exists also become multiple and interpenetrate each other. The mind formulates and authorizes ideologies and tests them against those with equal standing and authority. Paradox and contradiction characterize the testing process. The process is dialectical in nature. The distinct lines separating self and other blur, as do those between the self and the systems in which it exists, particularly the ideologies and institutions that formalize the relationships within these systems. The self, now less unitary, must still author, form, and regulate itself but it now does so with the aim of self-transformation through the dialectical transactions with other selves and other systems. Kegan has brought the new "chaos theory" in cosmology down to society and into the self.

Those who promote this fifth order consciousness long for, in Kegan's words, "the recognition of our multiple selves, for the capacity to see conflict as a signal of our overidentification with a single system, for the sense of our relationships and connections as prior to and constitutive of the individual self, for an identification with the transformative process of our being rather than the formative products of our becoming...."[219] These longings are an extension and intensification of those elements of fourth order consciousness that have unsettled individuals in our time. The demands on the individual are much greater in these two orders of modern consciousness. The world is more open and fluid, the authorities are themselves in need of support, the self, once moored firmly to enduring qualities defined and reinforced by society, is set adrift on a sea of self-consciousness and subjectivity where it must define by itself an identity. All that is good in the long quote earlier from Alice Miller is lost to individuals of this consciousness. Here we see a consciousness that is the logical consequence of the ideas and practices of modern liberal thought and society. In it we find both the blessing and the curse of modern life.

Kegan is aware of the problems these changes in consciousness pose for humans. He sees them as the natural challenges of a creature in a dynamic, evolutionary world. But Kegan also understands that the problem is deeper than the common dislocations or traumas of change.

As a developmentalist he acknowledges that in the evolution of structures of knowing and orders of consciousness differentiation precedes integration, conflict precedes re-solution. He is confident that integration and new order will emerge with time. Both modern and post-modern consciousness have great powers to dissolve existing structures and orders. It is not as clear or certain they possess the powers to create new orders to replace them that are capable of satisfying the needs of modern men and women.

Kegan is more confident than I am on this. He contends that while both orders of consciousness have destructive or deconstructive power, they both also have constructive or reconstructive power. Where we end up will depend on our ability to tap both their constructive and destructive powers. Differentiation is a fact of modern life. Integration can be too if we employ modern and post-modern consciousness, particularly the latter, to this end. His confidence comes from the naturalistic, evolutionary, and developmental framework of his thinking, his faith in the higher, more critical forms of intelligence associated with modern and post-modern consciousness, and his assessment of the nature and demands of modern life. In this modern life many of us are fish out of water and must evolve or die. There are fewer and fewer pools to save ourselves in. Modern forms of consciousness are slowly and inexorably draining them dry. If we must adapt or perish, then the critical issue is on what terms we will do so. To survive, Kegan argues, we must all become, to some extent, like Montaigne, Hume, and Freud, because the modern age demands it of us and we cannot escape the exigencies of the modern world in which we live.

But perhaps we need not, and cannot, completely put on the clothes of modern life. Kegan is sensitive to this issue and his position is an effort to find an accommodation of the demands of modern life and those of the humans who lived that life. He acknowledges that there are aspects of third order traditional consciousness that satisfy the basic needs of individuals and groups. These needs were described earlier in the quotation from Miller. The satisfaction of these needs comes into conflict with other needs of modern life, not met by the third order, that modern and post-modern consciousness satisfy. We are in the middle of the dilemma again. Kegan finds a resolution in the twin yearnings of humans: "the yearnings to be included, to be a part of, close to, joined with, to be held, admitted, accompanied" and "the yearnings to be independent or autonomous, to experience one's distinctness, the self-chosenness of one's directions, one's individual integrity."[220] He also cites David Bakan on the duality in our yearnings for both communion and agency. This is how Bakan says it in his book **The Duality of Human Existence**:

> I have adopted the terms 'agency' and 'communion' to characterize two fundamental modalities in the existence of living forms, agency for the existence of an organism as an individual, and communion for the participation of the individual in some larger organism of which the individual is a part. Agency manifests itself in self-protection, self-assertion, and self-expansion; communion manifests itself in the sense of being at one with other organisms. Agency manifests itself in the formation of separations; communion in the lack of separations. Agency manifests itself in isolation, alienation, and aloneness; communion in contact, openness, and union. Agency manifests itself in the urge to master; communion in non-contractual cooperation. Agency manifests itself in the repression of thought; communion in the lack and removal of repression. One of the fundamental points which I attempt to make is that the very split of agency from communion, which is a separation, arises from agency... and that it represses the communion from which it separates itself.[221]

Bakan's solution is "to mitigate agency with communion" but without violating it so that we achieve a delicate balance of these two sides of our nature.[222]

Any balance must respect both needs or it will not work. Highly individualistic communities will not satisfy the need for community. They will become an association or a group or a league and thereby lose the commonness and the sharing of ideas and values that hold community together. They are not able to demand the essential sacrifices of individual autonomy necessary to achieve community. In a community the individual is defined by the beliefs, morals, faith, commitments, tradition, rituals, and history of the community. When these do not shape the community, it becomes something less than a full, substantive community but instead a procedural or instrumental community held together by a political and social process and not by the substance of community belief and life. A method or process isn't enough. There are democratic communities whose principal interest and value is the protection and extension of the legal and social mechanisms that safeguard individual rights and freedoms. American democracy has become an example of this. In Dewey's philosophy, democracy will have the substance of community as well as the form. But in practice such concerns for democratic forms often undermine the essential elements of community life. This is so today in our democratic society. We have achieved the form without the substance and, as a result, do not have the community we need.

Kegan agrees that both are necessary and that integration is the goal. He describes the relationship of the two as one of foreground and background and sees it as a matter of emphasis and style. In his terminology, the reconstructive rather than deconstructive tendencies of post-modern thought should fill the foreground. The reconstructive "seeks to reelaborate and reappropriate modernist categories (such as reason, freedom, equity, rights, self-determination) on less absolutist grounds." The deconstructive is too determined to dissolve all of the fixed points in its consciousness and conceptual system, too intent on breaking-down and differentiating things, too little interested in defining what will be left when everything has been deconstructed. What will we do with a world of individuals whose cardinal virtue is the deconstruction of the widest range of subject matters, especially those dependent upon absolutes, hierarchies, generalizations, normative judgments, relations of power and domination, and uniformity. Kegan's reconstructive post-modernism takes the necessary step to a new integration by reopening the possibility "that some kinds of normativeness, hierarchizing, privileging, generalizing, and universalizing are not only compatible with a post-ideological view of the world, they are necessary for sustaining it."[223] He hopes for a reconstructive modernism in which the human needs satisfied in traditionalist consciousness may, in a modern way, be met by a different consciousness in a different world.

Kegan is aware of the dangers of an unbounded faith in the new orders of consciousness and the problems they pose for modern men and women. The difficulties of finding a modern alternative capable of balancing the competing claims modern life and human nature place upon us are great. They may prove too great. It is not a peculiarly modern problem. Plato once attempted to resist similar developments in Greek society and he failed to define an alternative persuasive enough to halt the development. Resistance in modern societies has been less single-minded and fierce than in Plato's Greece. We often, simultaneously, resist and encourage, hate and love, the new modern world. But we are as concerned as Plato was concerned about the kind of world the new ideas and consciousness are creating. If it is true, as Kegan claims, that we must evolve or die, and that this evolution means giving up traditional society and consciousness for some form of modern or post-modern society and consciousness, then it may be that we too, like Plato, will fail.

Kegan's reconstruction and integration is his name for a modern paideia. He argues for its necessity and acknowledges the difficulty of achieving it in our time. It may, in fact, be beyond us now, a specter of a past seen only as a scene in a twilight panorama of old times. It is just this paideia that we lose with traditional consciousness, with the communion of Bakan, and with deconstructive post-modernism. It may be better that it is in the past. Our age has prided itself on divesting itself of such dusty ancient ideas. The Enlightenment beat its chest to this theme, as do we of the twentieth century. Even Dewey, used earlier as a way beyond modern thought, sang this tune louder and longer than most in our century. In his spirit, neo-pragmatist philosophers like Richard Rorty have deconstructed almost everything, including the science in which Dewey placed such faith and the very philosophy he practiced.

The English essayist Walter Pater understood, I think, our modern dilemma and what is possible for us. The Greek paideia, he knew, was gone forever. We live and see the world differently now. It is in the nature of the incessant flow of human existence that the harmony, balance, and unity of the individual self and culture must pass away. For special eras it has been possible to create a culture imbued with these qualities, the Greeks and the Renaissance being Pater's chosen examples. In our time, he knew, they were not possible, except in art or for unusually perceptive and creative individuals. This is so because "to regard all things and principles of things as inconstant modes or fashions has more and more become the tendency of modern thought." All inner and outer life is a whirlpool and experience is "reduced to a group of impressions...ringed round for each one of us by that thick wall of personality through which no real voice has ever pierced on its way to us, or from us to that which we can only conjecture to be without. Every one of those impressions is the impression of the individual in his isolation, each mind keeping as a solitary prisoner its own dream of the world." The self is elusive: "a tremulous wisp constantly re-forming itself...—that continual vanishing away, that strange, perpetual weaving and unweaving of ourselves." What is possible in Pater's Heraclitean world? Only this: to seize each fleeting moment and, with our "passion or insight or intellectual excitement," give "nothing but the highest quality to our moments as they pass, and simply for those moments' sake."[224]

This is a faint light, indeed, a thoroughly modern and post-modern one. It offers a cold solace and a light with which to find our way through a dark age. Too faint and cold for most, certainly for me, for Kegan, and, I think, even for Rorty and Pater. Something resists the light with which it illuminates our world and its possibilities, and something persists, will not give way to a world without what paideia offers. There is an ancient wisdom and an eternal hunger behind this persistence, an awareness and longing that offers us, in Virginia Woolf's words, "a coherence in things, a stability; something, shines out...in the face of the flowing, the fleeting, the spectral, like a ruby" which bestows on us humans a feeling of peace and of rest. Of such moments, Woolf thought, "the thing is made that endures."[225] We have seen the desire for such enduring things in Kegan and in Dewey, and even in Rorty and Pater. For Rorty, as for Dewey, we reconstruct and reorder the world and our lives through community. In the modern age we have lost "metaphysical comfort" but have gained

> a renewed sense of community. Our identification with our community— our society, our political tradition, our intellectual heritage—is heightened when we see this community as **ours** rather than **nature's**, **shaped** rather than **found**, one among many which men have made. In the end, the pragmatists tell us, what matters is our loyalty to other human beings clinging together against the dark, not our hope of getting things right....Our glory is in our participation in fallible and transitory human projects, not in our obedience to permanent nonhuman constraints.[226]

While this may seem meager fare as reconstructions go, and paltry in comparison to Dewey's, it is Rorty's acknowledgment of the need to create something to replace the lost order of the ancient paideia and an invitation to reconsider Dewey's views.

For Pater the need was much stronger than for Rorty. Much of his later work, written after the hostile response to his conclusion to **The Renaissance** from which the quotes above are taken, was an attempt to temper the implications of his subjectivism and naturalism. The practical matter was to find the principle of unity and order in the flux of time and experience and to safeguard a place in our lives and society for the higher and finer expressions of our humanness: the ideal, the beautiful, the noble and good, and the sacred. He understood the difficulties of securing a place for these in a world pulled apart by the antinomies of modern existence in a world shaped by both centrifugal and centripetal forces. But it is possible. It may occur in those moments of passionate contemplation when experience, in all its unity and beauty, is present to us. With such moments experience becomes art and the flux is held still for an instant in our consciousness. It is this experience Virginia Woolf, who was influenced by Pater, captures in her experience. Pater's early writings offered little beyond these moments when, as we "burn always with this hard, gemlike flame," all the ecstasy and success possible for us is achieved.[227]

But this modern epicureanism, too, was not enough. He pushed to find, without denying his original understandings of human experience and life, deeper anchorage within the flood. One place he found it was in a long slow rapprochement with Christianity described in his novel **Marius the Epicurean**. Another was in his greater appreciation of Plato's thought, especially its insistence on the necessity of the claims of the absolute and the ideal on us, and of the order, stability, and continuity of the Dorian culture of Sparta. In both, the isolated self is freed from its solipsism, from being "shut into brief lives, cut off into this place and that place," and is able, through culture, tradition, and history, to experience that which is harmonious, beautiful, and good in both the self and the society. In this experience and a life built from it, we can define a modern paideia. William Butler Yeats, a famous disciple of Pater, in a poem for his daughter, prayed for this security and support, the deeper anchorage in a turbulent and dangerous modern world:

> And may her bridegroom bring her to a house
> Where all's accustomed, ceremonious;
> ....
> How but in custom and in ceremony
> Are innocence and beauty born?
> Ceremony's a name for the rich horn,
> And custom for the spreading laurel tree.[228]

In <u>Marius the Epicurean</u> Pater describes the house of St. Cecilia and the early ceremonies of the Christian church. In them, he finds a refugee and sees a way for the soul to be reborn out of itself into a different and better life:

> And from the first they could hear the singing, the singing of children mainly, it would seem, and of a new kind...; It was the expression not altogether of mirth, yet of some wonderful sort of happiness—the blithe self-expansion of a joyful soul in people upon whom some all-subduing experience had wrought heroically, and who still remember, on this bland afternoon, the hour of a great deliverance.[229]

And from what is this deliverance?

> Here was, if not the cure, yet solace or anodyne of his great sorrows—of that constitutional sorrowfulness, not peculiar to himself perhaps, but which had made his life certainly like one long 'disease of the spirit'. Merciful intention made itself known remedially here, in the mere contact of the air, like a soft touch upon aching flesh. On the other hand, he was

aware that new responsibilities also might be awakened—new and
untried responsibilities—a demand for something from him in return....At
least he suspected that, after the beholding of it, he could never again be
altogether as he had been before.[230]

So it is with us. Our hope must be that we can find a way beyond the
modern "disease of the spirit." If once we find our way to Yeats'
ceremonious house or hear the singing in St. Cecilia's, we will never be
modern in the same way again. The struggle to finding or creating this
way is our paideia agonistes.

Chapter Six
Education and Community

The democratic problem in education is not primarily a problem of training children; it is the problem of making a community within which children cannot help growing up to be democratic, intelligent, disciplined to freedom, reverent of the goods of life, and eager to share in the tasks of the age. A school cannot produce this result; nothing but a community can do so.

Joseph Hart

The difficulty is then dialectical: how shall you make a soul which is faithful to a lost yesterday and strong enough to meet a discontinuous tomorrow.[231]

Fred Inglis

As a first step in defining the implications of my argument for education, I will describe a model of education based upon the ideas of Dewey and Buber. This model will draw upon their similarities. The similarities I wish to use as the basis of my model are those that come from the general visions of each man that I described in chapter four. These visions provide the essential form and spirit of a good community and a good education. This form and spirit may assume various shapes in practice. It is capable of accommodating a range of possibilities; there is more than one type of community and there is more than one educational practice that achieves the ends Dewey and Buber seek.

The epigraphs to this section give a sense of their common vision. Hart insists on the inseparability of community and education. Only community can educate individuals as they should be educated. Inglis offers a hint of the dilemmas and tensions inherent in community and education. Community, that in some vital way is tied to the past and to tradition, must exist in an age of continuous change that threatens and often destroys the organic connections of past, present, and future. It must contain the friction generated when the freedom and autonomy of the individual rubs against the constraints of community. Education, when tightly bound to the fortunes of community, cannot avoid these dilemmas. They are in part characteristics of our age and in part the intransigent raw material of human existence. Any application of the conception of community to education must address and accommodate these dilemmas.

Dewey and Buber confronted these dilemmas and attempted, in their different ways, to resolve them. In doing so they have had to challenge some standard assumptions of modern thought. They have challenged an either/or approach to answers to these dilemmas and to the idea that apparent oppositions or contradictions must be mutually exclusive and incompatible. For Dewey, there is one reality and it is a complex integration of interlocking and overlapping dualities; for Buber there is the inveterate contradictoriness, a two-foldness, of human existence which must be both borne and hallowed. The task of both Dewey and Buber is to pierce the common understandings of the relationship between the individual and community and envision a new relationship. As we consider education these things must be kept before our eyes. The unity to be found in community and education will be one that daily faces the strains and incongruities of human existence but does so within a framework that reconciles and resolves, without obviating or violating, them. This framework is the key.

Dewey and Buber agree in enough ways to allow the construction, from their views, of a model of a good education. The cardinal components of this model are these:

1. Modern educational practices are lifeless and have blocked out or ignored vital needs of humans and essential ingredients of human existence. Specifically, they are out of touch with the life process necessary to a complete and good life. Education must embody this process. In Dewey the process is that of human experience and in Buber it is the life of dialogue and mutuality.

2. There are two aspects of these processes that are vital to education. One is their rhythmic nature. This rhythm allows for the existence of different and conflicting tendencies within the process and for their reconciliation. They present themselves as polarities. The two

of particular importance here are stability-change and community-individual. Both Dewey and Buber insist that humans need all four and that the process of human existence regulates and modulates their interdependencies. In education this means that the process of education must liberate the individual within community and create stability in the face of the imperatives of change. Inglis' quote captures this process in the specific tension between the past that moors and the future that cuts free. The second aspect is community-individual. The essential life process is realized in community and therefore education may only be good education in community. Good education occurs when the rhythmic pattern resolves itself into an ordered and stable existence, fulfilling individuals and binding them in a communion, rooting itself in the past and flowering in the future.

In the final paragraph of **A Common Faith** Dewey affirms this critical connection:

> We who now live are parts of a humanity that extends into the remote past, a humanity that has interacted with nature. The things in civilization we most prize are not of ourselves. They exist by grace of the doings and sufferings of the continuous human community in which we are a link. Ours is the responsibility of conserving, transmitting, rectifying, and expanding the heritage of values we have received that those who come after us may receive it more solid and secure, more widely accessible and more generously shared than we have received it[232]

Here is the whole image: individuals in community conserving and expanding the accumulated wisdom and values of human experience. This is the natural process of human existence and it is a paradigm for good education. Buber would agree with it; Dewey's view could be a description of Buber's "living tradition."

The precise relationship of education and community may be expressed in a simple syllogism: the life process realizes itself in community; education must embody the life process; therefore good education must possess the qualities of a good community. Good community is inherently educational; good education is inevitably within a community. The meaning of this relationship is important but less than self-evident and therefore requires some elaboration.

Its first meaning, captured by Hart in the epigraph to this section, is of the community as educator. This is straightforward enough. The life of the community is the means and the end of education; daily life is the organization, administration, and curriculum of education. The conditions of everyday life provide the methods of instruction. The goal is the preservation and renewal of the community and its way of life.

Both Dewey and Buber support this meaning, tacitly at least, in the models they describe and endorse: nineteenth century New England farm life, science, kibbutz, and Hasidim. They both seek the education that takes place beyond the walls of formal schooling. The lure of this natural and informal education is powerful for them and it rests upon a simple truth they hold in common: the aim of education is to immerse the young in the fullness and richness of human existence—in the world of relation and experience. Community, when it is whole and healthy, is where this human existence is found.

This first meaning is about informal education. The second is about formal education. This formal education is in the school. There are several different relationships between formal education and community. The first is the relationship of the healthy and good community with its schools. The community would dominate the educational process and the work of the school would be filled with the spirit and life of its community. Buber contends that schools in such communities have no separate or special identity but are extensions of the community. Dewey's ideal is one in which schools and communities are bound as closely as they are in Buber. But he, more than Buber, focuses on the tendency of the relationship to fissure and pull apart. The second relationship is the one that emerges with this pulling apart. The cause of the pulling apart may be the weakening of the community which, for Dewey and Buber, would result from the deterioration or loss of the qualities necessary to a good community. If the community weakens, two things can happen. One is the withering away of the community as the formative influence on the school and the emergence of the school as a semi-autonomous and distinctive institution. The other is that the characteristics of the weakened community may become the guiding and shaping force in the schools. In both cases there is a tendency for the schools to become more important and independent parts of the educational process. In either situation the school must take up the educational responsibilities the community no longer meets. The most destructive consequence of this loss of community is the separation of the school from the larger and essential processes of human life. Schools become places where teaching takes place but not genuine education. Buber, for instance, considers the teaching of skills and content to be mere training, of technical and secondary importance. Teaching is not education. It teaches students to think "while education is meant to influence their character and behavior." Buber believes that

teaching itself does not educate, it is the teacher that educates. A good teacher educates when silent as well as when speaking, during recess, during an occasional conversation, and through his own behavior, provided he really exists and is really present. He is an educator by touch. The...school is based upon the encouragement of contact between teacher and student—upon the principle of dialogue; dialogue of questions from both sides, and answers from both sides, dialogue of joint observation of a certain reality in nature, or in art, or in society, dialogue of true fellowship, in which the breaks in conversation are no less of a dialogue than speech itself.[233]

Community may be substituted for teacher in this quote. The effect is to reinforce the idea, common to Dewey and Buber, that only the expansive view of education captures their meaning and is the correct conception of a good education.

But this still leaves us with the reality of the modern condition of society and education. Community has been badly eroded in modern society and this erosion has affected the schools. They reflect the conditions in which they operate and they display the tendency to set themselves up as semi-independent and technical institutions, narrowly functional, tooling the specific components for the larger social system. These schools aren't nurtured, propelled, and directed by the life of a genuine community. What is to be done in this situation? Is educational practice capable of any significant progress in the face of the breakdown of community? Does school reform make any sense when the critical and determinative problem exists beyond school walls? Does meaningful and effective school reform require social transformation? And finally, what may schools do while awaiting the creation of community and the transformation of society?

The answer to these questions is that the schools can do important things to create community, both within the school and in the society at large. Dewey and Buber believe that schools can take steps to restore and renew community and good education. They can do so by laying the foundation for community in the relationships and activities—the life—of the school. The schools should not be written off as the simple and unwitting pawns of larger forces, although in some ways they are. They should instead be defended and promoted as a source of regeneration and hope. The blend of realism and optimism—of pessimism in the face of the conditions of the times and a fervent and inextinguishable faith in the possibilities of each new day, generation, and era—is present in both of their educational philosophies. In a dark time, Dewey and Buber see the schools as one potential source of light. What schools must do is this. They must begin to bring the elements of the life process back into the school. They must do what Buber and

Dewey consider necessary for good education: create small communities within the schools as the building blocks of a future community beyond school walls. The keys are the return to genuine relation through dialogue and the reconstruction of experience in all its fullness. This implies a different connection between community and education. Education here becomes a source of change rather than merely a reflection of existing conditions. To envision less for education, in the eyes of Dewey and Buber, is to underestimate its power to transform human life and society. In this they are more optimistic than Mead's quote suggests they should be, and more than I think realistic.

There is also an argument for community and education on pedagogical grounds. It states that there is only good education when teaching is based upon and driven by the processes of life that are the essence of Dewey's and Buber's visions. Since those processes both require and create community, there may not be a good educational process that doesn't create a necessary link between the ideas of community and education. When Dewey and Buber call for the reform of education they are calling for the creation of community in the schools and the growth, from these seeds, of community in society.

3. Education must contain the common characteristics of community in Dewey and Buber's works. Their community requires the protection and liberation of the individual, a democratic social life (defined by equal and active participation, openness and extensive communication, freedom of inquiry, and a commitment to the shared experiences and relationships that are the foundation of collective life), a common faith, and a "living tradition." Some of these characteristics, when applied to education, may not, however, apply in the same way or to the same extent as in community. Education, in its larger meaning as part of the process of human existence, will and should possess all of these qualities; education, in its narrower sense as the instruction of the young and as schooling, will not possess some of these qualities. The model of community assumes a maturity commensurate with the obligation of full and free participation in the life of the community. Education, in the narrower sense of schooling the young, is the process of leading the young into full participation, of preparing them for the life of the community. The young must be nurtured by and socialized into the community if they are to renew and reconstruct it.

Specifically, this nurturing and socializing entails the curtailment of some of the powers and decision-making responsibilities of the young. Dewey and Buber stand together in rejecting an egalitarianism of age.

The young are by nature immature and education is the process of planning and directing their development. The process must, however, be of a specific type. It must require the immersion of the young in the living experience of the group and in the life of dialogue. While the young may not define and direct this process, they must be active participants in it. They must actively interact with the environment and enter into the life of relation between humans. Their end is also specific. It is the creation of free individuals who renew, recreate, reaffirm, and take responsibility for the community in which they live. Put in terms of the rhythmic pattern of existence, education of the young is the preparation for the fullness of human existence and as such it teaches both the perching and the flight, the I-It and the I-Thou. If it leans in one direction it is toward the construction of a stable perch from which the maturing individual may fly when it is able. But the goal is always the full process of existence and those moments of consummation when human experience is stable, complete, and inspirited by the living presence of the Thou.

The teacher plays a special part in this process. He or she is the one who assumes the power of decision-making and guidance, and is the instrument through which the school and the community realize their goals. In schools it is the teacher who must embody the life of the community and direct the life of the school in accordance with the larger rhythm of community life and human existence. The teacher is the person who lives in relation, in the I-Thou, in inquiry—in the fullness of experience and community. Dewey and Buber, in their own ways, make this point.

To understand this relationship of democracy, education, and community two things must be clear. One is that schools and communities are not the same things. Schools are peculiar parts of communities and regardless of how closely communities are attached to them they remain peculiar. The peculiarity comes from the specific mission of the schools—to educate and socialize the young—and the biological and cultural facts of slow and gradual maturation of the human being into adulthood and society. The second is a congruence in Dewey's and Buber's thought on the correct understanding of democracy. For both men democracy is social before it is anything else. To conceive of democracy as a political concept or philosophy misses its main meaning. In arguing for the "democratic conception in education" Dewey says that "a democracy is more than a form of government; it is primarily a mode of associated living, of conjoint communicated experience." This is another way of saying community.[234]

4. The end of education is to produce individuals who are active participants in the living experience of their community and of the world. They are open, engaged, live a life of inquiry and relation, seek to live in the vital and continuous ebb and flow of experience and relation. It is not a body of knowledge or a set of skills that are the principal objectives of education but the quality of the life of schools and the character of the individuals who emerge from that life.

The specific content of education, its curriculum, possesses two qualities. One is the centrality and indispensability of the method of interacting or relating to the world, people, and knowledge. There is a spirit, which comes from the method, of inquiry that embodies the fullness of experience and of relation that reveals the reality of the Thou. This spirit is more important than any specific content; it is the point around which all content revolves. The second aspect is knowledge and skills. These are inescapable in human existence. Education, whether formal or informal, must impart the knowledge and skills appropriate to the particular time and place. But, and this is the critical point, knowledge and skills without the spirit, without the correct stance toward the world and an involvement in the essential processes of existence—of experience and relation—are worthless. All good education is the confluence of content and spirit. It is always contemporary in that it requires all content to be given life by the spirit; the study of content is, in fact, the study of the spirit-in-action and not rather the mere mastery of a body of knowledge. All content serves the end of the living present.

5. Teaching is the act of ushering individuals into this living present. It introduces them to the elemental processes of human existence. The teacher is the model, for Dewey, of inquiry and the life lived in the fullness of lived experience, and, for Buber, of the life of relation. The only way to usher others into this life is to embody and live it, and to participate in it with those to be taught. The teacher must make the process of experience the fundamental method of educating and enter into relation with those to be educated. Those specific methods of teaching that operate within the parameters set by Dewey's conception of experience and Buber's I-Thou relation are permissible, those that don't aren't. The heart of education in Dewey is reflective inquiry, the search for meaning, and the method of science; in Buber it is the way of the zaddik and his disciples. These are the paradigms that a good education must emulate and embody.

6. The organization of the school, both its physical plan and the

routine of its operation, must make possible the realization of the ends of education. Specifically, it must be small enough to nurture human experience and to foster communication, dialogue, and community. This does not mean that all organization be small, but that, if it is large, smallness be preserved within the larger structure. The operations of the organization, its conception and way of doing its work, must also abide by the process and in the spirit of a true community.[235]

These are the key elements of an alternative vision of education. Community is at its center. Its first principle is that good social and educational practices must be responsive to the realities of human life that underlie them. It gives "a local habitation and a name" to realities that, too often, have been considered "airy nothing" and have been omitted from conceptions of social life and educational practice.

II

This Dewey-Buber model provides us with a general model, but it does not, I think, give us a feeling for the lived experience of the individual in such a community and educational process. In this section I will discuss the implications of the model, some of which move beyond what either Dewey or Buber might have believed. My intention is to add some flesh and blood to the highly abstract model of section I.

I will begin with a quotation from Buber:

> Socratic man believes that all virtue is cognition, and that all that is needed to do what is right is to know what is right. This does not hold for Mosaic man who is informed with the profound experience that cognition is never enough, that the deepest part of him must be seized by the teachings, that for realization to take place his elemental totality must submit to the spirit as clay to the potter.[236]

What is essential for Buber is that members of the community believe, commit themselves, and allow the life of the community to give their existence its general shape and order, its meaning, and the richness of its everyday experience. More is demanded than mere knowing. All must live the knowledge and affirm a faith that binds them steadfastly to each other and the community. Buber's Mosaic man is the man of community. This community does not allow for the kind and amount of openness we prize in the modern age. It demands closure, choice that excludes, a commitment that doesn't include all possible choices in a completely open realm of possibilities.

It also involves saying specific things are right and wrong and saying them with conviction and authority. The type of community being discussed here is a moral community and moral communities define a moral universe and a moral order. In the modern world such a universe and order have been besieged by the ideas of the Enlightenment and a pervasive relativism. To step into such a community requires, for us moderns, a blind and difficult leap of faith. It demands that we make a world for ourselves out of the broken idols and discredited authorities of modern life. This world must be strong enough to provide the order, stability, ideals, and meaningfulness of life we need to be whole and free individuals and live rich fulfilling lives, ones where freedom, independence, and reason are defined by the larger community and become integral parts, in the fullest and best sense, of each individual life and the life of the community.

This approach, in contrast to that of the Enlightenment, does not rely on a view of humans as primarily or quintessentially rational. This is Buber's point: not Socrates, but Moses, not knowing, but submission to the teachings, not Athens, but Jerusalem. But is there a place for reason in the life of Mosaic man and his community? Buber is a modern enough man to prize reason and reject the idea of discarding it. One reason he, and most modern thinkers, insist on freedom for individuals is so that they may use their reason to understand and bring alive the living truths of the past, of custom or tradition, of dominant opinion. Reason is the great liberator. Reason, science, and critical intelligence are very good at this and make possible wonderful things for humans. Buber is not Martin Luther. Reason is not a whore, it is simply, in itself, not the most important thing and it is never by itself enough.[237]

Are reason, science, and critical intelligence dangerous if they become ends in themselves? Do they create monsters? Do they get so good at smashing things apart that we end up with a ruined house filled with the remains of their good work? Yes, says Buber, if they are not seized by the teachings and shaped by the spirit. When reason becomes destructive, it is not reason itself we should blame, not Socrates or the champions of the Enlightenment, but what we in modern society have allowed it to create. Our failure has been to recognize that cognition, while vitally important, is never enough. Societies make decisions and use reason and science to do their bidding. Reason may be narrow, reductionist, and analytic but it need not be. All science need not be positivistic. Reason and science are ways of thinking and conceiving the world. They readily, but not inevitably, become positivistic and conceive worldviews in their own images when the culture permits them to do so. When they do, the world they envision is often a narrow and inhuman one, all physics, mechanics, technical and rational, cold and machine-like—all parts without a whole, all body without a soul. They can be more and different from this, but often are not. This is due, perhaps, to their materialism and to their need to take things apart, to discredit and dissolve all that is solid. They work to undermine the capacity of humans for faith, commitment, belief, and the security and confidence that come with certitude.

Our modern dilemma, then, is this: if we find truth only by turning our backs on reason then we lose one of our great faculties and a hallmark of our humanness, but if we hold onto reason then we may lose our capacity for faith, belief, and commitment. But, as Buber contends, cognition need not have this effect if it is guided by the spirit of the community. This guidance is a difficult and delicate art. In most communities it is the responsibility of formal and informal education. We see an example of this guidance in the Dewey-Buber model's process of socialization. Socialization may be understood to be two related but distinct processes. One involves teaching new members of society, through a government agency, their basic social responsibilities: to be good citizens and to understand and abide by the society's basic values. The other goes further to describe a community process in which individuals become adults through participation in the full life of a small, intimate, and unified community. The first prepares the young to function in a society, the second to become the living expressions of the life of their community—to become citizens of a community. The first is the more modern, technical form of socialization, the second an older, more traditional form. It is the second that is relevant here and that is present in the Dewey-Buber model described above. One or the other is a necessary and inescapable condition of human existence. As social beings, we depend upon it, in some form, to prepare us for life in community and society; as biological organism, born helpless and incomplete, we require the group to nurture and complete our development. The differences between cultures are not between those who socialize and those who do not. They are, instead, the result of differences in the methods and contents of socialization which reflect the differences between the cultures into which they socialized their young.

In modern thought the idea and the practice of socialization is itself a problem. Respect for the individual, for individual freedom and especially freedom of thought, all demand that individuals, both the mature and immature, be free enough to autonomously select or create the ideas and beliefs constitutive of their distinctive selves and lives. Socialization, particularly the more traditional forms of it, infringe on this freedom. If socialization is in fact inescapable and necessary, as I contend it is, and if freedom too is necessary, as we insist it is today, then the critical issue is the place and treatment of the individual and freedom in the process of socialization. Since constraints on the individual are inevitable in any form of socialization, any accommodation must begin from the understanding that the inevitable constraints of socialization do not make it, by its nature and ineluctably, anti-individual and oppressive. Communities will socialize in accordance with their basic beliefs and values, with some being more, some less, restrictive of the individual and of freedom. It does not follow

> that all schooling is repressive, **ipso facto**, any more than it means all other forms of community expression are repressive simply by virtue of their being expressive. It is difficult to conceive a form of expression that would not require some sort of constraint for its coherence and transmission: All of us blurting simultaneously anything at all may well be unconstrained, but it is not clearly an example of expression that has any significance in a discussion of education."[238]

The determinative factor is the community that expresses itself through the school and raises its young to live in its community. When schools fail, or engage in activities some deem wrong or harmful, it is the community that is both the source of the problem and of the solution.[239]

What of our socialization? Of our community? In chapter three I used Colin Turnbull to suggest some answers that I will develop more fully here. Turnbull begins from the conviction that two things are wrong with our current modern American and British process: we do a sloppy and incomplete job of it and we produce the wrong kind of people when we are finished muddling through. His sharpest criticism is directed to the latter failure: of the people and the world we produce with our misconceived notions of individualism and individual freedom, which inculcate a habit of independence, a preoccupation with individual achievement and success, a belief in the paramount position of individual rights without the tempering habits and beliefs in the duties and responsibilities of social obligations and commitments beyond the narrow range of the self and its interests. We do a poor job of teaching our young to care for others, to have a sense of collective responsibility or concern, and to respect the nature, place, and value of community in individual and social life. Our socialization is a socialization out of social commitments, an attenuating of the bonds that hold individuals together, and a weakening of the forces that make group living a form of community. In contrast, primitive societies envision life as a "constant process of socialization and binding the various stages of life together, just as it binds individuals into communities and communities into societies...."[240]

We socialize people to be free. But no matter how successful we are in this socialization they are still in a cage, one made of the bars that define the individual and freedom as the first and sacred principles of a good life. These bars are real, but invisible, for how is it possible for freedom and independence to restrain us. But they can. Are we freer than the Mbuti? Is our life better? Turnbull thinks we are not and it is not. In our willingness to condone an individualism that defines itself by weakening social bonds, we undermine the strength and unity of both the individual and the group. We socializing the young to be free, independent, indifferent to all but immediate personal relationships, to see social obligations as an infringement on or impediment to the exercise of personal freedom, to relate to each other through a code of laws and system of rights, to envision the world as an incessant struggle of each against every other for the fruits of the natural liberty of the individual, and to define life in the terms set by political, social, and economic life. In doing so we offer them one kind of freedom and one kind of cage. Turnbull is convinced the Mbuti are just as free, in their own way, and their cage is a finer one in which to live.

What good is our freedom? What do we use it for? What kind of individuals and societies does it create? A partial answer to these questions has been given. We use it to make new lives, lives of our own individual designs, stamped with our distinctive desires, abilities, and beliefs. These new lives are better lives for they vouchsafe each person a better chance to be happy, to maximize pleasure, to achieve control and security, and to attain personal goals or ends. In these new lives we hope to achieve human fulfillment, to realize the distinctiveness of each individual in a life of his or her own making, and to permit the emergence or efflorescence of the authentic or natural self of each individual.

Few would deny this freedom to be a boon of our age and one of the prized legacies of the Enlightenment. Our consciousness is indelibly marked by it. The difficulties we have with agreeing on a definition of good and bad, and the pervasive relativism of our thinking, do not disturb our settled and tenacious belief in freedom. Both the popular and the academic mind acknowledge its primacy in both our personal and social lives. While there is debate about its precise meaning and definition, there is little argument over its importance and place in any society that considers itself enlightened and dedicated to the betterment of its people. Betterment, in fact, has become inseparable from the demand for freedom and the progressive liberation of individuals and groups from the hegemony of others. No call to action is more powerful than that to liberation: of races or peoples or women or young and old or workers or poor people or gays or any individual who see things differently and wishes to be left alone to think, believe, and live as he or she wishes.

But Turnbull thinks there is a more complete and better way. Like almost everyone else, he favors freedom. But not freedom as we in the West have defined it. Freedom, like cognition for Buber, must be shaped by the teachings and by the spirit of the society; freedom, like reason, must be an instrument of some greater purpose or means to an end beyond itself. The apotheosis of freedom and its definition as independence and liberation from oppression has made it easier to break the bonds that hold people together than to create new ones. It has cut us loose, which is generally seen as good, armed us with modern tools of thought that allow us to take apart our world, from the deconstruction of our cultures, social systems and ideologies to the hermeneutics of our modern consciousness, and declared this all progress. When freedom severs individuals from the group or society it harms them and misunderstands the social nature of all human existence; freedom that pits the individual against the society is just another social belief in a different kind of social system that socializes its members in a different way. The outcome of such a society, though, is bad for the individual who is too often severed from necessary sources of meaningfulness and purpose and for the society which too often becomes selfish, competitive, and mean-spirited. These were the fruits of Turnbull's own modern education in Britain—isolation, coldness, self-absorption, and spiritlessness—and they are, in his view, of most modern educations.

Our humanness drives us to be free but it also urges us to union with or submergence into a larger whole. We are impelled to assert a place for ourselves in a world and universe that recognize our importance and gives greater meaning to our lives than those we wring from our daily autonomous existence. We long to rest in an encompassing source of power and meaning that lifts us beyond the petty cares of our self seeking. We satisfy this need by losing ourselves in groups, organizations, communities, or nations; or in devotion to a belief, philosophy, cause, or religion; or in meditation of mystical union or to poetry or art or, for some, science. Whatever the route, we are propelled down it by an apprehension of what might become of us without it. Insecurity is inherent in our condition as creatures who do not fit neatly or completely into a world seemingly better suited for turtles or ants. The more we remove ourselves from the intimate relations that bind us into a world the more we feel the chill of our natural estrangement and homelessness in the world, our being-at-odds with the world, being out of joint, an oddity in a natural order that is both part of us and alien to us at the same time.

Turnbull argues for a conception of freedom and independence that acknowledge this fact of life. It is based upon a social ethic of sharing, caring and responsibility in which the intimate bonds of community nurture and direct our freedoms, and the integration and unity and richness of individual lives are built upon these foundation stones. To pursue these things is to pursue a reordering of our society. To effectuate the necessary transformation we will have to change our basic values, our institutions, the process and content of education and socialization, and our vision of who we are as human beings and what our society can and should be. Turnbull is convinced that without such a transformation we will remain broken and lost, mangy birds in an iron cage.

Turnbull's alternative offers us an insight into a different way of looking at the world and of understanding the needs of its human inhabitants. It is this insight and understanding that is the integrating force holding all his particular ideas and beliefs together. It both expresses his vision of things and describes the essential attributes of any vision which hopes to successfully integrate or unify human existence. In the Bushman's life, for all its primitiveness, we see these attributes. He seeks something beyond the concerns of ordinary routine or everyday life that, when affirmed and followed, transforms that life and fills it with the higher purposes of life: the pursuit of beauty and truth, an awareness of the transcendent and spiritual nature of human existence, a devotion to an ideal, and a dedication to a vision more encompassing than one defined by getting and spending, cultivating our own individual gardens, or enlarging our modern sort of freedom.

What is essential to human life and culture, that which makes possible the rich and whole life of the Bushman, is a community of belief, a sense of the sacred in the world, mutual interdependence, social responsibility, and obligation, an appreciation of the whole range of human needs and powers, a conception of self and society that makes these possible, and a socialization of the young into a community built upon all of these. In celebrating the cultures that possess these attributes, he also criticizes those that do not. He is particularly critical of modern societies because they lack these things. A world built on a "mechanics of fragmentation and isolation" in which individuals achieve success either outside of social life or in opposition to it leaves too much of the human out. We have lost the idea that humans become fully human as social selves who achieve individuality through society, who live in a world that is both secular and spiritual, who can have free and full lives through the obligations and responsibilities defined by the community and affirmed by individuals who find the greatest fulfillments in life in the richness and the miracle of human life in community.

With these things in mind, the modern dilemma of the individual and the community can be conceived as follows. With liberation from the infantile state of the tribe and the collective superstitions of traditional societies, humans have taken to the sea, and striven tirelessly to explore and expand the horizons of human existence. Estrangement and a sense of loss have come in the wake of this liberation. Humans need to belong somewhere and to something, something higher and grander than themselves and their secular existence. The modern world has made the satisfaction of these needs both more difficult and less acceptable. The open sea hasn't supplied all that humans must have; to sail out, humans must have a home and harbor from which to depart and to which to return. Some soil must nourish their seaward strivings, some fixed firmament balance the slip and slide of the deck, and roots must hold them to the certainty and contentment of an ordered universe of ideas and values embodied in a specific time, place, and community. They must be seized by these ideas and values, and the virtues of reason and freedom must be shaped by the spirit of the time, place, and community. This seizing and shaping are the responsibility of education. When a society is successful, as the Mbuti and Hindu were, socialization integrates the individual and community, making both whole and healthy. When it fails, the individual is cut from the vital lifeline that sustains a full and rich life. In modern secular societies, it is commonplace for this education and socialization to either not occur or to be so thin and technical that the young are set adrift trained only in the modern rosary of individual, freedom, independence, and "doing your own thing." We have failed to create a rich and fulfilling experience for our young capable of instilling in them a determination to pursue the highest and noblest ideals of the culture and community.

III

Dewey, Buber, and Turnbull give us ways to conceive an alternative form of education and community. In this section I will describe three more, all of which attempt, in different ways and to varying degrees, to envision an education in the light of the issues raised in this and the preceding chapter. The three are of the British educational philosopher John White and the American educational philosophers John Bremer and C. A. Bowers.

In his book **Education and the Good Life,** White attempts to define the characteristics of an education acceptable to our modern liberal democratic society.[241] He begins by asserting that the end of education is well-being. Well-being in modern society requires autonomy. White's conception of autonomy is more than being left alone. The proper end of liberal and democratic society is an individual who can define his or her own conception of the good life and act upon the definition. This is achieved when the individual reflects on the nature of his society, develops a critical awareness of the forces within it that work to either limit or liberate the individual, and acquires the ability to make decisions based upon these reflections. White rejects the conception of education as transmission of tradition, custom, and the received opinion of the groups. The cardinal virtue to be cultivated in education is the critical reflection of the individual. In order to be autonomous, which means being critically reflective, the individual needs freedom to choose, knowledge of choices, an understanding of one's desires and their hierarchical relationship to one another, a definition of what is valuable, and the dispositions and virtues—the character—that allow one to be autonomous. The last requires some form of moral education since character is necessary for the exercise of autonomy.

White insists that his position does not lead to a radical or asocial individualism. Humans are social by nature and are therefore able to agree, on the basis of either reason or intuition, that basic moral principles should be taught and that the core principle would be altruism. He is advocating a specific type of autonomy, one tempered and guided by altruism—an altruistic autonomy. The specific virtues he associates with altruism are courage, temperance, practical wisdom, and self-control. With these, the individual has the means—the strengths and abilities—necessary to be altruistic.

White's path to the good life is not an easy one. He is aware of the conflicts of desires and the power of an untutored and unrestrained egoism. The task of education is to develop the virtues and, more importantly, the dispositions of character that rank desires and determine what is more and less valuable. In all of this, White's view is expansive: he wants a reflective and autonomous life devoted to morality. His autonomous and free individual is possible only if the foundation of character is solid.

Well-being, then, requires more than an autarchic individualism where the individual is free to do as he or she wishes (within the minimal limits set by legal obligations), to be rational or not, to be moral or not, to be self-consumed and indifferent to others or not. White wants, instead, a well-being that demands much more of both the individual and the society. He acknowledges that well-being may be possible without altruism but it is also possible with it. So he chooses it as best suited to our society, to our individual and social needs, to the health of both individuals and society, to our basic ethical and political principles, and to our traditions. It is the better, the more rational, choice for us.

This altruistic autonomy will not develop by itself. Left to their inclinations and experience, individuals may not become either altruistic or autonomous. To insure that they are both, White proposes an education in altruism. Through it, altruism would be instilled, which means it must be imposed. Instilling and imposing is tricky when the overarching aiming is autonomy. Such a balancing act requires that education not be a process of indoctrination of systems of ideas or beliefs, as are most traditional programs of moral education that include altruism. Rather, it will be one that shapes the basic dispositions and virtues in such a way that the individual becomes free, autonomous, and altruistic. The goal is a type of upbringing or education that achieves these aims without engendering a sense or consciousness of individual isolation and separateness. White hopes to accomplish this through the cultivation of the dispositions he considers necessary to such an upbringing: the awareness and appreciation of personal pleasures, interests, and projects, the enjoyment of others, the willingness to help those close to you and to work toward shared goals, the pursuit of the general good and well-being, and the personal qualities of truthfulness, promise keeping, justice, and non-harm to others. The creation of these dispositions should be the primary aim of education. In his education, knowledge is secondary and must be tailored to suite the larger ends of education: altruistic autonomy and the creation of proper dispositions.

White claims this education will not infringe on or undermine his larger aims of well-being and autonomy. The dispositions and virtues he makes central to education are to be understood narrowly, as instruments necessary to achieve his ends and the ends of a democratic society. Education will produce an individual who is a "radical chooser" living a life of abundant choice, including the choice of life ends. There is no definition of the good life imposed in this education. Democracy demands that the group not define and impose such a single definition. Only individuals can plan their lives and determine the good life. But he resists the idea, common in liberal democratic thought, that these individuals must therefore embody a radical, autarchic conception of individualism based upon a sharper separation of the individual and society, a consuming self-interest, and an expansive conception of freedom and individual self-creation and autonomy. In tempering each of these, White claims he is removing the excesses and misconceptions of one form of liberal individualism, the negative and unhealthy form, and replacing it with one that protects the autonomous person and creates the conditions for that person to achieve the greater good and the true end of both education and life: well-being.

White's approach to education is an attempt to restrain the natural tendencies and raw energies of modern culture. While accepting its basic premises, he is concerned about the possible consequences for individuals and society. But the logic of his philosophic position does not allow him to qualify or temper very much the emphasis on individual autonomy and freedom. Altruistic autonomy is an attempt to do so, but a modest one, and one he is unable to adequately justify because he does not move outside the bounds of traditional modern liberal thought. He is, in fact, more vulnerable from his own philosophical tradition than from others. Operating within liberal thought, the defense of the imposition of altruism is a difficult one to make. He does so by infringing on autonomy and imposing on the individual an attitude towards and a conception of what the individual must be to achieve a good life and well-being. He demonstrates an awareness of the shortcomings of liberal thought. But his corrections to these shortcomings, however thoughtful and interesting, fail. It is his awareness of the problem and his effort, however successful or unsuccessful, to address it that is of most interest here.

John Bremer in **A Matrix for Modern Education** is more successful because he is willing to go further.[242] The difference is in his fuller understanding of the problem, an understanding closer to the one developed in this book. He begins his book by praising those societies "which have kept life and learning in a continuing and interdependent relationship—which have no specialized education out of all contact with the way of life of the group, in which education is thought to be everybody's business and not just the concern of professionals."[243]

These societies have what White argues we can not have: a common conception of the good life. Bremer agrees that we are without such a unifying conception. We have an abundance of specific goods but not a singular, unifying vision, knowledge, and moral order. As a result our society fragments and disintegrates. Our modern conception of the good, and it is White's, is each individual doing as he or she pleases and the common good is all doing as they please together. Bremer's view contains, at the least, a paradox and, at worst, no common good at all. He envisions, instead, a community in which the individual transcends individual wants and goods to find a common good. Through this transcendence the individual and, through the individual, the society achieve true well-being.

Education is the way we achieve this end: it creates community, a common good, and a conception of the good life. Great teachers are those who invest knowledge with moral value. The fundamental problems of education are moral, not technical: education and morality are inseparable (a point I think White tacitly affirms). Societies renew themselves and raise their young through education and the morality it embodies, not through the transmission of the content (knowledge and skills) of the curriculum or the creation of intelligence. There is, in fact, no education without morality. Intelligence, like knowledge, is social and has a social function. It is always connected, in education and in society, to morality. There is not, as the pragmatists knew, a merely instrumental intelligence or rationality because the means and ends are inseparable. Intelligence and education are both active agents, not tools or observers, in the world. As an integral part of social life they define and serve ends and are therefore social and moral.[244]

The individual is not to be submerged or lost in Bremer's education and community. He wishes to avoid both extremes of child-centered and society-centered education. Good education is found between them, in the space where they interact to preserve the culture and enrich the student without overwhelming either. The middle space may be maintained by creating community and a framework of ideals and beliefs that define and liberate the individual. Education will always reproduce its society. A good education does so by creating in all its members altruism, friendliness, and commitment to community while, at the same time, it is liberating the energies and resources of individuals and the group. Learning itself is an interaction or dialogue of the individual and the community. It occurs where desires and duties, the choice of one action and another, one way of life or another, resolve themselves within a community that preserves and recreates itself. We live fully only in the tension created by this dialogue. The curriculum of education is always the society itself and teaching always an illumination of the interplay between the individual and society that reveals the permanent amid change, the free individual within community.

C. A. Bowers in **Elements of a Post-Liberal Theory of Education** comes to many of Bremer's conclusions.[245] He arrives at them after a review of contemporary liberal educational thought. He begins by challenging the dominance of liberal thought, a dominance that has "delegitimated" other forms of thought and experience in modern culture. He next challenges the assumptions of this dominant liberal thought that progress and change are inevitable and good, that the power and authority of the individual must be expanded, that critical rational thought must replace traditional forms of authority, and that the rational individual stands above the partisan interests of group or culture as the possessor of truth and authority. Taken together, these assumptions mark a deep divide between modern and traditional thought. Bowers thinks the divide is too deep, leaves us ignorant of much that is true and vital in human life, and has unjustifiably excluded all earlier ways of thinking from contemporary discourse.

What in particular has been excluded? We have already discussed most of what Bowers is concerned about. His central and unifying concept is embeddedness. Individuals do not exist outside of a linguistic and cultural context. Each is embedded within these contexts, defined and identified by them, and dependent upon them. This is a fact of human life and is therefore necessary to human beings. It is also, when not oppressive, good for us. To insist on this point is to call for a reconsideration of our common understanding of individualism. Bowers sees the task of a post-liberal philosophy as "de-centering individualism." To de-center we must acknowledge the weakness of the liberal "**telos** of progressive change and rationality as the basis of emancipation," of the idea of the "possibility of the autonomous, self-directed individual," and of the shared "assumption that education should empower people to transcend their embeddedness in traditional patterns of thought and behavior."[246] Bowers' challenge to liberalism is to "renew a sense of social and moral relationships essential to the interdependent community."[247] A realization of our embeddedness is the way forward and the destination is a certain kind of place—a community. He argues that the liberal separation of individual and society is an inaccurate portrayal of human experience, which is never wholly either one or the other, as it is for liberalism, but both at once.

Such a position brings with it all the tension that exists in asserting both as necessary and valuable. This tension is particularly intense when we acknowledge, and accept as necessary and good as Bowers does, that the true definition of an individual is only within the context of a culture that extends before and after the individual in the form of stable but evolving traditions and communities.

Bowers develops and supports these contentions at greater length. His pressing concerns and principal solutions are much the same as those of White, Bremer, and this book. But he moves beyond either White or Bremer in calling into question the central tenets of liberalism and in the definition and defense of an alternative. That alternative is an educational system and process rooted in community. This education would reflect Bowers' social ecology of the classroom, school, and community; it would be based upon an ideal of civic humanism and an "image of the individual as a social-cultural being" rather than a lone, autonomous individual. Language membership, a communal product, is the essence of education. We begin as members of a community and become fully human through its higher and finer features, especially "its moral foundations, its vision of good and evil, and its ability to adjust the daily routines, institutions, and structural characteristics to the requirements of its moral aspirations."[248]

IV

All three of these conceptions move toward a full and satisfying theory of education for modern society. They stop short, however, of the vision of education and community required here. We need to go a little further than they do. In this final section I will use Ernest Becker to carry their ideas a step further.

The critical issue for a full view of education, as we have seen, is its conception of a fully human and good life. But it is an issue that can not be addressed without considering the contents of our culture, for it is in culture that we find the ends and the means, the faith and belief, that make possible a full and good life. Is such a life possible in modern society? When Becker asks if modern societies have created a rich and fulfilling life, with cultural forms and ways of life filled with profound and beautiful meanings, the answer is an emphatic no. Modern rituals are shallow, without deep connections and rich associations. In comparison to primitive societies, one of Becker's models for the good community, our culture fails to address our most fundamental needs. Enamored with technical solutions, we miss the central and crippling dilemma of our time: we have substituted mechanical, technical, and scientific approaches and solutions for the mythical-ritual-communal approaches and solutions humans need if they are to be fully human.

What must be done to address this problem? Becker suggests, moving beyond Bowers' solution of civic humanism and ecological consciousness, that we must do something along the following general lines. Some of these suggestions may seem foreign or anachronistic, out of place in a age of science, advanced technology, and a more hard-headed and secular view of things. But the fact that they rub against our modern grain is precisely the problem; like the Ik, we find humorous or absurd those very elements of humanness we have forgotten in the press of everyday modern life. Briefly, we must do these things:

First, we must give each individual a sense of the part he or she plays in the cosmos. Our existence has become so insignificant in the order of things postulated by science that we cannot give ourselves what we most need: a sense of meaningful participation in a universe that has a place and role for human beings. With this, we will instill a sense of the serious and self-transcending nature of human life.

Second, we need to define and transmit an ideal to which the young may commit themselves, take responsibility for, and believe in. The belief and ideal are goods in themselves, but they are also instrumental in satisfying a deeper urge in humans. William James argued that "mankind's common instinct for reality...has always held the world to be essentially a theatre for heroism" and Becker agreed: "our central calling, our main task on this planet, is the heroic."[249] If a culture fails to define a heroic sense of life and to mark off some realm for heroic endeavors, then it fails, in a critical way, its members.

Third, we need to reconceive the relationship between the individual, the community, and freedom so that their "ideal and fullest form is the fullest development of each individual in the community of other individuals. It will be a community where unlimited knowledge is the goal, and where the mystery of life is the guiding principle of communal action." It will teach the individual "the need to know the self-constraint and social constraint to which he is subject as a member of the human family." With "the mystery of life the guiding principle of communal life, man will resanctify himself and his fellows... which is the only hope for rediscovering human dignity." Through the self-transcendence of mystery and community, we will liberate the energies of all humans to make communal life "a celebration of the broadest and deepest meanings of the universe."[250]

Fourth, human existence, even without assistance from modern culture, generates flux, instability, and uncertainty. Humans have a penchant for associating these with freedom, adventure, and excitement, thereby romanticizing their virtues and ignoring their costs. The costs are in fact great. When change becomes endemic in a culture and when certainty and stability become defined as either impossible to attain or undesirable, then the culture has become inhospitable to its people. Humans require and will insist upon certainty and stability in some form at all levels of their lives, from the everyday routines to the grander systems of thought and belief.

Possessing these elements of a whole and healthy society, Becker contends we can overcome the shortcomings of our age; without them and the qualities they bring to life, we will stay "modern." Staying modern, at the least, means sensing some unmet need and feeling dissatisfied with our lives. If this was all it cost us, some dissatisfaction and an unmet need, its many benefits would seem a bargain. But it isn't. What it does to us, slowly and inexorably, is make us, like the Ik, less than human. It starves our spirit instead of our body, and slowly dismembers us until we become, in Emerson's words, "so many walking monsters—a good finger, a neck, a stomach, an elbow, but never a man."[251]

When in the course of daily discussions of social and political life so many call for policies focused on jobs, or international competition, or scientific and technological advancement, what are we to make of a view insisting, as Becker's does, that our real problem is that we have lost the willingness or the vision "to fight on the edge of the cosmos" in the struggle to bring into existence a new moral order. And what, too, can we do with a vision which proclaims freedom, self-reliance, self-knowledge, and critical inquiry as the pillars of a good community when it is clear that each of these, when put into practice in the modern world, will make a habit of menacing and undermining the integrity and viability of the indispensable underpinning of the community—its transcendent myth or religion. And what, finally, of the place of these very values—freedom, individualism, inquiry, and knowledge—in a world where humans readily cast them aside to meet the more elemental need for a secure and meaningful home vouchsafed them by community. The answer is that Becker's view of our nature and condition offers us, along with his vision, all the intractable problems the modern world places before us. His conception offers few easy solutions. There are none. The value of his analysis is its attempt to bring us to an awareness of the ancient urges and needs of the human heart. It is up to us to find a way to refashion our world so that whole humans, rather than monsters, may inhabit it.

Becker had cause to hope that we could do so. We have liberated humans to create a new world. Liberation will bring more and better understandings of humans and the world. Upon these we can build a new synthesis of knowledge, a new science of man which is a moral science. This new science must offer modern culture a grounding in some transcendent source of and justification for life. Only with this grounding can humans affirm and live by their meanings; only in the community based upon this grounding can humans be free and self-reliant, and only by giving up the headstrong and destructive individualism of the modern ages can humans find a firm footing for their ideals and highest strivings.

Can we find models of what we need to guide us? Becker found them in primitive societies and the Middle Ages. While each exemplifies attributes of the culture and community we need today, they are in too many ways different from our basic conceptions of the world to act as guides for us. A secular, materialistic culture, prizing freedom, individualism, open inquiry, exploration, dynamism and change is too different from these earlier cultures to make them credible models.[252] Is there a model that better captures what is needed. I think the Greeks aspired to an ideal close to the one Becker passionately sought to resurrect for our age. They called it paideia. For them, and for us, it is through culture that humans become fully human; for them, and for us, culture is the most complete and perfect embodiment of the substance, the curriculum perhaps, of this education. All those issues defined here as important but missing in modern life were central to paideia: the unity of culture, a consciously pursued ideal, the central place of the spiritual life in the development of individuals and groups, and the cultivation of the character and the soul of individuals by the ideals and the spiritual life of the culture. For the Greeks, "the ultimate justification for the existence of both the individual and the community...was the creation of a higher type of man." The creation was the task of education, which at its heart was "deliberately moulding human character in accordance with an ideal." This educational process is inseparable from the idea of culture:

> It starts from the ideal, not from the individual. Above man as a member of the horde, and man as a supposedly independent personality, stands man as an ideal; and that ideal was the pattern towards which Greek educators as well as Greek poets, artists, and philosophers always looked.[253]

Where does their model come from? The subjective self is too narrow and too modern a conception to be the source for it. They look, instead, to the "universal law of human nature" as it takes a specific form in their culture. The goal of culture is to shape the individual "into his true form, the real and genuine human nature."[254] That nature demands we pursue the highest ideals and insists that virtue and the heroic life guide and ennoble each individual. Since humans can never escape the influences of time and place, our human nature manifests itself through the cultures we create and that, in turn, create us. The Greek conception is therefore not a static one but dynamic: it takes different shapes and changes across cultures and eras. But its essence remains always the same. It is thoroughly anthropocentric and humanistic, its consummation coming when the great man—noble, virtuous, and heroic—embodies the ideals of the culture and affirms them through his life and words.

This Greek view may not be as modern as it at first seemed. Neither the dynamic nature of its culture nor its humanism, both of which are congenial to our modern temper, should be seen as ancient reflections of the dynamism or the humanism of our time. They are different. Their dynamism operates within a unified conception of humans and is constrained by the ideals of the culture; their humanism insists upon the higher man and his self transcendence and affirmation through the culture and its ideals. All that religion made possible in primitive culture and the Middle Ages is here accomplished by classical humanism.[255]

Greek paideia merged the humanistic ideal of the greatness of the individual human being with the older, primitive practice of embedding the individual within the life of the community. For the Greeks the ideals that inspired the culture arose from the collective life of the group but took form in the unique individual educated to achieve greatness. Their ideal was thoroughly aristocratic. Becker's was also. He called for a new aristocracy, a "mass-elitism." The humans he, and the Greeks, wished to mould were to be noble, virtuous, and great. They were to be individuals who fully realized all their powers and achieved excellence in their characters and lives.

Perhaps paideia is not possible for us. We are too uncertain of our ideals and common culture. Education has become instrumental in the narrowest and meanest ways. But we have lost something even more essential for a modern paideia: we have no agreed upon understanding of human nature, no ideals of culture that embody this understanding, and no sense of education as the creation of human beings in the image of these ideals. We further compound our dilemma with our modern conceptions of individualism, freedom, and autonomy. Paideia becomes, therefore, not just something we lamentably no longer have but something we wonder whether we want at all.

I am convinced we must have it or something close to it if we are to realize the possibilities, and escape the terrors, of our human estate. I am also convinced that education, to warrant the name of education, must become fully engaged in the struggle over the meaning and possibility of a modern paideia. The ambiguities and paradoxes of human existence may not be washed away in this paideia. It will be a paideia agonistes: a struggle with our times and our selves.

Perhaps such a synthesis is impossible for us. However long the odds, it must be ventured for it arises out of a desperate longing and need of the human heart. It may seem too hard and dark and uncertain a voyage, too hopeless and grim a modern predicament. Is there any overcoming or resolving it? Can we find a way out of the darkness and pessimism of our modern condition? Can the barbarians be driven from the gates? Is there some new light to lead us out of the wilderness of modern life? There is cause for hope. The course of modern thought and life has carried us through the earlier bright light into dusk and now darkness. Along the way it brought us a fuller understanding of ourselves and our human and modern conditions. On our modern way we have become turned around, as was Ishmael in **Moby Dick,** and can see only "a jet gloom, now and then made ghastly by flashes of redness" and feel that we are not bound for some haven ahead but "rushing from all havens astern." In the beginning "a stark, bewildering feeling, as of death," came over us as our early and sunlit life slipped into night. But also like Ishmael we have reoriented ourselves, turned back from darkness to the light, but one that is not and never can be the same. It is a light that knows the dismal heart of things and the dark places of the earth. Melville's conclusions are ours: "The truest of all men was the Man of Sorrows, and the truest of all books is Solomon's, and Ecclesiastes is the fine hammered steel of woe." In this he discovers a resignation which is a way forward and "a wisdom that is woe," but not a resignation that is despair or madness. He, with us, is like a Catskill eagle "that can alike dive down into the blackest gorge, and soar out of it again and become invisible in the sunny spaces. And even if he for ever flies within the gorge, that gorge is in the mountains; so that even in his lowest swoop the mountain eagle is still higher than other birds upon the plains, even though they soar."[256]

Notes

Introduction

[1] This applies most directly to formal education. But it also holds true for most forms of informal education. Informal education, for example that which takes place in the family, church, or social group, is based upon the interconnection of these organizations and the society in which they exist. The organizations themselves exist within, are a part of, and have been shaped by the society and culture in which they exist. This connection of education to a larger, superordinate social group or institution is inescapable in both formal and informal education.

[2] Benjamin Barber in Harper's, November 1993, pp. 39-46. The essay comes from his book Aristocracy for Everyone (New York: Oxford University Press, 1992). The theme is common in modern educational thought and criticism. The anti-modern tradition of thought is particularly enthusiastic in its development of this idea. John Ruskin, Thomas Carlyle, and Matthew Arnold each found our problem in the larger culture rather than specific institutions, ideas, or individuals. More recently, Jackson Lears, No Place of Grace (New York: Pantheon Books, 1981) and Christopher Lasch, True and Only Heaven (New York: Norton, 1991), make the case against twentieth century culture. It has always been a central theme of the left that we suffer from the inhumane society created by capitalism.

[3] Margaret Mead in From the South Pacific (New York: Morrow, 1939), p. 277.

[4] Crime is an example. As is often the case, schools are called upon to solve the problems. More money for education and less for prisons-- "spend it now or spend it later"-- is the slogan. More education, fewer drop-outs, higher skill levels, special programs for at-risk children are the best approach to the national problem. But schools can't address the immediate problems on the streets. So we turn to another quick and relatively easy solution: more police. The problem with this remedy is that there is little evidence that more police will reduce crime (above a baseline per capita number that most urban areas with crime problems have already reached). There is here an old and deep difference in our approach to social problems, where one side sees the system as essentially sound but in need of some adjustment or fine tuning and the other finds basic problems in the system itself and calls for reform of

the organization and operation of the primary institutions of the society.

Chapter One

[5] Ernest Becker, The Denial of Death (New York: The Free Press, 1973), p. 200.

[6] Robert Pirsig, Zen and the Art of Motorcycle Maintenance (New York: Bantam Books, 1984), p. 8.

[7] From the poem "The Rose" by W. B. Yeats.

[8] Muir is like Kierkegaard in this. Belief is for Muir what faith was to Kierkegaard. They are the highest passions and the most pressing needs of humans. But in themselves they are never enough,. They can be, as many have said, idle or useless. They have become idle and useless for us, wasted in the pursuit of the most trivial or destructive modern lives. They are vibrant and important when tied, as they are for Muir and Kierkegaard, to a binding belief and faith, a vision of the nature and possibilites of existence, and a command to live in accordance with their demands. For both men, their work gained its power and authority from their belief and faith born out of their intense personal struggles. Belief and faith arise from a first principle of human existence expressed in reformulations of the Cartesian axiom: "I believe, therefore I am" and "I have faith, therefore I am."

[9] Carl Becker, The Heavenly City of the Eighteenth-Century Philosophers (New Haven: Yale University Press, 1932), pp. 15-6.

[10] Michael Harrington, Politics at God's Funeral (New York: Penguin Books, 1983), p. 202.

[11] Allan Bloom, The Closing of the American Mind (New York: Simon & Schuster, 1987).

[12] Ernest Becker, Beyond Alienation (New York: George Braziller, 1967), pp.46 and 210. He goes on in the same passage (p. 46) to say this: "This is another part of the vision that modern man has lost: having abandoned ideals, he also abandons their active realization. Then, when he sees that ideals do not come about, he scoffs at them as idol dreams! Impeccable logic." The quote connects the ideas of vision and ideals. It also suggests an issue that will come up later. There are deepseated ambivalences, contrary impulses, or contradictory tendencies in the modern mind. In this instance, the tension is between our desire for ideals, often as strong and important as in the past, and our modern realistic and hard-headed scoffing at the naive views of the past.

[13] From T. S. Eliot's "The Waste Land."

[14] William James, "The Will to Believe" in The Will to Believe and Other Essays in Popular Philosophy (New York: Longmans, Green, and Co., 1908), p. 3. There are other ways to use the word believe. For example, you may say that you believe something to be true--that the sun will rise tomorrow morning or that Caesar was assassinated. But these are different in that they make statements about what you can know and, depending upon your allegiances in the wars of epistemology, that may be considered facts rather than beliefs. It is different when we ask about God, the good life, or love. These have a more difficult time achieving the status of fact. Mired forever in the world of mere belief, they are nevertheless of vital importance to humans attempting to understand themselves and live their lives. You may be thoroughly uninterested in the sun or Caesar but it is unlikely you escape some interest in God or the good life or love. While these often earn little standing or use in epistemology, they are of the highest standing in the matters of our hearts and lives.

[15] Edwin Muir, An Autobiography (London: Hogarth Press, 1954). Muir's conversion to Catholicism and a mystical faith was his resting place in the struggle to believe and to be. It is not the only place. You may end up a rationalist or a scientist or a hedonist or a stoic or an atheist (these are not mutually exclusive) so long as what comes to be believed coils around the soul and defines who we are and what we believe. It must be strong and vital enough to permit us "to be."

[16] Gide in his forward to Antoine de Saint-Exupery's Night Flight (New York: New American Library, 1945), pp. vii-ix.

[17] W. B. Yeats, "A Prayer for Old Age."

[18] Quoted in the review of Wartime Writings in Time, August 4, 1986 by Paul Gray.

[19] Ruskin, "Traffic" in Selections and Essays (New York: Charles Scribner's Son,1918), p. 296.

[20] Their is no vacuum in human life. Something always rushes in to fill the silent empty human space. The law of our needs and nature is as strong and regular as the physical laws of nature. It will not be ignored or spurned. Confronted by the vast lacunae of our modern world, we have gone on living and the empty spaces of modern life filled up. We have done so with a certain pride in the new world we have created, in our virtuosity and extraordinary progress, in our wealth and health, and in our possessions and longevity. We have even come, in those

unrestrained, ebullient moments, to think ourselves blessed and happy
in the best of times and worlds. Like Camus' Sisyphus, or more likely
Voltaire's Pangloss, we imagine ourselves happy. Yet not really, and
not without doubt and the nagging suspicion that the sort of life that has
rushed into the void is inadequate. But most of us, most of the time,
hold firmly to what we have and push our reservations aside. We are
like a brain-injured patient who has lost his ability to abstract himself
from his immediate concrete situations and is tied to these situations by
a compulsion to hold onto them, to compulsively order and limit his
realm of action and range of possibilities. Such a person, when asked to
write his name "typically write in the very corner, any venture out from
the specific boundaries of the edges of the paper representing too great
a threat. It was as though they were threatened with dissolution of the
self unless they remained related at every moment to the immediate
situation, as though they could 'be a self' only as the self was bound to
the concrete items in space." (Existence, ed. by R. May, E. Angel, and
H. Ellenberger [New York: Basic Books, 1958], p. 72-3) We, too, are
afraid and compulsive. We create safe havens by limiting our world,
ignoring its shortcomings through a self-imposed blindness, unwilling
and eventually even unable to abstract and transcend it, thereby
condemning ourselves to be less than fully human. And in those
moments when we awake from our modern sleep, and see and think
clearly about our condition, we find consolation in the writers and
philosophers, especially the existentialists, who whisper in our ears, as
slaves whispered in the ears of conquering heroes and emperors in the
ancient world, that it is all fleeting and vain and, in the larger scheme of
existence, worthless. No matter how grand our illusions, the final text is
always the reality therapy of Ecclesiastes.

   [21] For those who come through with their belief and faith intact,
modern pilgrims, they must avoid the peril, commonplace in many
areas of modern life, of the divided self or the compartmentalized life.
This can signify, as it did for Ruskin when addressing his countrymen,
that we have separated our religion from our life, our faith from our
ideals, and our beliefs from the everyday affairs of our life. It may
mean separating the worlds of politics and business from the ethics of
private life, or having the public self and the private self occupy
different realms ruled by different beliefs. But in the end it leads to not
believing, really believing, anything at all.

   [22] A culture's idea of the heroic is a part of its larger myth-ritual

system. Modern societies, suspicious or contemptuous of this old fashioned language, suitable in describing primitive societies but not for modern ones, would prefer to call it a political and social system, an ideology or public philosophy, a common culture and its symbols. Regardless of the differences in terminology, the basic elements are present in both: a way of life and an elaborate public system of ideas embodied in symbols, ceremonies, celebrations, festivals or holidays, that make tangible the complex of beliefs of the society.

Modern society is peculiar in that it must first consider whether it has a hero system and a functioning conception of the heroic. If we have one, then we must ask whether it is a rich or healthy one. I contend ours is so poor and unhealthy that it effectively leaves us without a vital or viable hero system. There is little comfort in this: it seems either we go without or we go with what is incomplete and inadequate. Specifically, our options are either not having heroes or having heroes so unworthy or undeserving as to make a mockery of even the minimal demands of modern heroics. We have athletes, entertainers, successful entrepreneurs, the beautiful and the successful, all selected without consideration of any but the most ephemeral and superficial criteria, all reflecting, in our image conscious culture, not the virtues responsible for success but only the glitter of fame and money.

Ernest Becker argues in the The Denial of Death that the "great perplexity of our age...is that the youth have sensed...a great social-historical truth: that just as there are useless self-sacrifices in unjust wars, so too is there an ignoble heroics of whole societies."(op. cit., p. 6) He wrote this during the 1960s which explains, in part, its meaning. But I think it is true too in our far deader days when the young, rather than rebel, play dead in the face of what Herbert Read described as the exceptional "boredom... the horror vacuii; a fear of being alone, of having nothing to do, a neurosis whose symptoms are restlessness, an unmotivated and undirected rage, sinking at times to vapid listlessness." (Adventures of the Mind, ed. by R. Theulsen and J. Kobler [New York: Knopf, 1959], p. 150) He was writing of the 1950s but it is a good description of today's young.

[23] John Ruskin, op. cit., pp. 303-04.

[24] Ernest Becker, The Denial of Death, op. cit., p. 8.

[25] Interesting studies of the lives of children during junior and senior high school have shown a lack of adult contact and influence. It is as if

adults have stepped out of the lives of young people during the vital
years of their passage into adulthood. This is both extraordinary and
peculiar to modern culture. It has also been found that the adult world
has far less influence or impact on these children than the world created
for them by television, by music and movies, and, most of all, by living
in a world populated and created by their peers. Such an abdication by
adults reflects either indifference, misplaced values and priorities,
insufficiency of time and energy, or a lack of the necessary resources--
beliefs, ideals, heroes-- to counteract the variety and attractiveness of
the available alternatives. While all are a part of the current situation,
my emphasis here is on the last and most critical of these: beliefs,
ideals, and heroes.

[26] Jackson Lears, No Place of Grace (New York: Pantheon, 1981),
ch. 1.

Chapter Two

[27] The first quote is from "Dover Beach" by Matthew Arnold and
the second is the final line of "The Circus Animals' Desertion" by
William Butler Yeats.

[28] For two hundred years we have experienced the systemic
dismantling of earlier systems of thought and views of the world. Our
age has demonstrated tremendous ability in this business,
dismemberment being its forte. This process of clearing away long
settled habits of thought and fixed ways of thinking about and seeing
the world is traumatic. It is also a common and inevitable part of
existence. Human history has not been as static and sleepy as primitive
cultures envisioned it to be; the millennia of human existence not the
seemingly eternal, unchanging rhythm of a simple life ordered by the
stars, seasons, and immortal gods. Contending with change has
preoccupied cultures as it has individuals. It has led to the creation of
schemes to deny it, or to accommodate it to the existing, honored ways,
or when these fail to condemn it as a corruption or the work of the evil
one, or to escape it through nostalgia for the past and wailing over the
present. But in the end humans, being realists and pragmatic, acquiesce
and through a series of tactical retreats or accommodations, transform
their world, sometimes utterly and beyond recognition, sometimes only
in small but important ways. Against all the dams and dikes and levees
we construct to keep it in the channels we are accustomed to, history
floods and rages, cutting new courses and altering the river basin

forever. Or perhaps it is like the great geological ages that make up prehistory or the plate tectonics of the earth's surface that shift and slide slowly reshaping the surface of the planet or, with earthquakes, suddenly jump to alter a landscape in one violent cataclysm.

However calm or cataclysmic, a conversion of some sort takes place. As is the case in conversions, either religious or secular, "a passage into nothing" must occur in which "a critical point is turned within one. Something must give way, a native hardness must break down and liquefy...."(William James in The Varieties of Religious Experience (New York: Modern Library, 1902), p. 99) In the centuries that created the modern age much gave way and liquefied, the old order was transformed, and the foundation for a new one was laid. Wordsworth spoke for the first generations: the world was born again, all was suffused with a new and better light, all was possible for the new vision of human beings and its nearly boundless faith in the human prospect. The conversion was complete: the old fell away like an old and useless garment, the new was swaddled in the robes of a new age.

Only for saints is the conversion so clean and final. They alone seemed blessed with the simple and direct revelation, with the clean conversion that burn the old out forever and imprint indelibly the new faith and truth, beyond the possibility of a doubt. On this side of sainthood it happens otherwise; it is a longer, more tortured and convoluted process, fraught with uncertainties, subject to interpretations and endless doubting, where the old won't melt away but lingers to tease or trouble the mind, peeking around corners or awakening us in the middle of the night, and the new light is not so powerful and pervasive that the world shines whole and eternal in its glow. It is Rembrandt's chiaroscuro for most of us, or the haunting, empty light of Edward Hopper, but rarely the clear, holy light of Botticelli or Raphael. While the modern world's initial explosion of faith in progress, science, and the triumph of the human genius and will may have convinced some that the modern age would be a golden secular age with its secular saints and crystal and steel palaces, it has not been so simple or easy for the rest of us.

The original consensus, a reasonably unified and coherent view of man, society, and the cosmos, gave way in the nineteenth century to the attacks of conservatives and romantics, Christians and anti-modernists. The resistance grew as it became clear that the break with the past envisioned by the Enlightenment world view might be complete and

final, and that the critical eye of the new thought might smash all the
old idols, raze all the old sacred places, as the Christians before them
had destroyed the sacred groves of the classical world. This resistance
reflects the unusually deep and mixed feelings stirred by change and by
the nature of the new modern order. But it has been more than a
rearguard action of reactionary forces wedded to the past and fearful of
the new world of reason, science, and liberalism. There has been a
sense, from the beginning, that this new world was a dangerous and
uncertain enterprise capable of unleashing forces beyond our control
and destroying the essential elements of human well-being. This
premonition or suspicion has become, in our time, the belief that there
is something seriously wrong with us and our age. The resources for the
creation of a new order, so formidable and admired in the beginning,
have come to be seen, after the nature and logic of their new order
began to define itself, as too narrow and incomplete.

[29] We have, in some ways, become accustomed to our illness, and even
come to see it as the only good and reasonable way to live. The anthropologist
Colin Turnbull tells the story of a tribe, the Ik tribe of western Kenya, who did
just this. As a result of generations of hunger and desperate struggles to prevent
starvation, they slowly became, in Turnbull's view, degraded to the point of
being less than human. Many of their normal human impulses had disappeared.
The natural feelings of love or affection and the intimate bonds that hold friend,
kin, and lovers together were gone. After months with them, he

> had seen no evidence of family life such as is found almost
> everywhere else in the world. I had seen no sign of love, with its
> willingness to sacrifice, its willingness to accept that we are not complete
> wholes by ourselves, but need to be joined to others. I had seen little that
> I could even call affection. I had seen things that made me want to cry,
> though as yet I had not cried, but I had never seen an Ik anywhere near
> tears of sorrow-- only the children's tears of anger, malice and hate.

The brute facts of life had reduced them to a state as grim as that of the
grimmest of the contract theorists. And yet, and this is the important point here,
they had lost any sense that their way was abnormal or somehow a fall from
some earlier, more fully human, life. Instead, they affirmed their life in the face
of Turnbull's questioning and dismissed derisively his ideas as peculiarities,
laughable and foolish. Pressed to the limits of humanness, the human qualities
and behaviors Turnbull had observed in every other culture he had studied were
in fact beyond the realm of the possible or thinkable. For them, locked into
their ways by time and place, recollection of some other times and life, had
vanished and the crude, ineluctable reality of the present shaped their world and
made it the only world there was for them. See Colin Turnbull, The Mountain

<u>People</u> (New York: Simon & Schuster, 1972), p. 129.

The psychologist R. D. Laing makes the same point. Mental health and illness are entangled in the relationships between the patient and the norms of behavior and thought of his or her society. The diagnosis of mental illness may reflect as much the illness of society as the illness of the patient. The limitations of understanding, the partial and self-imposed blindness, the obsessions and neuroses, of the society may find their logical and full expression in those it claims are sick. Seeing and understanding too clearly and well the world in which they live may, ironically, place them beyond socially condoned madness of normal life.

[30] Ernest Becker, <u>Escape From Evil</u> (New York: Free Press, 1975), p. 71 and <u>Structure of Evil</u> (New York: Free Press, 1968), p. 264.

[31] Loren Eiseley, "The Brown Wasps" in <u>The Norton Anthology</u>, 4th ed.. (New York: W. W. Norton & Co., 1977, pp. 78-84.

[32] Peter Berger, Brigitte Berger, and Hansfried Kellner, <u>The Homeless Mind</u> (New York: Random House, 1974), p. 82.

[33] Joan Didion, "On Going Home" in <u>The Norton Reader</u>, op. cit., pp. 75-7.

[34] Jackson Lears, <u>No Place of Grace</u> (New York: Pantheon, 1981).

[35] These ideas are common in James' writings. He calls vision many things: sentiment, ideals, dispositions, moods, and temperaments. They all stand for a general frame of mind or way of conceiving experience and the world that defines the limits and possibilities of both. The early chapters in <u>Varieties of Religious Experience</u>, the first three essays in <u>The Will to Believe</u> (New York: Longmans, Green, and Co., 1908), and "On a Certain Blindness in Human Beings" in <u>Selected Papers on Philosophy</u> (London: Everyman Library, 1947) each in their own ways make the points I make here.

[36] Kenneth Benne, "If Schools are to Help Build Communities" in <u>Philosophy of Education: 1988, Proceedings of the Forty-Fourth Annual Meeting of the Philosophy Society</u> (Normal: Philosophy of Education Society, 1988), pp. 18-20.

[37] Bruce Catton, <u>Waiting for the Morning Train</u> (Detroit: Wayne State University Press, 1987), pp. 18-9.

[38] This chapter may be seen as another indulgence in the perennial human pastime of bemoaning the woeful condition of its present state. We moderns are fully, perhaps superlatively, human in this regard, bewailing our condition with an energy and inventiveness characteristic

of our age. Most of us are, to one degree or another, implicated in this congenital modern malcontent. Political and ideological differences, regardless of how wide and violent, do not separate us on this; my in-laws, conservative Republicans and fundamentalist Christians, think we are in terrible shape, but so do the critical theorists with whom I have worked; Allan Bloom and Alisdair MacIntyre complain about our troubles but so do Michael Harrington and Richard Rorty. Even those who find themselves searching in the middle, like Christopher Lasch in his last work or the communitarians, find our times deficient in important ways; among the warring parties there is a point of agreement on our bleak condition, albeit one ranging from the merely upset to the thoroughly depressed, from hard times and the reforming spirit to prophetic thundering and the apocalypse.

This is a monstrous ingratitude when considered in the light of the many blessings of modern life. It is certainly true that the extraordinary transformation of human life in the modern era has altered and, in many important ways, improved the lot of those fortunate enough to live in societies that have modernized. Wealth, health, knowledge, power, control, expanded possibilities and opportunities, leisure, mobility, and freedom have altered the lives of the average person in modern societies, and alterations have improved the condition of individuals and societies. In the aggregate these alterations constitute a revolutionary change in the way we moderns live, one that has been, when fairly judged, salubrious.

There are those who dismiss this moderate, commendatory stance, its tone and tacit acceptance, insisting on a radical and thoroughgoing condemnation and rejection of all things modern. They form a band of interesting and irascible activists. John Ruskin, some of whose ideas I agree with, was one of these, never more so than when he categorically denied the usefulness or necessity of ever traveling faster than the speed of a good horse and chaise.

The choice, though, need not, and isn't for most, either an appreciation of the benefits of the age or a wholesale rejection of it. Most fall somewhere in between and struggle to understand why amid so much they often feel so lost or empty. They do not need to read Ruskin to know this. They simply live it and come to know it as a bird knows the air in which it flies. It is a part of the modern world in which we live. Each knows, in his own way, that at the very heart of the modern enterprise, that which has made possible all its advances and is the engine of its progressive transformation of the world, is the worm that undoes it. In this paradox lies the problem and the tragedy of modern life. It is at the center of the discussion to come.

While a reasonable degree of agreement on this very general condition exists, there is less when we attempt to be clear about what exactly it is in the air that ails us. It is variously attributed to the inhuman world created by modern capitalism, or the dominance of a rational-scientific-technological world view, or the loss of tradition, custom, and established truths, or our brutish materialism and mindless consumerism, or the triumph of a clinical, therapeutic, behavioral, bio-medical approach to human personality and life, or the erosion of religion, or the loss of good, meaningful, skilled work, or the failure to make a reality of republican ideals of citizenship, civic virtue and participation, or the failure of modern societies to be rich and good communities. All of these, and others, have set off all of these alarms.

Chapter Three

[39] Walker Percy, Signposts in a Strange Land (New York: Farrar, Straus, & Giroux, 1991), p. 260.

[40] William Barrett, The Illusion of Technique (Garden City: Doubleday Anchor, 1962), p. 245.

[41] Ernest Becker, Beyond Alienation (New York: George Braziller, 1967), p. 170.

[42] From John Keats' poem "On Looking into Chapman's Homer."

[43] Ernest Becker, Escape From Evil (New York: Free Press, 1975), p.xviii.

[44] Soren Kierkegaard in A Kierkegaard Reader, ed. by Robert Bretall (New York: Modern Library, 1946), p. 6.

[45] Alfred North Whitehead, Science and the Modern World (New York: Mentor Book, 1960), p. 83.

[46] Ibid., p. 74. The lines are from Alfred Lord Tennyson.

[47] Ibid., pp. 79-80.

[48] D. H. Lawrence, Phoenix, ed. by Edward McDonald (New York: Penguin Books, 1978), p. 293.

[49] Blake's Newton is the great hero of modern science. He is portrayed as a beautifully proportioned and muscular figure, sitting at the bottom of the "Sea of Space and Time" bent over his diagrams, calculating the shape of the world. It is, though, the face, and particularly the eyes, where Blake deviates from modern myth: they are

arresting, even disturbing. There is little in them, except their anatomy, that is human. He is possessed by the "Single vision" of the new science, by the "catatonic fixity of the single vision." He has fallen into "Newton's sleep."

[50] William Barrett, The Death of the Soul (Garden City: Doubleday Anchor, 1986), p. 6.

[51] Morris Berman, The Reenchantment of the World (New York: Bantam, 1984). Berman relies on Frank Manuel's A Portrait of Isaac Newton (Cambridge: Harvard University Press, 1968). Manuel traces Newton's extraordinary self-conception to his early experiences of loss, first of his father and then of his mother through estrangement after her remarriage, and to other dislocations and uncertainties that plagued his early years. These experiences were reinforced by the sense of loss, isolation, and sin (of a broken and fallen world separated from God) of his Puritan religion. Pascal's cold and silent heavens were less abstract for Newton; the heavenly home Pascal saw receding into an empty astronomical infinity was for Newton a matter of his immediate personal life. Newton, plagued both by visions of his own shipwreck and by the belief that his abandonment and insecurity were the sign of his special mission and status, sought a new order upon which to build his life. He found it through an aggressive assertion of himself, a projection of his own ego onto the world, a determination to make the world bend to his will and genius and grant him the place, respect, and security he demanded of it. This new world, created from his drivenness and genius, was an orderly, predictable, rational world in which certainty was accessible to human understanding and an indelible fixture of nature. It had to be so, according to Manuel, because it arose from his "anxiety before and a fear of the unknown" and his need "to force everything in the heavens and on earth into one rigid, tight frame from which the most miniscule detail would not be allowed to escape free and random...." Having created this grand order of the universe, he and others convinced his age and our whole culture to accept his "grand obsessive design." (Berman, p. 111)

[52] Morris Berman, The Reenchantment of the World (New York: Bantam, 1984), Chapters 3 and 4.

[53] Carl Becker, The Heavenly City of the Eighteenth Century Philosopher (New Haven: Yale University Press, 1932), p. 31.

[54] Ibid., pp. 16-17.

[55] Ernest Becker, The Structure of Evil (New York: Free Press,

1968), p. 230-36.

[56] Carl Becker, op. cit., pp. 15-16.

[57] Erich Heller, The Artist's Journey into the Interior (New York: Farrar, Straus and Cudahy, 1957), p. 181-2.

[58] Richard Rorty's Science and the Mirror of Nature (Princeton University Press, 1979) makes this case for science and philosophy, the philosopher Paul Feyerabend demonstrates the somersault of self-annihilation in his work on epistemology, deconstruction offers it in literature and as a general tool for understanding life as collection of texts, and moral philosophy long ago slipped below the surge of modern thought, as Alisdair MacIntyre argues in After Virtue (South Bend: University of Notre Dame Press, 1981). In education, Henry Perkinson's recent book Teachers without Goals/Students without Purposes (New York: McGraw- Hill, 1993) shows us the poor man's feast modern thought has prepared for us.

[59] C. S. Lewis, The Abolition of Man (New York: MacMillan, 1965), p. 90.

[60] Frank Manuel in Morris Berman, The Reenchantment of the World, op. cit., chapter 4.

[61] Blaise Pascal, "Thoughts" in Thoughts and Minor Works, Vol. 48 of the Harvard Classics (New York: Collier & Son, 1938), entries 277 and 282, pp. 98-100. Entries 267 tp 290 are all concerned with the nature of reason, intuition, and the heart. He also begins the "Thoughts" with this topic (entries 1-4).

[62] Diderot in Peter Gay, The Enlightenment: The Science of Freedom, Vol. 2 (New York: Norton, 1977), p. 191.

[63] D. H. Lawrence, Studies in Classical American Literature (New York: Viking Press, 1966), p. 31.

[64] Ibid..

[65] Albert Levi, Philosophy and the Modern World (Chicago: University of Chicago Press, 1977), p. 31 and Robert Hughes, Consciousness and Society (New York: Vintage Books, 1961), pp. 16-7, 24.

[66] Albert Levi, Philosophy and the Modern World, op. cit., pp. 39 and 41.

[67] Friederick Nietzsche, The Gay Science in W. Kaufmann, The Portable Nietzsche (New York: Viking Press, 1954), section 125, pp. 95-6.

[68] King Lear, III, iv, 26-31.

[69] I draw from Archibald MacLeish's poem "Dr. Sigmund Freud Discovers the Sea Shell" in this paragraph.

[70] Jacob Bronowski, Science and Human Values (New York: Harper Torchbooks, 1959), pp. 60-1.

[71] Ibid., p. 29.

[72] Walker Percy Signposts in a Strange Land, op. cit., p. 260.

[73] Jacob Bronowski, Science and Human Values, op. cit., p. 90.

[74] Jacob Bronowski, William Blake and the Age of Revolution (New York: Harper & Row, 1965).

[75] Stephen Toulmin, Cosmopolis (New York: Free Press, 1990).

[76] Ibid., p. 186.

[77] Peter Gay, The Enlightenment, The Rise of Modern Paganism, Vol. 1 (New York: Norton, 1977), pp. 418-19.

[78] Ernest Becker lived from 1924 to 1974. He received his Ph.D. from Syracuse University in 1959 in cultural anthropology. He taught at the University of California, Berkeley, San Jose State University, and Simon Fraser University after leaving Syracuse. From 1963 until his death he published seven books including Beyond Alienation, The Structure of Evil, and The Denial of Death. His final work, Escape From Evil was published posthumously.

[79] Ernest Becker, Escape From Evil (New York: The Free Press, 1975), p. 168.

[80] Ernest Becker, The Structure of Evil (New York: Frre Press, 1968), p. 12.

[81] Ernest Becker, The Lost Science of Man (New York: George Braziller, 1971), p. 111.

[82] Ernest Becker, The Structure of Evil, op. cit., pp. 8-10.

[83] Alfred North Whitehead, Science and the Modern World, op. cit., p. 52.

[84] Ernest Becker, The Birth and Death of Meaning (New York: Free Press, 1962), pp. 148-49.

[85] Ernest Becker, Beyond Alienation, op. cit., p. 220.

[86] Ernest Becker, Escape From Evil, op. cit., p. 71.

[87] Ernest Becker, The Lost Science of Man, op. cit., p. 4.

[88] Ibid., p. 6.

[89] Ibid., p. 7.

[90] Ibid., p. 16.

[91] Ibid..

[92] Ibid., p. 20.

[93] Ernest Becker, <u>Beyond Alienation</u>, op. cit., p. 126.

[94] Ibid.. Dilthey quote is from <u>Patterns and Meaning in History</u> (New York: Harper Torchbook, 1962), p. 105.

[95] Ernest Becker, <u>The Structure of Evil</u>, op. cit., p. 317.

[96] Ernest Becker, <u>The Lost Science of Man</u>, op. cit., p. 145.

[97] Ernest Becker, <u>The Structure of Evil</u>, op. cit., p. 366.

[98] Ibid., p. 362.

[99] Ibid., p. 363.

[100] Ibid., pp. 372-73.

[101] Ernest Becker, <u>Beyond Alienation</u>, op. cit., p. 30.

[102] Ernest Becker, <u>The Lost Science of Man</u>, op. cit., p. 116.

Chapter Four

[103] Jurgen Habermas argues this same thing: our aim should be to humanize the modern age, not reject it. We cannot turn back. We do not want to turn back. But we cannot accept modern ideas and institutions in their present form. See his <u>Toward a Rational Society</u> (Boston: Beacon Press, 1970).

[104] Alfred North Whitehead, <u>Adventure of Ideas</u> (New York: Mentor Books, 1955), p. 32.

[105] Hans Jonas, <u>The Phenomenon of Life</u> (New York: Dell Publishing, 1968), p. 196.

[106] Alfred North Whitehead, <u>Adventure of Ideas</u>, op. cit., p. 48-9.

[107] Ernest Becker, <u>Beyond Alienation</u>, op. cit., p. 72.

[108] Huston Smith, "Excluded Knowledge", <u>Teachers College Record</u>, v. 82, 3, Sp 81, p. 432.

[109] Michael Polanyi makes this argument in his works. See <u>Personal Knowledge</u> (New York: Harper Torchbook, 1964), <u>The Study of Man</u> (Chicago: University of Chicago Press, 1969), and <u>The Tacit Dimension</u> (Gloucester, MA: Peter Smith, 1983).

[110] Johann Wolfgang von Goethe quoted in Armine, "Goethe's Science in the Twentieth Century", <u>Toward</u>, p. 23. Also see Douglas Sloan's "Insight-Imagination" in the same issue of <u>Toward</u> and in two books he edited, <u>Toward the Recovery of Wholeness: Knowledge, Education, and Values</u> (New York: Teachers College Press, 1984) and <u>Education and Values</u> (New York: Teachers college Press, 1980).

[111] Mathematics is intentional in its construction of a system of axioms held together by the mind. It exists only in the act of cognition and achieves unity only through the power of the intentionality that

conceives it. It is so powerful a tool not because of its objectivity but because of its intentional, rational, and systematic nature and method. What we need in the human sciences is an equally powerful method--clear, systematic, rational, and self-conscious.

[112] Armine, Toward, op. cit., p. 25 . Thomas Kuhn's view of scientists who toil away on the dominant paradigm is not possible in Goethe's science where transformations are continuous and science itself is a "permanent revolution."

[113] Michael Polanyi, Personal Knowledge (New York: Harper Torchbook, 1964), p. 380.

[114] Peter Gay, The Enlightenment: Volume 1, The Rise of Modern Paganism (New York: Norton, 1977)p. 230.

[115] See my dissertation on this point: Education and Community in John Dewey and Martin Buber, Washington University, 1989.

[116] William James, "The Will to Believe" in The Will to Believe and Other Essays in Popular Philosophy (New York: Longmans, Green, and Co., 1908). At the end of his essay James quote Fitz James Stephens as follows:

In all important transactions of life we have to take a leap in the dark....If we decide to leave the riddles unanswered, that is a choice; if we waver in our answer, that, too, is a choice: but whatever choice we make, we make it at our peril. If a man chooses to turn his back altogether on God and the future, no one can prevent him; no one can show beyond a reasonable doubt that he is mistaken. If a man thinks otherwise and acts as he thinks, I do not see any one can prove that he is mistaken. Each must act as he thinks best; and if he is wrong, so much the worse for him. We stand on a mountain pass in the midst of whirling snow and blinding mist, through which we get glimpses now and then of paths which may be deceptive. If we stand still we shall be frozen to death. If we take the wrong road we shall be dashed to pieces. We do not certainly know whether there is any right one. What must we do? 'Be strong and of a good courage.' Act for the best, hope for the best, and take what comes.

[117] From William Butler Yeats' poem "Lapis Lazuli".

[118] William James, Selected Papers on Philosophy (London: J. M. Dent & Son, 1947), p. 130.

[119] Three of William Barrett's books, in different ways, address the issues considered in this book: Irrational Man (Garden City: Doubleday/Anchor Books, 1962), The Illusion of Technique (Garden

City: Doubleday Anchor Books, 1979), and Death of the Soul (Garden
City: Doubleday Anchor Books, 1986).

[120] William Barrett, The Illusion of Technique, op. cit., p. 307.

[121] Ibid., p. 296.

[122] Ibid., pp. 304 and 295.

[123] Ibid., p. 230.

[124] Ibid., p. 247.

[125] Ernest Becker, The Denial of Death (New York: Free Press,
1973), p. 50.

[126] Quote from Otto Rank in Ernest Becker, The Denial of Death,
op. cit., p. 158.

[127] Ernest Becker, The Structure of Evil (New York: Free Press,
1968), p. 230.

[128] Becker, Beyond Alienation, op. cit., p. 46.

[129] Becker, Escape From Evil (New York: Free Press, 1975), p.88.

[130] Ernest Becker, The Structure of Evil, op. cit., p. 271.

[131] Ibid., p. 264.

[132] Ibid., pp. 241 and 246.

[133] Ernest Becker, Beyond Alicnation, op. cit., p. 220.

[134] Ernest Becker, Escape From Evil, op. cit., p. 71.

[135] Ernest Becker, The Structure of Evil, op. cit., p. 264. He is using
Max Scheler from The Nature of Sympathy.

[136] Colin Turnbull, The Human Cycle (New York: Simon &
Schuster, 1983).

[137] Ibid., pp. 29-45.

[138] Ibid., p. 133ff..

[139] Ibid., p. 147.

[140] Ibid., p. 15.

[141] Ibid., p. 266.

[142] Ibid., p. 267.

[143] Ibid., p. 268.

[144] Ibid., p. 277.

[145] Ibid..

[146] Ibid., p. 280.

[147] Ibid., p. 283.

[148] Ibid., p. 184.

[149] Ibid., p. 283.

[150] ibid., p. 266.

[151] Ernest Becker, The Denial of Death, op. cit., p. 6.

[152] Colin Turnbull, <u>The Human Cycle</u>, op. cit., p. 107.

[153] Ibid., p. p. 188.

[154] Ibid., p. 243.

[155] Ibid., p. 244.

[156] Ibid., p. 246.

[157] Ibid., p. 108.

Chapter Five

[158] Margaret Mead, <u>Growing Up in New Guinea</u> in <u>From the South Pacific</u> (New York: William Morrow, 1939), p. 277.

[159] Joseph Hart, <u>Education and the Humane Community</u> (New York: Harper & Brothers, 1951),p. 48. There are, of course, many forms or types of education. In addition to the formal educational system, there are the informal and private realms of education: the realms of the private world where we are all to some extent autodidacts of our peculiar selves, or in the idylls of a country life where nature tutors us through the communion of field and spirit, or in the social struggle, acute in our time, of individuals to free themselves from the oppressions of culture, class, race, or gender that define and limit the range of their powers and lives. Such realms, if they do in fact escape or transcend the cultural contexts in which they emerge, and I doubt they do, would fall, in a technical sense, beyond the scope of my assumptions. But the point is really only a technical one, acknowledging that there is a private world, circumscribed admittedly by the public and cultural ones, and that educators and social scientists make a mistake when they, in moments of enthusiasm and self importance, claim too great or exclusive a power for social, cultural, and institutional forces in making people what they are. It can be as truly said that all education is self-education and all such education, while inescapably within a cultural context, is self-education shaped by the imperatives of our individual natures and needs in their silent conversations with themselves. To the extent that this is true, education is in fact beyond the culture and beyond the assumption of this work. Regardless, it remains for us to wrestle with the basic concerns shared by both views about the relationship between the individual and the culture and about the preoccupation with the liberation of the individual from culturally imposed limitations and intrusions that is a cardinal tenet of the modern faith. It is the development of a modern individualism that posits, in Jules Henry's phrase, "culture against man"

or seeks a Rousseauean neo-primitivism that is at the heart of the matter in this study. Furthermore, the idea of reasons of the heart used in the book aims at uncovering the private realm of life and self that has been severed, to our great loss, from the public life of modern society. Turnbull's main concern is with this separation: we moderns have exiled part of ourselves from the suzerainty of society and culture. The Mbuti experienced far less of this splintering of the self into public and private realms than moderns do. Their virtue, according to Turnbull, is in just this ability to bring into the public this private realm to the enrichment of both.

[160] Harry Boyte, Community is Possible (New York: Harper and Row, 1984).

[161] Robert Nisbet, The Quest for Community (New York: Oxford University Press, 1953). There is irony in such a quest: it is within community that such qualities are most likely to develop and flourish. Quests begin and end in community, even if the community is suffering through a time of trouble. To quest outside of community is to do something very different from the prototypical quest of the Greek or medieval worlds, of Jason or Perceval. Yet we moderns do quest, in our own way. Our heroes are common and unheroic, a low form of hero, ironic and absurd, but nonetheless they quest. What is it they are after? It is after what earlier heroes and quests already had-- a community that sends them into the forest or across the seas armed with its strengths and fired by its mission. We, in contrast, wander in the forest and on the seas seeking not the grail or the fleece, but a community in whose beliefs and ideals give meaning and purpose to our lives.

[162] To talk about community is a tricky business for two reasons. One is the common and vested interest people have in such a commonplace concept and the quick heat generated when one steps off the straight and usually narrow line of each individual's special and indisputable understanding of its meaning. The other is that community is a contested concept. It has too many definitions (once calculated to be ninety four). Few concepts are as protean as community. It changes shape so often in the scholarly literature and everyday discourse that running it to ground would have been a fitting labor for Hercules. But some sense can be made of the concept. What sociologists and philosophers can't figure out in their heads, people experience and understand in their lives and feel in their hearts. All inquiry into community should begin at this elemental level of experience and

understanding.

[163] Irving Singer, <u>Meaning in Life</u> (New York: Free Press, 1992), p. 129.

[164] Mortimer J. Adler, <u>The Paideia Proposal</u> (New York: Collier Books, 1982).

[165] J.J. Chambliss, <u>Educational Theory as Theory of Conduct</u> (Albany: SUNY Press, 1987), p. 47.

[166] Lawrence Cremin, <u>American Education: The National Experience</u> (New York: Harper & Row, 1980), pp. 52 and 55.

[167] Werner Jaeger, Paideia: <u>The Ideals of Greek Culture</u>, Volume 1 (New York: Oxford University Press, 1976), p.xxii.

[168] Ibid..

[169] This discussion assumes a general knowledge of the thought of both men.

[170] Martin Buber, <u>Between Man and Man</u>. (New York: MacMillan, 1975), p. 91.

[171] For detailed sources on the various arguments of this essay see chapters two and three of my unpublished dissertation, <u>Community and Education in John Dewey and Martin Buber</u> (Washington University, St. Louis, 1989). Some selected sources are as follows. See Dewey's rousing conclusion to <u>The Public and Its Problems</u> (Denver:Alan Swallow, 1954), pp. 211-19. On the social nature of self see Paul Pfuetze, <u>Self, Society, Existence</u>. (New York: Harper Torchbook, 1961), chapters one and three for a discussion of Buber's view and S. Hook, (ed.), <u>John Dewey</u>. (New York: Barnes and Noble, 1950), p. 107 for a quote by Dewey. The rhythmic nature of existence is described in Dewey's <u>Experience and Nature</u>. (New York: Dover Publications, 1958), pp. 47 and 312; Buber develops it as a theme of <u>I and Thou</u>. The first seven chapters of <u>Democracy and Education</u> make the connections between community and democracy. Buber's commitment to democratic socialism is articulated in <u>Paths in Utopia</u>. Dewey attempts a new definition of freedom and individualism throughout his works, and specifically in <u>Individualism Old and New</u>, <u>Freedom and Culture</u>, and <u>The Public and Its Problems</u>. The religious aspect of experience is pervasive in Buber's works; Dewey considers it in <u>A Common Faith</u>. The best way to understand the position I have developed, though, is to read the works of each author that capture their visions of human existence, the world we live in, and the lives we can and should create together. For Dewey, this includes <u>Experience and Nature</u>, <u>Art as</u>

Experience, and Democracy and Education; for Buber, I and Thou, Between Man and Man, and The knowledge of Man. The common conception of community presented in this essay is fashioned from the visions expressed in these works.

[172] Martin Buber, Paths in Utopia, op. cit., pp. 108-09. He is referring here to a debate over the nature of socialism. He stands in opposition to centralized forms. He adheres to the slogan "Local Communes, complete regional autonomy, independence, no police, no officials, sovereignty of the armed masses of workers and peasants."

[173] Ibid., pp. 13-5.

[174] In On Judaism, pp. 211-13, Buber makes a connection between love and local community: "...the higher, the decisive principle, which alone can knit together the relationship to God and the relationship to man--the principle of love--requires neither organizations nor institutions but can be given effect at any time, at any place. The will to realization was not, however, confined to individuals. Within the communal form of life adopted in place of a state--that is, the local communities--active love, in the guise of mutual help, recurs as a basic social element. This structure found its perfection about two centuries ago in Hasidism, which was built on little communities bound together by brotherly love." This same sentiment is expressed in a quote Buber uses from Landauer: "transformation of society, can only come in love, in work and in stillness"(p.52 in Paths in Utopia). Love is a word for the relation of I-Thou. All that comes with this relation comes in and with love. Another interesting quote is this one: "True art is a loving art....True science is a loving science....True philosophy is a loving philosophy.... Every true deed is a loving deed." A last one: "In all love to man...there shines forth perfected relation." These two are from Pointing the Way, pp. 29-30 and The Knowledge of Man, p. 164, respectively. Buber's use of love is another example where he operates from a lived experience of humans that Dewey rarely touches upon. Love is a stranger in most of Dewey's work. It is found often, however, in his poetry.

[175] Martin Buber, Paths in Utopia, op. cit., pp. 27-9, 21, and 75.

[176] See the following: Israel and the World, pp. 42, 47, and 121-2; On Judaism, pp. 142 and 154; Between Man and Man, pp. 92 and 160; Paths in Utopia, pp.48 and 52-3.

[177] Martin Buber, Paths in Utopia, op. cit., p. 132.

[178] Ibid., pp. 133 and 136.

[179] Ibid., pp. 130-33. Here is a somewhat more concrete expression of Buber's vision of such a community: "Wherever historical destiny had brought a group of men together in a common fold, there was room for the growth of a genuine community; and there was no need of an altar to the city deity in the midst when the citizens were united round-- and by--the Nameless. A living togetherness, constantly renewing itself, was already there, and all that needed strengthening was the immediacy of relationships. In the happiest instances common affairs were deliberated and decided not through representatives but in gatherings in the market-place; and the unity that was felt in public permeated all personal contacts. The danger of seclusion might hang over the community, but the communal spirit banished it; for here this spirit flourished as nowhere else and broke windows for itself in the narrow walls, with a large view of people, mankind and the world."(pp. 135-6)

[180] Martin Buber in Bernard Susser, Existence and Utopia, op. cit., p. 60.

[181] Martin Buber, Paths in Utopia, op. cit., p. 140.

[182] Martin Buber, "Three Theses of a Religious Socialism," in Pointing the Way, op. cit., pp.112-14.

[183] Ibid.. See also pp. 229-32 in Hasidism and Modern Man and chapter IV in On Zion, in particular the sections on Ahad Ha'am, Rav Kook, and A. D. Gordon. Buber's views on the meaning of Zion and Zionism would be another good model of his vision of community. In the section on Gordon, Buber describes, and I think affirms, Gordon's vision of the need for connection with Nature, the land, and the soil. The village commune that works the land and lives the agricultural life participates in the cosmos in the distinctively human way. Gordon is Buber's model of the "man who realizes the idea of Zion."

[184] John Dewey, Experience and Nature (New York: Dover Publications, 1958), p. 202.

[185] Ibid., pp. 204-05. This includes the long quote before it.

[186] On Mill's dilemma see Dewey's Liberalism and Social Action (New York: Capricorn Books, 1963), pp. 29-31.

[187] John Dewey, Art as Experience (New York: Paragon Books, 1979), p. 81.

[188] Ibid., p. 104. See also pp. 244 and 334-36.

[189] Ibid., pp. 270-71.

[190] John Dewey, Freedom and Culture (New York: G.P. Putnam's

Sons, 1939), pp. 10 and 150-51.

[191] John Dewey, Human Nature and Conduct (New York: Modern Library, 1922), pp. 330-32. Dewey makes a similar statement at the end of Reconstruction in Philosophy (Boston: Beacon Press, 1965), pp. 210-13.

[192] John Dewey, Art as Experience, op. cit., p. 338.

[193] John Dewey, Reconstruction in Philosophy, op. cit., p. xxix.

[194] Ibid., pp. viii-ix.

[195] Ibid., p. 173. See also Individualism Old and New (New York: Capricorn Books, 1963),p. 154.

[196] John Dewey, Liberalism and Social Action, op. cit., p. 50.

[197] Ibid., p. 53.

[198] John Herman Randall in The Philosophy of the Common Man, ed. by Sydney Hook (New York: Greenwoood Press, 1968), pp. 110-11. See also John Blewett, John Dewey (New York: Fordham University Press, 1960), p. 37.

[199] See Dewey's chapter "Democracy and American" in This Is My Best, ed. by Whit Burnett (New York: Dial Press, 1942).

[200] John Dewey, Intelligence in the Modern World, ed. by J. Ratner (New York: Modern Library, 1939), p. 400.

[201] Dewey said this in an early article, "Ethics of Democracy": "Democracy, in a word, is a social, that is to say, an ethical conception, and upon its ethical significance is based its significance as governmental. Democracy is a form of government because it is a form of moral and spiritual association." And later this: "Democracy does not differ from aristocracy in its goals. The end is no mere assertion of the individual will as individual; it is not disregard of law, of the universal; it is complete realization of the law, namely of the unified spirit of the community." These ideas endured after the early Hegelian and religious language and influence faded. Both quote are in John Dewey: The Early Works, 1882-98, eds. F. Bowers and J. A. Boydston (Carbondale: S.I.U. Press, 1967-71), vol. 1, p. 240 and vol. 4, p. 367.

[202] Richard Bernstein, Praxis and Action (Philadelphia: University of Pennsylvania Press, 1971), p. 218.

[203] See R. W. Sleeper, The Necessity of Pragmatism (New Haven: Yale University Press, 1986), pp. 116ff.

[204] John Dewey, The Public and Its Problems (Denver: Allan Swallow, 1927), p. 184. See also the end of Reconstruction in Philosophy, pp. 210-13, Art as Experience, pp. 335ff., and chapter 7 of

Democracy and Education.

[205] Jean B. Quandt, From Small Town to the Great Community
(New Brunswick: Rutgers University Press, 1970) and M. and L.
White, The Intellectual Versus the City (New York: Oxford University
Press, 1977).

[206] Ibid., pp. 5-17. See p. 17 for the quote from W. A. White. See
also Sally F. Griffith, Home-Town News: William Allen White and the
Emporia Gazette (New York: Oxford University Press, 1988).

[207] Ibid., p. 133. The argument in these paragraphs is based upon
Quandt and White. For a different, and often opposing, view see
Thomas Bender Community and Social Change in America (Baltimore:
John Hopkins Press, 1978).

[208] John Dewey, The Public and Its Problems, op. cit., p. 148.

[209] John Dewey, Freedom and Culture, op. cit., pp. 159-60.

[210] See Dewey, Individualism Old and New,and Quandt.

[211] John Dewey, Freedom and Culture, op. cit., pp. 160-61.

[212] John Dewey, The Public and Its Problems, op. cit., pp. 211-19.
Other rousing conclusions may be found in Reconstruction in
Philosophy, Experience and Nature, Art as Experience, A Common
Faith, and The Quest for Certainty.

[213] Ibid..

[214] Nietzsche thought the solution to the human problem was in the
ubermenschen who affirmed himself by throwing off the limitations of
his condition and asserting his individual self as the source and
authority of his existence. The view offered here seeks the same escape
from the limitations and problems of human life but finds it in the
absorption of the individual by external sources of power and authority.
What Nietzsche advocates is what most humans, however much they
may desire it, cannot tolerate or achieve. The human way is that of the
untermenschen. It may be, as Nietzsche contends, that we are weak,
stupid, pusillanimous pawns of ideologies and religions that enslave
and degrade us. But this is so because something inside of us wishes or
needs it, in spite of our doubts and a certain native resist, to be so.

[215] Floyd Matson in The Broken Images (Garden City: Doubleday Anchor
Book, 1966) describes the traumas of freedom in his discussion of post-
Freudian psychology:

> In this perspective the achievement of freedom-- the act of liberation-
> - is always an estrangement, both biographically and historically. From
> the traumatic emancipation of birth onward-- or from the traumatic

emergence from the tribe-- freedom is encountered in fear and trembling.(p. 216)

Richard Tarnas, in "The Transfiguration of the Western Mind", a paper presented at the conference on "Philosophy and the Human Future" (Cambridge University, England, August, 8, 1989) elaborates on this idea:

> Thus the Cartesian-Kantian condition begins as a Promethean movement toward human freedom, toward autonomy from the encompassing matrix of nature, toward individuation from the collective, yet gradually and ineluctably it evolves into a Kafka/Beckett-like state of existential isolation and absurdity-- an intolerable double-bind leading to a kind of deconstructive frenzy. And again, the existential double-bind closely mirrors the infant's situation within the birthing mother: having been symbiotically united with the nourishing womb, growing and developing within that matrix, the beloved center of an all-comprehending supportive world, yet now alienated from that world, constricted by that womb, crushed, strangled, and expelled in a state of extreme confusion and anxiety-- an inexplicable incoherent situation of profound traumatic intensity.(p. 16)

[216] Martin Buber, The Knowledge of Man (New York: Torchbooks, 1965), p. 71.

[217] Robert Kegan, In Over Our Heads (Cambridge: Harvard University Press, 1994), p. 103.

[218] Ibid., p. 100ff..

[219] Ibid., p. 351 and 321.

[220] Ibid., pp. 217-218 on the two yearnings of humans.

[221] David Bakan, Duality of Human Existence (Boston: Beacon Press, 1966), pp. 14-5. For a bleaker view of our two-sidedness see Arthur Koestler's Janus: A Summing Up (New York: Vintage Books, 1979). He depicts human beings as a failed experiment of nature and a pathological creatures destined for self-destruction.

[222] Ibid..

[223] See Kegan, op. cit., pp. 331 and 324ff., for his full discussion of this point.

[224] Walter Pater, The Renaissance (New York: Modern Library, 1919), pp. 194-99.

[225] Virginia Woolf, To the Lighthouse (New York: Harcourt, Brace, & World, 1955), p. 158.

[226] Richard Rorty, Consequences of Pragmatism (Minneapolis: U. of Minnesota Press, 1986), p. 166-68. Bold is italics in original.

[227] Pater, op. cit., p. 197.

[228] William Butler Yeats quoted in Gerald Monsman's <u>Pater</u> (Boston: Twayne Publishing, 1977), p. 164.

[229] Walter Pater, <u>Marius the Epicurean</u> (New York: Everyman's Library, p. 1968), p. 196.

[230] Ibid., p. 201. So much in modern art, philosophy, and literature expresses this great sorrow. We seem congenitally vulnerable to it in our modern times.

Chapter Six

[231] Joseph Hart, <u>Education in the Humane Community</u> (New York: Harper & Brothers, 1951), p. 48. Fred Inglis, <u>The Promise of Happiness</u>. (London: Cambridge U. Press, 1981), p. 32.

[232] John Dewey, <u>A Common Faith</u> (New Haven: Yale University Press, 1961). Here Dewey is more encompassing and expansive in his use of the term community. It is not uncommon for him to use it in this way. The best and most common example of this use of community is in his conception of the "Great Community" of modern society. The human community is the international or global version of the "Great Community." The local community, however, remains the essential community and is the foundation for these others.

[233] Martin Buber, 'The Dialogue Principle in Education" in Kalman Yaron, ed., <u>Lifelong Learning in Israel</u> (New York: Schocken Books, 1959). He is talking about the people's school, an adult education school in Israel.

[234] See Dewey's <u>Democracy and Education</u>, p. 87, Buber's "Society and the State" in <u>Pointing the Way</u>, pp. 161-176, and <u>Paths in Utopia</u>, chapter 10.

[235] See Raymond Callahan's <u>Education and the Cult of Efficiency</u> (Chicago: University of Chicago Press, 1963) for the antithesis of this-- school administration and operation that violate the spirit of this process. The intimate connection of education and institutional arrangements is made explicit in this quote from Buber's <u>A Believing Humanism</u>, p. 95: "As in everything else, so also here the institutional and educational influence must supplement each other. The secret longing of man for a life in reciprocal mutual confirmation must be developed through education, but the external conditions it needs in order to find its fulfillment must also be created. The architect must be set the task of also building for human contact, building surroundings

that invite meeting and centers that shape meeting."

[236] Martin Buber, Israel and the World (New York: Schocken Books, 1976), p. 141.

[237] Turnbull has an interesting discussion of reason in Part Three of The Human Cycle. He argues that youth, the period immediately after adolescence, is the time when the "art of reason" is developed. This art is the "the art of the right application of knowledge" by which we "convert mere knowledge to wisdom."(p. 128) It is learning what to do with the facts and how to turn what you know into what you are. It is the rational ordering of knowledge and the self in light of the ideal and the greater values of the individual and the culture. The art of reason is part of the larger socialization into the community but, being developed at an older age, it utilizes reason rather than conditioning, habit, blind obedience, emotion, or ties of affection and loyalty. It is the strongest voice in the soundless conversation within ourselves about how we should live and who we will become. It is all the reasons we give to ourselves for what we do and what we are, reasons that make sense for us of what we believe, value, and live for. Reasons or logic or facts by themselves are never enough. They are vital when part of the art of "recognizing and interpreting the symbols and learning what to do with your life rather than your mind."(p. 158) Turnbull, in insisting on the rational ordering of self and world in accordance with the teachings and the spirit of the community, is, in a different way, saying much the same thing as Buber.

[238] David Nyberg, "Education as Community Expression" Teachers College Record, Vol. 79, 2, December 1977, p.217-18.

[239] Ibid.. In making this point, Nyberg concurs with Barber and Mead:

> In this proposed conception, schools reflect descriptively, after the fact, what the communities that support them are like. If the community changes, then the school changes eventually to reflect a new description. It is implied here that when schools are perceived as unsatisfactory, the community must not blame the schools first, nor should the community or benevolent outsiders assume that changing schools will solve the problem. When it is remembered that education is a mediating agency maintained by a community, and that the school is an expression of a method by which individuals become communities, and through which these communities describe themselves, then it becomes clear that problems in the school reflect problems in the community. The solution to the problem in the school lies in the community more than in the school itself. Interracial fighting is not basically a school problem. Lack

of sensible discipline or too much insensitive discipline are not primarily a school problem. The humiliating desecration of literature, philosophy, and the humanistic studies in general that we are forced to endure in the media, in our educational institutions, in our lives, when they occur in schools, are reflections of the communities that support them.(p.219)

[240] Colin Turnbull, The Human Cycle (New York: Simon Schuster, 1983), p. 277.

[241] John White, Education and the Good Life (New York: Teachers College Press, 1991).

[242] John Bremer, A Matrix for Modern Education (Toronto: McClelland & Stuart Ltd., 1975).

[243] Ibid., p. 1.

[244] Daniel Calhoun in The Intelligence of a People (Princeton: Princeton University Press, 1973) argues that intelligence is a "function of the whole experience of the individual, of the family conditions in which he is raised, of the formal learning he meets in schools, and of the public ideas that surround, sustain, and even express his mind." (p.ix)

[245] . C. A. Bowers, Elements of a Post-Liberal Theory of Education (New York: Teachers College Press, 1987).

[246] Ibid., p. 53.

[247] Ibid., p. 54.

[248] Ibid., p. 142-43.

[249] William James, The Varieties of Religious Experience (New York: Modern Library, 1902), p. 356 and Ernest Becker, The Denial of Death (New York: Free Press, 1973), p. 1. The central place of the heroic in human life and its loss in modern society are the main themes of Becker's The Denial of Death.

[250] Ernest Becker, Beyond Alienation (New York: George Braziller, 1967), pp. 218-19.

[251] Ibid., p. 248.

[252] Becker often used eras or types of cultures of the past as a foil to our age and as models of what we have failed to achieve in modern culture. His favorites were medieval and primitive cultures. On the appropriateness and accuracy of such a use of the past, a topic that generates fierce partisanship, I will say only that the turn to the past to discover a way out of problems and confusions of the present has been commonplace since people amassed the resources necessary to know about the past. Societies throughout history have done so in times of

trouble or in the face of social change. The tendency to distort the past to exemplify just those qualities absent in the present is powerful and humans often succumb to the temptation of using a glowing past to satisfy the longings of the present. This acknowledged, there is still something valuable in the use of the past as a mirror in which we can see and understand the present and to show us other ways of ordering individual and social life. For many in the twentieth century the medieval world has offered a perfect foil for all our modern faults. Whether the Middles Ages were any or all of the things we have ascribed to it, and putting aside all sentimental or romantic images of the age of chivalry, courtly love, crusades, and Catholicism, it at the least offers moderns the material with which to construct a model of all that we lack and long for in our lives, society, and culture. The question of historical accuracy and the true nature of medieval, or any other, society is beside the point when used in this way. I would add only that I think medieval culture and society did create and put into practice, however imperfectly, a unified system of thought, a cosmology that placed humans in an ordered universe and society, a meaning to personal existence, and a moral order that aimed to guide both individual and social life. It envisioned a human existence whose richness, breadth, and depth make ours appear sallow and jejune.

Peter Laslett's The World We Have Lost (New York: Charles Scribner's Sons, 1971) touches these issues. In discussing the seventeenth century in England he both rejects the idea that we can look to the past as a good or golden time free of the problems of the present and accepts that this particular period of history did possess a unity of life and experience that so many declare absent in our world today. Christopher Lasch in his recent The True and Only Heaven argues that Laslett's book is nostalgic and elegiac and thereby distracts us from the reality of the past and the pressing needs of the present. I think Lasch is wrong about Laslett's book, which is clear about the nature of the past it discusses, but agree with him that we too often substitute critical consideration of our present condition with mournful yet glowing accounts of the good old days. For an interesting study of the historiography of the Middle Ages see Norman Cantor, Inventing the Middle Ages (New York: William Morrow, 1991).

Those we call antimodernists are especially guilty of this approach to the past. They cull it for examples of a way of life that was good and is now gone, and then use them to flail away at the corruptions of the modern world. Jackson Lears' No Place of Grace deals with American antimodernism at the beginning of the twentieth century and, in chapter four, discusses the place the medieval world had in its thought. The argument of this book has been influenced in many ways by antimodernist thought and can be fairly categorized as an antimodernist critique of contemporary, late-modern society.

[253] Werner Jaeger, Paideia: The Ideals of Greek Culture, Vol. 1 (New York: Oxford University Press, 1976), pp. xvii-xxii.

[254] Ibid., p.xxiii.

[255] This same point is made by H. I. Marrou in A History of Education in Antiquity (Madison: University of Wisconsin Press, 1982), p. 251ff..

[256] Herman Melville, Moby Dick (Indianapolis: Bobbs-Merrill, 1964), pp. 541-43.

Index